books**online**

Read this book online today:

With SAP PRESS BooksOnline we offer you online access to knowledge from the leading SAP experts. Whether you use it as a beneficial supplement or as an alternative to the printed book, with SAP PRESS BooksOnline you can:

- Access your book anywhere, at any time. All you need is an Internet connection.
- Perform full text searches on your book and on the entire SAP PRESS library.
- Build your own personalized SAP library.

The SAP PRESS customer advantage:

Register this book today at *www.sap-press.com* and obtain exclusive free trial access to its online version. If you like it (and we think you will), you can choose to purchase permanent, unrestricted access to the online edition at a very special price!

Here's how to get started:

1. Visit *www.sap-press.com*.
2. Click on the link for SAP PRESS BooksOnline and login (or create an account).
3. Enter your free trial license key, shown below in the corner of the page.
4. Try out your online book with full, unrestricted access for a limited time!

Your personal free trial **license key**
for this online book is: gyi7-j28z-vfsk-pwbc

100 Things You Should Know About
Sales and Distribution with SAP®

 **PRESS**

SAP PRESS is a joint initiative of SAP and Galileo Press. The know-how offered by SAP specialists combined with the expertise of the Galileo Press publishing house offers the reader expert books in the field. SAP PRESS features first-hand information and expert advice, and provides useful skills for professional decision-making.

SAP PRESS offers a variety of books on technical and business related topics for the SAP user. For further information, please visit our website: *www.sap-press.com*.

Luis Castedo and Matt Chudy
Sales and Distribution in SAP ERP—Practical Guide
2011, 406 pp. (hardcover)
ISBN 978-1-59229-347-6

Ashish Mohapatra
Optimizing Sales and Distribution in SAP ERP—Functionality and Configuration
2010, 517 pp. (hardcover)
ISBN 978-1-59229-329-2

D. Rajen Iyer
Effective SAP SD
2007, 265 pp. (hardcover)
ISBN 978-1-59229-101-4

D. Rajen Iyer and Suresh Veeraraghavan
Effective Pricing with SAP ERP
2012, 423 pp. (hardcover)
ISBN 978-1-59229-380-3

Matt Chudy and Luis Castedo

100 Things You Should Know About
Sales and Distribution with SAP®

Galileo Press

Bonn • Boston

Galileo Press is named after the Italian physicist, mathematician and philosopher Galileo Galilei (1564–1642). He is known as one of the founders of modern science and an advocate of our contemporary, heliocentric worldview. His words *Eppur si muove* (And yet it moves) have become legendary. The Galileo Press logo depicts Jupiter orbited by the four Galilean moons, which were discovered by Galileo in 1610.

Editor Laura Korslund
Technical Reviewer Ricardo Lopez
Copyeditor Anne Stewart
Cover Design Graham Geary
Layout Design Graham Geary
Production Kelly O'Callaghan, Graham Geary
Typesetting Publishers' Design and Production Services, Inc.
Printed and bound in the United States of America

ISBN 978-1-59229-405-3

© 2012 by Galileo Press Inc., Boston (MA)
1st edition 2012

Library of Congress Cataloging-in-Publication Data
Chudy, Matt.
100 things you should know about sales and distribution with SAP /
Matt Chudy, Luis Castedo. -- 1st ed.
p. cm.
ISBN 978-1-59229-405-3 -- ISBN 1-59229-405-7 1. Sales
management--Computer programs. 2. Inventories, Retail--Data processing.
3. Inventory control--Data processing. 4. SAP ERP. I. Castedo, Luis.
II. Title. III. Title: One hundred things you should know about sales
and distribution with SAP.
HF5438.35.C477 2011
658.8'10028553--dc23
2012005005

Contents at a Glance

Dear Reader,

Have you ever found yourself staring at the computer screen in the middle of a sales activity and thought to yourself, "If only there was an easier way to ...?" With this book, you'll find the answers to many of those questions, and also find different (and hopefully better!) ways of accomplishing tasks you find challenging. With information ranging from how to manage customers with less than stellar credit ratings to comparing your company's products to a competitor's, you'll be sure to find helpful tidbits and expert tricks that will give you that "Aha!" moment.

It's been a pleasure working with Luis and Matt, who were already SAP PRESS pro authors when their manuscript landed on my desk. They've put a lot of thought and energy into coming up with the best tips and tricks they've learned from their 30+ years of professional experience. With attention to detail combined with their insider knowledge of the Sales and Distribution component, I'm sure you'll find yourself holding on to this essential book for a long time!

We at SAP PRESS are always eager to hear your opinion. What do you think about *100 Things You Should Know About Sales and Distribution with SAP*? As your comments and suggestions are our most useful tools to help us make our books the best they can be, we encourage you to visit our website at *www.sap-press.com* and share your feedback.

Thank you for purchasing a book from SAP PRESS!

Laura Korslund
Editor, SAP PRESS

Galileo Press
Boston, MA

laura.korslund@galileo-press.com
www.sap-press.com

Contents

Part 1

Master Data

Things You'll Learn in this Section

Master data is the foundation on which all SAP transactions are executed. This data is accessed when you create a sales order or a delivery, pick transfer orders and execute shipment documents, or when you process billing. Because of the dynamic nature of master data, it's very important that it's accurate and up-to-date. In order to ensure this, you need to invest time up front when the master data is created and use maintenance transactions to keep it clean. In the following tips, we'll share a few little-known transactions to consider for your day-to-day data maintenance operation, making it easier and more efficient.

Customizing the Fields in Customer Master Screens

You can ensure the most relevant fields are always available and irrelevant fields are removed from the screens in the customer master.

The customer master is the foundation on which your SD configuration rests. When master data records are created, many times users don't enter values in fields that are needed to obtain the results you expect. Other times, they enter data in fields that needed to remain blank so that they don't interfere with the configured functionality.

This tip shows you how to customize the customer master to suit your specific needs, allowing you to hide unnecessary fields, make entries that are mandatory in critical fields by changing the field status settings, and allow users to either enter information or not in fields that don't affect the resulting functionality.

✓ And Here's How ...

To make changes to the field status settings, use Transaction OVT0 or follow the IMG menu path:

> LOGISTICS GENERAL • BUSINESS PARTNER • CUSTOMERS • CONTROL • DEFINE ACCOUNT
> GROUPS AND FIELD SELECTION FOR CUSTOMERS

In the resulting screen, select which fields are mandatory or required entries, optional, or suppressed for each customer's account group. To do this, select the account group you want to change. It's a good practice not to change the standard-delivered account groups; if you want to do that, make a copy of that account group so you can make changes to it.

When you double-click on the selected account group, you'll see a screen with the general settings for the account group. In the middle part of this screen, you have a section labeled FIELD STATUS. Figure 1 shows these field statuses; they group the different views you have in the customer master and within them the fields you want to customize.

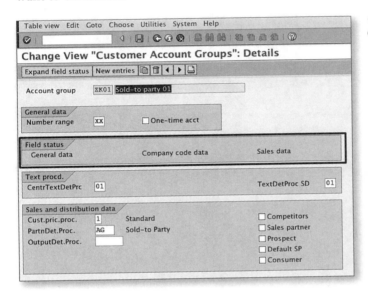

« *Figure 1* Account Group Details Screen

To start customizing the field statuses, double-click on the STATUS GROUP name; from there, you'll be taken to the FIELD STATUS GROUPS screen. Now you see a more familiar description for the groups. The field status groups are organized in the same way as the field groups in the customer master screens. Each section of the different views of the customer master corresponds to this classification (see Figure 2).

Double-click again on the groups in the list and that will take you to the settings for each of the fields in the group (see Figure 3). This screen allows you to make a field invisible, mandatory, or display only. Note that some fields carry through several screens; for example, TRANSPORTATION ZONE in the STREET ADDRESS section of the ADDRESS tab.

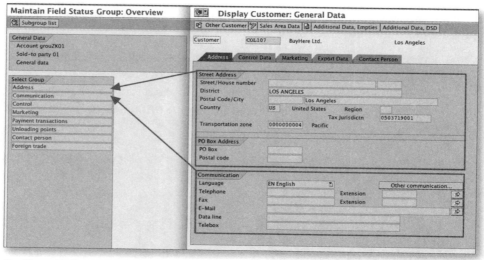

⊼ *Figure 2* *Organization of the Field Status Groups*

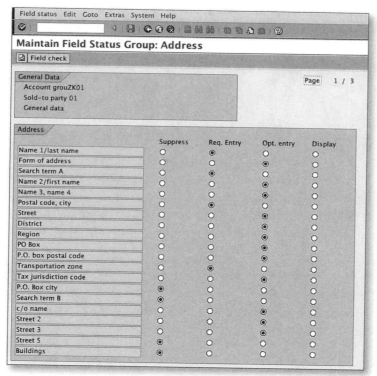

⊼ *Figure 3* *Selecting a Status for Every Field*

In these cases, you'll find that the settings you make may work differently in different tabs. In this case, TRANSPORTATION ZONE is a mandatory field in the ADDRESS tab, and display only in the CONTROL DATA tab. Let's look at the different statuses you can have in Table 1.

Field Status	Description
SUPPRESS	When you select this setting for a field, it will disappear from the screen.
REQUIRED ENTRY	These fields are mandatory and appear with a check mark when empty, indicating that data must be entered in them.
OPTIONAL ENTRY	These fields appear blank when they have no data.
DISPLAY	These fields appear "grayed out" and won't allow data to be entered or changed.

≫ *Table 1* Field Status Meanings

After you make changes to these settings, you'll see how fields in the customer master appear, disappear, become display only, or become mandatory, as shown in Figure 4.

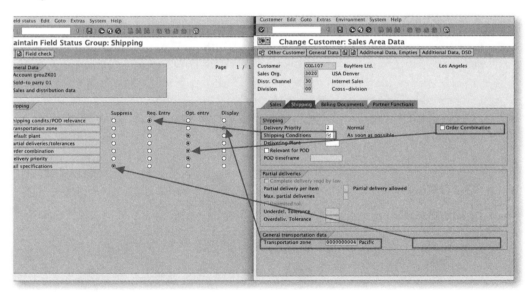

≫ *Figure 4* Field Status Settings in the Customer Master Screens

Tip 2

Understanding Cross-Company Sales

You can easily go through the steps for cross-company sales when you know the proper sequence, as well as troubleshoot missing configuration steps.

A cross-company sale occurs when you create a sales document in which the sales organization and the delivering plant belong to different company codes; in this case, the system checks the company codes of the sales organization and of the delivering plant and automatically carries out intercompany billing processing for different outcomes.

If you find that customer and intercompany billing documents aren't listed in the *document flow* (ENVIRONMENT • DISPLAY DOCUMENT FLOW or F5) for the customer's sales order, then you missed configuration steps and your business transaction is incomplete. In this tip, we'll go through a multi-step solution that can be used as a checklist in order to complete all the steps in setting up cross-company sales, or to discover whether you missed any.

And Here's How ...

Create Customer for Plant

> LOGISTICS • SALES AND DISTRIBUTION • MASTER DATA • BUSINESS PARTNER • CUSTOMER • CREATE

Create a customer using account group PLNT. Enter all customer information and save your data to get a customer number, then define the internal customer for the plant.

Define Internal Customer for Plant

> SALES AND DISTRIBUTION • BILLING • INTERCOMPANY BILLING • DEFINE INTERNAL CUSTOMER NUMBER BY SALES ORGANIZATION

In the VIEW FOR INTERCOMPANY BILLING: OVERVIEW screen, enter the customer number that you just created in the line for the company code number of the receiving plant. Save your data and proceed to the following step.

Define Sales Order Type for Intercompany Billing

> SALES AND DISTRIBUTION • BILLING • INTERCOMPANY BILLING • DEFINE ORDER TYPE FOR INTERCOMPANY BILLING

Click on your document type entry and type "IV" in the INTERCO column. Save your data and continue to the following step.

Maintain the Copy Control for the Delivery Document to the Billing Document

> SALES AND DISTRIBUTION • BILLING • BILLING DOCUMENTS • MAINTAINING COPY CONTROL FOR BILLING DOCUMENTS

1. Choose COPYING CONTROL: DELIVERY DOCUMENT TO BILLING DOCUMENT in the CHOOSE ACTIVITY dialog box.
2. On the DISPLAY VIEW HEADER: OVERVIEW screen, choose DISPLAY • CHANGE (or press Ctrl+F1), then choose NEW ENTRIES.
3. On the NEW ENTRIES: DETAILS OF ADDED ENTRIES screen, enter the following values:
   - TARGET BILLING TYPE: IV (Intercompany billing)
   - FROM SALES DOCUMENT TYPE: LF (Delivery)
   - COPYING REQUIREMENTS: 014 (Header delivery to intercompany billing)
   - Check the COPY ITEM NUMBER checkbox
4. On the CHANGE VIEW ITEM: DETAILS OF ADDED ENTRIES screen, enter the following values:

- ▶ COPYING REQUIREMENTS: 015 (Item delivery to intercompany billing)
- ▶ BILLING QUANTITY: B (Delivery quantity less invoiced quantity)
- ▶ DATA VBRK/VBRP: 001 (Inv. Split (sample) Pos./neg. quantity)
- ▶ PRICING TYPE: G (Cumulative batch quantity minus invoiced quantity)

Save your data and continue to the next step.

Create the Material Intercompany Sales Price

> SALES AND DISTRIBUTION • MASTER DATA • CONDITIONS • CREATE

On the CREATE CONDITION RECORDS: FAST ENTRY, enter:

- ▶ CONDITION TYPE PR00
- ▶ MATERIAL NUMBER
- ▶ SALES PRICE (to the end customer)
- ▶ VALIDITY PERIOD

Remember to save your data and then continue to the next step.

Create the Transfer Price Condition at the Deliverying Plant

> SALES AND DISTRIBUTION • SALES • CONDITIONS • SELECT USING CONDITION TYPE • CREATE

On the CREATE INTERCOMPANY PRICE CONDITION (PI01): FAST ENTRY, enter:

- ▶ SALES ORGANIZATION OF ORDER: Your sales organization
- ▶ PLANT (from where goods are shipped): Your plant
- ▶ MATERIAL: Your material
- ▶ SALES PRICE (TRANSFER PRICE TO ORDER SALES ORG): Your price
- ▶ VALIDITY PERIOD

Save your data.

After completing these steps, you can create a sales order in the ordering company code, then a delivery in the supplying plant. After picking, PGI, and billing, the result should show one invoice for the customer in the ordering company code and an invoice to the ordering company code in the supplying company code, as shown in Figure 1. The latter is the intercompany billing document.

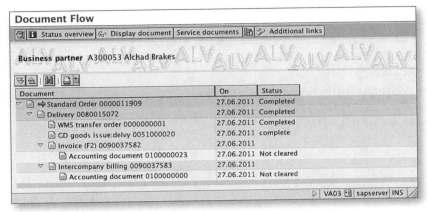

⌃ *Figure 1 Display the Document Flow by Pressing F5*

Tip 3

Changing Customer Master Data en Masse

You can save time and a lot of tedious, repetitive work by performing a mass update for your customer master data with a single transaction.

When you need to modify a large number of master data entries, there's nothing like a mass update transaction to save you time (to say nothing of your sanity!). In this case, the SAP system offers one for customer master data, which we'll discuss in this tip.

When you change master records, they aren't available for transactional work. If possible, you should try to use these transactions only at times when disruption will be minimal, and only after communicating that the master data will be locked for a certain period of time.

✔ And Here's How ...

To get to the customer master mass update transaction, use Transaction XD99 or follow the path:

> LOGISTICS • CUSTOMER SERVICE • SERVICE AGREEMENTS • ENVIRONMENT • SALES AND DISTRIBUTION • MASTER DATA • BUSINESS PARTNER • CUSTOMER MASTER MASS MAINTENANCE

Note that you'll see warning screens almost every time you move into the next step in the process. Read each warning carefully and then press [Enter] to continue.

In the initial screen shown in Figure 1, you're presented with two tabs: TABLES and FIELDS. The TABLES tab shows you the tables that are available for mass maintenance. You'll have to choose these tables based on the key fields required for searching the relevant records.

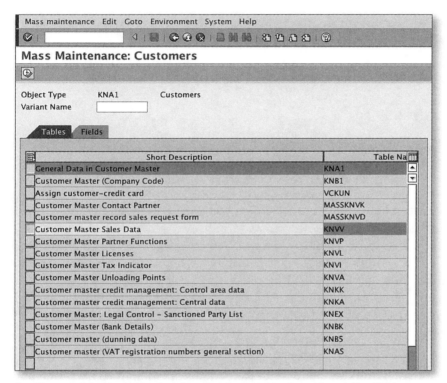

⌃ *Figure 1 Selecting Tables Based on Maintenance Needs and Search Key Fields*

When you're done selecting the tables, click on the FIELDS tab, which shows you the fields that are available for maintenance. Choose all the fields for which values need to be maintained en masse so that they're included in the maintenance screen.

Once you've selected the fields, press F8 to continue to the search screen. In the selection screen shown in Figure 2, you'll see all of the key fields for the tables you selected; enter your search criteria and press F8. You may receive a warning based on the number of records that match your search criteria.

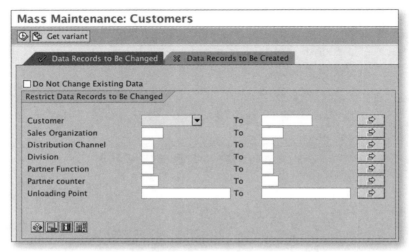

Figure 2 Search Screen with the Key Fields for the Selected Tables

In the MAINTENANCE screen (see Figure 3), you'll see a list of all the records that match your search criteria. Here you could still select just a few records, but try not to select the records manually. Because you'd need to go through a very long list and it could lead to errors, it's better use the SELECT WITH CONDITION BUTTON or use different search fields. This functionality allows you to refine your search by allowing you to use additional fields. When you push the button you will be presented with a pop-up window that where you can select extra search fields and enter search values.

At the top you'll see a MODEL line, where you'll enter the new values you want to maintain for each field you selected. Whatever values you enter on this model line will be copied to all the selected records that appear underneath.

To perform the copy, click on the CARRY OUT A MASS CHANGE button (▦).

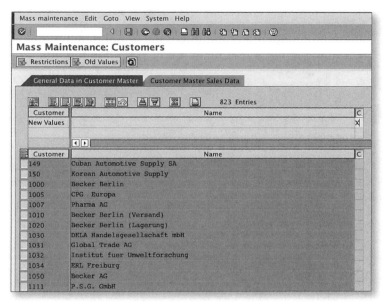

⤊ *Figure 3* *Values are entered on the Model Line*

At this point you should check that the values were copied to all the records on the screen, and that the selected records are the correct ones. If you're completely sure, you can proceed with the actual change to the database by saving your work ([Ctrl]+[S]).

The system will take a while to process, depending on the number of records, and will return a screen with traffic lights indicating the result of attempting the change (see Figure 4).

⤊ *Figure 4* *Results of the Mass Change*

Tip 4

Changing the Account Group for a Customer

You can change the account group for a customer after it has been created, which will define what information is needed in a specific master record and which partner functions will be available.

When you create a master record for a business partner in the SAP ERP system, you need to enter an account group. This account group helps determine which fields are mandatory when entering the data, which fields are hidden, and which are display only (see Tip 1). The account group also determines number range assignment and, maybe the most important, which partner functions are valid. Sometimes it's necessary to accommodate changes in our customer's hierarchy by making changes to the account group. Let's explore how to make these changes.

 And Here's How ...

Prerequisites

Unfortunately, you can't switch account groups indistinctively. You can only start at a lower level and move upward in the partner role hierarchy, and you can't change the account groups in reverse order because the higher level partner roles have more fields in the database than the lower levels. If you try to change back to a lower level account group, the system won't normally allow this; if it's configured to do so, then it will list all the fields that would be affected or lost.

Procedure

To change the account group for a customer, use Transaction XD07 or follow the path:

> SALES AND DISTRIBUTION • MASTER DATA • BUSINESS PARTNER • CUSTOMER • CHANGE ACCOUNT GROUP

On the CHANGE ACCOUNT GROUP screen, enter the customer number for which you want to change the account group. Press the [Enter] key, and the system will look up the current account group and will display it in a pop-up window (see Figure 1) and ask you for the new account group.

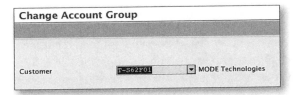

« *Figure 1* Change Account Group Screen.

Select a new account group and press the [Enter] key. The screen will change to a series of warning messages related to the switch from one account group to another, as shown in Figure 2.

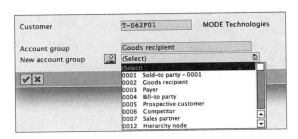

« *Figure 2* New Account Group Selection Pull-Down Menu

Alternatively, you can click on the OVERVIEW button to the left of the new account group field and you'll see a list of the assignments for this customer (shown in Figure 3).

If you're using different number ranges for each account group, for example, you may receive a warning message saying that the partner number isn't in the target account group's number range.

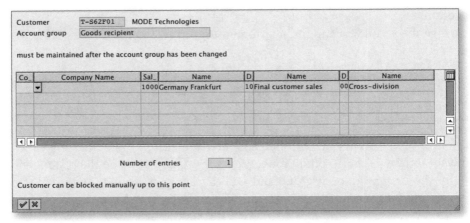

⤷ **Figure 3** *Overview Screen for Sales Structure Assignment for the Partner*

Next, you'll see another screen with a complete list of the relevant fields that have to be maintained because of the change to a new account group. Then you'll be taken to the CUSTOMER MASTER CHANGE screen (shown in Figure 4) where you maintain those fields and save them. If you don't see that window, it means there are no fields to maintain.

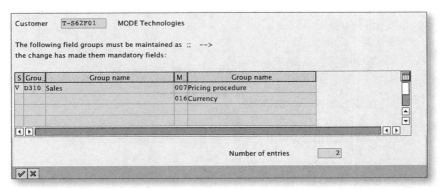

⤷ **Figure 4** *Fields to Be Maintained in the Customer Master after Changing Account Group*

Once you're taken to the CUSTOMER MASTER CHANGE screen, you can complete the information for those critical fields listed on the previous window. After completing the information, save the customer and you're done!

Blocking or Unblocking a Customer Account

You can suspend or reactivate your customers' business activities due to reasons like embargo or an outstanding debt relationship.

You may run into a scenario where your customer filed for bankruptcy or you have to suspend all business activity due to political instability or embargo. This could be a temporary measure that may have to be reversed at a later time. In this situation, you need to apply a block status to a customer master for just one of the specific sales organizations without disrupting business activities in others. To suspend or reactivate business with a customer for a specific sales organization, you can maintain customer blocks. These blocks can be applied to block sales orders, deliveries, billing, and sales support activities, but not the accounts receivables transactions—allowing you to collect payments.

And Here's How ...

To maintain blocks for a customer account, run Transaction VD05 or follow the menu path (see Figure 1):

> LOGISTICS • SALES AND DISTRIBUTION • MASTER DATA • BUSINESS PARTNER • CUSTOMER • BLOCK

If you need to restrict business activities for all sales organizations you can run Transaction XD05 (block centrally) and add the company code as another selection and blocking criteria.

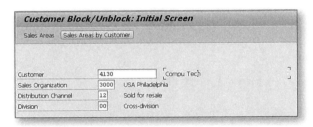

≪ *Figure 1* Customer Block/
Unblock Initial Screen

On the initial screen of the transaction, specify the customer account number and use the SALES AREAS BY CUSTOMER button or press F5 to choose the specific sales organization for which you want to maintain blocks.

Once you select your sales area data, press Enter or the ⊘ icon to continue. On the following screen, shown in Figure 2, you can maintain blocking reasons for each sales activity for which you need the controls to be applied.

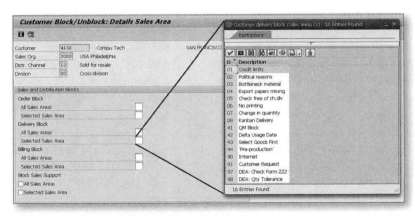

⌃ *Figure 2* Customer Block/Unblock Details

Restrict Future Orders

To restrict a customer's ability to place future sales orders, maintain the ORDER BLOCK. You can do this for every sales area or just a specific one; select the blocking reason using the drop-down selection list. Repeat for DELIVERY BLOCK and BILLING BLOCK, assuming that all necessary configuration exists to support these blocks. They're defined in Customizing; for further details you can refer to DEFINE REASONS FOR BLOCKING IN SHIPPING and DEFINE BLOCKING REASON FOR BILLING nodes in SAP IMG. You can also maintain blocks for sales support activities, such as promotions, sales calls, and cross matching by using BLOCK SALES SUPPORT and selecting tick boxes for ALL SALES AREAS or choose SELECTED SALES AREAS (see Figure 3 for an example of completely maintained customer blocks).

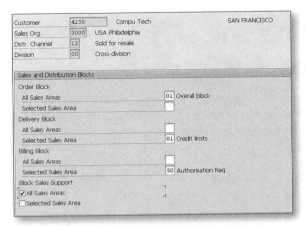

« Figure 3 *Customer Block/ Unblock with Selected Block Reasons*

View Change History

With your cursor on the specific block reason, you can use the pull-down menus and access ENVIRONMENT and choose FIELD CHANGES (or use F8 on your keyboard). This option will show you the change log for that field and can help you establish the historical trace of changes if any have been applied before. To save your data, click on the SAVE icon or press Ctrl + S. You can now run a test by attempting to create a sales order using VA01, a delivery using Transaction VL01N, a billing document using Transaction VF01, or a sales activity using Transaction VC01N. Assuming that you do have all configuration mentioned above in place to support this process, you should get an error message if your customer was blocked as shown in Figure 4.

« Figure 4 *Sales Support Block Error Message*

Tip 6

Troubleshooting Missing Sales Areas for Customers

You can easily check for and fix missing configuration if the system tells you that sales areas don't exist when you're trying to create or extend a customer.

The error message you get when you want to extend a customer into a new sales area can sometimes be misleading and many times frustrating. You've already assigned the sales organization, distribution channel, and division in Customizing under ENTERPRISE STRUCTURE • ASSIGNMENT • SALES AND DISTRIBUTION • SET UP SALES AREA, but the error still persists. To solve this problem, you can look at the assignments in Transaction OVXG, but you also need to look in two more places for missing configuration to make sure that the reference distribution channels and reference divisions are set up.

✓ And Here's How ...

The solution for this problem takes two steps:

Define Common Distribution Channels

Use Transaction VOR1 or follow the path:

> SALES AND DISTRIBUTION • MASTER DATA • DEFINITION OF COMMON DISTRIBUTION CHANNELS

In Transaction VOR1, define which distribution channels have common master data within a sales organization (see Figure 1). Indicate which one is the main or "reference" distribution channel for all the other distribution channels.

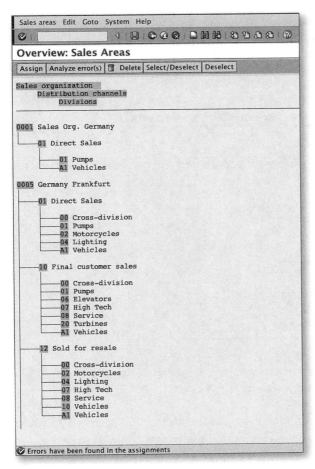

« *Figure 1* *Set Up Reference Distribution Channels in Transaction VOR1*

If you have several distribution channels in a sales organization and the customers are shared among them, select one of these to be the reference distribution channel and assign it as that to the rest, or to those to which it applies.

On the other hand, if the distribution channels don't share customers, then each distribution channel can be the reference to itself.

Definition of Common Divisions

To define common division, use Transaction VOR2 or follow the path:

SALES AND DISTRIBUTION • MASTER DATA • DEFINITION OF COMMON DIVISIONS

Define which divisions have common master data within a sales organization by indicating which is the main or "reference" division for all the other divisions (see Figure 2).

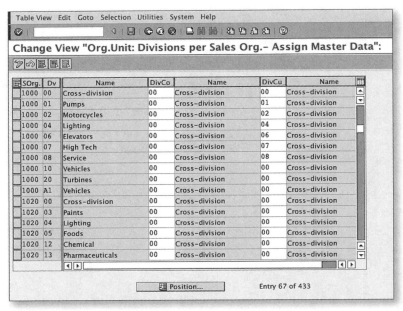

Table View   Edit   Goto   Selection   Utilities   System   Help

Change View "Org.Unit: Divisions per Sales Org.– Assign Master Data":

SOrg.	Dv	Name	DivCo	Name	DivCu	Name
1000	00	Cross-division	00	Cross-division	00	Cross-division
1000	01	Pumps	00	Cross-division	01	Cross-division
1000	02	Motorcycles	00	Cross-division	02	Cross-division
1000	04	Lighting	00	Cross-division	04	Cross-division
1000	06	Elevators	00	Cross-division	06	Cross-division
1000	07	High Tech	00	Cross-division	07	Cross-division
1000	08	Service	00	Cross-division	08	Cross-division
1000	10	Vehicles	00	Cross-division	00	Cross-division
1000	20	Turbines	00	Cross-division	00	Cross-division
1000	A1	Vehicles	00	Cross-division	00	Cross-division
1020	00	Cross-division	00	Cross-division	00	Cross-division
1020	03	Paints	00	Cross-division	00	Cross-division
1020	04	Lighting	00	Cross-division	00	Cross-division
1020	05	Foods	00	Cross-division	00	Cross-division
1020	12	Chemical	00	Cross-division	00	Cross-division
1020	13	Pharmaceuticals	00	Cross-division	00	Cross-division

Position...   Entry 67 of 433

⌃ *Figure 2 Set Up Reference Divisions in Transaction VOV2*

If you have several divisions in a sales organization and the customers are shared among them, then you select one of these to be the reference division and assign it as that to the rest, or to those to which it applies.

On the other hand, if the divisions don't share customers, then each division can be the reference to itself.

Tip **7**

Checking for Incomplete Customer Master Data

There's an easy way to make sure that master data for the customer or vendor has been correctly maintained before creating a sales order.

When organizations maintain the vendor's master data using Transactions VD01 and FD01, there's some risk of customers not being completely maintained by the time a sales order is created. This could be due to a few different factors—you may have identified a customer that hasn't been maintained at all, and a message will indicate that the customer doesn't exist for the combination of SALES ORGANIZATION/DISTRIBUTION CHANNEL/DIVISION; or the system has redetermined the sales area because the customer exists but not for the area indicated in the CREATE SALES ORDER initial screen. Instead of painstakingly searching through all of your records, there's an easy way to generate a list of customers that are missing data. Let's go over how to do this in this tip.

And Here's How ...

Before you start with this tip, you need to make sure that you've identified that there *is* missing master data while creating a sales order (listed in the Log for Incompleteness). To check for incompletely maintained customers, use Transaction OV50 or follow the menu path:

> LOGISTICS • SALES AND DISTRIBUTION • MASTER DATA • BUSINESS PARTNER • CUSTOMER • MASTER DATA COMPARISON

In the generated report (see Figure 1), enter a list of customers and check for either missing accounting data or missing sales data. Alternatively, enter the company code number and the sales organization/distribution channel/division for which you want to find incomplete data.

Near the bottom of the screen, there's a radio button that allows you to show the customers that are missing accounting data or the customers that are missing sales data.

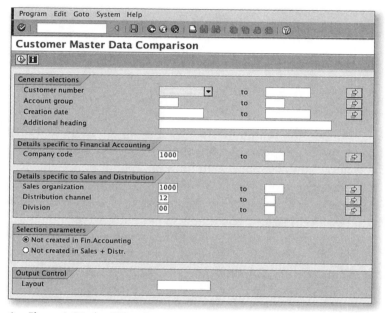

⨠ *Figure 1* Display Either Customers' Missing Accounting or Sales Data

The result of executing the report will be a list of all the customers that fulfill your search criteria, and that are missing the step of creating either the financial accounting data or the sales area data (see Figure 2).

List Edit Goto Settings System Help

Customer Master Data Comparison

| IDES-ALE: Central FI Syst | Customer Master Data Comparison | Time 16:12:43 | Date | 20.09.2011 |
| Frankfurt - Deutschland | | RFDKAG00/CASTEDOL | Page | 1 |

Customers not created in Financial Accounting

SOrg. DChl Dv Customer	Customer Address Line 0 Customer Address Line 1 Customer Address Line 2	Created on
1000 12 00 1098	Productos Argentinos Imp. S.A PO Box LS15 1401 BUENOS AIRES	13.07.1999
1000 12 00 1960	K.A.P.A GmbH Wernerstrasse 45a D-30519 HANNOVER	19.06.1997
1000 12 00 2005	SudaTech GmbH Filiale Karlsruhe Kaiserallee 115 D-76185 KARLSRUHE	28.11.1996
1000 12 00 2400	Firma 2400 I- MILANO	15.05.2001
1000 12 00 6701	e-Lumination Automotive Modules Edisonstraße 110 D-01309 DRESDEN	07.01.2004
1000 12 00 10000	IDES AG Postfach 1342 D-60231 FRANKFURT	05.03.2001
1000 12 00 14000	Werk 1400 Stuttgart Rotebuehlstrasse 121 D-70178 STUTTGART	11.06.1997
1000 12 00 99999	Postal Customer I- BARI CA	20.02.1997

Figure 2 Customers Missing Either the Accounting or Sales Views

The report is a very simple list indicating the company code or the sales area for which the customer was created, the customer's number, the address data, and the creation date. Now that you've identified what information is missing, you can navigate to the correct customer or area and maintain that information.

Tip 8

Extending the Material Storage Location View

If you have several new storage locations that you need to extend material master views to, you can extend several materials to these new locations.

In any business environment, organizational structures are added and removed, and new prototype materials are transferred to full product line offering. All of this requires you to maintain material master extensions in the most efficient way. If your system isn't set up for auto-extension of storage location views when material movement transactions are performed, you'll have to perform the extend function multiple times for multiple storage locations and materials, which is time consuming and error-prone.

✅ And Here's How ...

There are several ways to extend the storage location view starting with the simple Transaction MM01 (Material Master Create) or MM50 (Mass-Extend Material Master View; see Tip 9 for details), but these are time-consuming or designed for mass-processing of data.

To extend the material master storage location view in a quick and simple way, run Transaction MMSC or follow the menu path:

> LOGISTICS • MATERIALS MANAGEMENT • MATERIAL MASTER • OTHER • ENTER STORAGE LOCATIONS

On the initial screen, enter the material number and the plant number you want to extend storage locations for. We recommend that you use the LIST ALL EXISTING STORAGE LOCATION option from the LIST CONTROL section—it shows you where the material is already extended so you can avoid unnecessary duplicate entry attempts. If you're maintaining material masters in the master client and distributing your data centrally, select the CREATE CHANGE DOCUMENTS checkbox. This is very important for your ALE (Application Link Enabling) distributed data—you only have one shot at it because change documents are required. Remember one of the restrictions for this transaction is that you have to have at least one storage location view already extended during material master creation using Transaction MM01; this view will be used as a base for other storage location extensions.

Once you've maintained the relevant information, click on the ENTER icon or press [Enter] on your keyboard. On the following screen (see Figure 1), you'll see the list of storage locations already maintained.

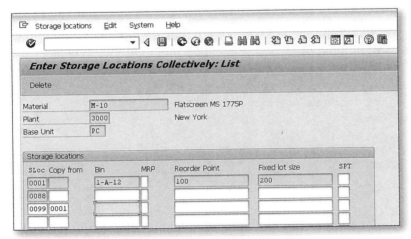

⌃ *Figure 1* *Extend Storage Locations View Detail List*

To extend the basic view, use one of the new storage locations given to you for extension. Type in the storage location number in the SLOC column and press [Enter]. If you want to copy data from another storage location that has already been maintained, specify the source data location in the COPY FROM column before you press [Enter]. This will copy all the data including BIN (code for a fixed storage bin of the storage location); do not confuse with WM fixed bin location and MRP related data (like reorder point [triggers MRP to create replenishment requirements] and fixed lot size [the quantity the replenishment requirement will be generated for]). See Figure 2, where storage location 0001 is used as a source of extension data for location 0099, where BIN column data was changed. If accepted, the source will copy to the destination location data fields. Bin data and MRP data will still be available for editing before you click on SAVE.

Enter Storage Locations Collectively: List						
Delete						

Material	M-10		Flatscreen MS 1775P			
Plant	3000		New York			
Base Unit	PC					

Storage locations

SLoc	Copy from	Bin	MRP	Reorder Point	Fixed lot size	SPT
0001		1-A-12		100	200	
0088						
0099		12-B-3		100	200	
0055						

« *Figure 2* Extend Storage Location Data List Maintenance

If any of your data has changed and you need to make adjustments (you cannot make them in MMSC), this transaction won't allow you to update MRP, bin data, or delete the storage location views. If you need to make any modifications after you save your data, you need to use either a mass update transaction like MM17 or MM02 to make corrections individually.

Tip 9

Extending the Material Master Views

To make existing material master records fully usable, you can perform a mass update to provide them with required views.

Let's say that you have a large number of material master views to maintain. You know that there are several views that need to be completed for several organizational units as quickly as possible to avoid loss of business opportunities and procurement disruptions. To help you accomplish this, we'll show you how to maintain all missing views of the materials en masse, making the extension process more efficient. Note that to use mass-extend, any material master data, basic data views, and reference plant views must already exist.

And Here's How ...

To extend material master views en masse, run Transaction MM50 or follow the menu path:

> LOGISTICS • MATERIALS MANAGEMENT • MATERIAL MASTER • OTHER • EXTEND
> MATERIAL VIEW(S)

On the initial screen choose MAINTENANCE STATUS if you want to maintain a specific view, or simply leave it blank and all extendable views will be pulled into the report when you execute.

Enter already-maintained plants to narrow down your selection. If the material master record hasn't been previously extended to the desired plant, even if selected, the view extension won't occur.

Specify the sales organization data, material type, industry sector, and material numbers to make your report look cleaner, as well as easier to manage. Choosing the options in the SELECTION LOGIC section will also alter the report behavior. If you set the indicator to:

▶ AND: You'll get materials that match all specified maintenance statuses and other selection parameters.

▶ OR: You'll get maintenance statuses that satisfy one of your selection parameters.

Once the suggested fields are populated, click on EXECUTE or press ⌅F8⌅. On the next screen, you'll see a list of materials that are ready for processing. To simplify the extension process, you can use the reference function that allows you to copy data from a reference material—simply click on the REFERENCE/ORGANIZATION button or press ⌅F9⌅. This action will display a reference popup window where you can specify the reference data that will be used in the extension process. Select the lines you want to process and click on MAINTAIN MATERIALS or press ⌅Shift⌅+⌅F1⌅ (see Figure 1). You can see that the material master views are grouped logically, so maintenance selection master data is displayed in the order of alpha key designation (for example A [Work Scheduling] through V [Sales]).

Extend Material View(s): Overview

S	Created	Material	MTyp	I	CoCd	Plnt	SLoc	SOrg	DC	WhN	Material Description
☐ Q	01/24/1996	1300-1400	FERT	M		3000					MSI 1200 cc Touring Bike
☑ Q	01/24/1996	1300-1400	FERT	M		3100					MSI 1200 cc Touring Bike
☑ Q	02/13/1996	1300-1401	FERT	M		3000					MSI 750 cc Touring Bike

⌃ *Figure 1* Extend Material Views Overview

Choose all relevant lines to process and you'll cycle through the views for each individual material before continuing to the next. If you maintained the reference data, the popup window will be displayed for your confirmation (see Figure 2).

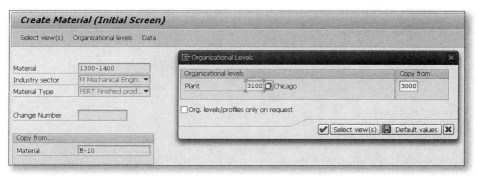

⌃ *Figure 2* Create Material View Reference Data Confirmation Popup

Next, review or update the data on the detailed material master screen (in our example the QUALITY MANAGEMENT tab is shown; see Figure 3). Be careful if you want to exit or save your data before completing the entire data set extension of individual material master records.

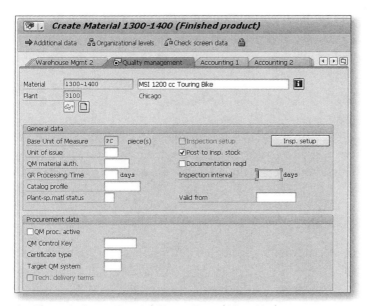

⌃ *Figure 3* Create Material Master Extend View Mode

When all of the selected views for material you're processing are maintained, click SAVE or press $\boxed{\text{Ctrl}}$+$\boxed{\text{S}}$ to store changes. At this point, all requested views for the first selected plant have been updated and saved. You can now perform transactions using materials in plants you've just maintained.

Blocking Sales Orders for Obsolete Materials

You can easily block obsolete materials from being allowed in sales orders when you find that these materials are still being included.

Many times users set a material as OBSOLETE in the X-PLANT MATL status from the BASIC DATA view of the material master, and then they find that sales orders that contain these materials can still be entered. When this happens, it causes frustration for the users and will generate work on the part of the IS support team, who will be called to help.

Users may try to flag the material for deletion, but they'll find that doesn't help either. When a material is flagged for deletion, all you get is a warning message in the sales order. In addition, flagging a material for deletion should only be done when you plan to archive it, not for status change. In this tip, we'll show you how to keep obsolete materials from being included in sales orders.

✓ And Here's How ...

To prevent an obsolete material from being included in a sales order, go to Transaction MM02 or follow the path:

> LOGISTICS • MATERIALS MANAGEMENT • MATERIAL MASTER • MATERIAL • CHANGE • IMMEDIATELY

Enter the material number, select the SALES 1 view, and enter the values for the sales area you want to change. In the DCHAIN-SPEC. STATUS field, select 12-SALES ORDERS NOT ALLOWED, as shown in Figure 1, and save your changes.

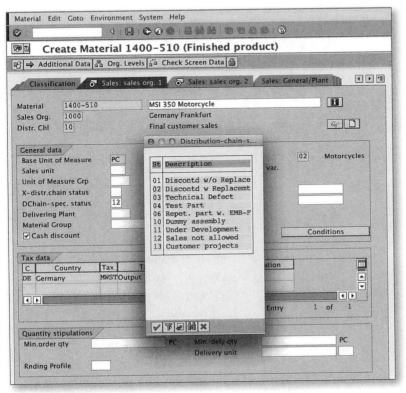

⌃ *Figure 1* DChain-spec. Status Changed to "Sales Not Allowed"

Now when the material is entered in a sales order, the user will receive an error message, indicating that the material can't be sold. This will force the user to remove the material number from the item just entered (see Figure 2).

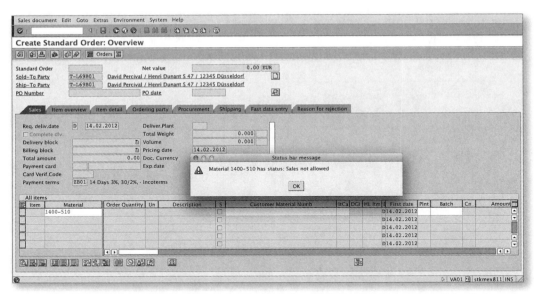

Note that the value 12 we're using is a standard delivered SAP value. If you use different statuses, make sure that you have one value configured to send an error upon sales order creation. You configure this in the IMG path:

> LOGISTICS - GENERAL • MATERIAL MASTER • SETTINGS FOR KEY FIELDS • DATA RELEVANT TO SALES AND DISTRIBUTION • DEFINE SALES STATUSES

Here, configure a status that has the value B in the BLOCK FOR ORDER field.

Tip 11

Maintaining Serial Number Records

You can maintain a large number of serial numbers with a single transaction to keep your information current.

Your organization uses serial numbers for internal and external purposes. You need to update this data periodically to make sure that warranty data is up-to-date, and other details, such manufacturer information, remains current. If you don't have all the selection criteria down to an individual serial number, you need to expand your search criteria.

The transaction we show you in this tip allows you to search for the records that need to be updated and helps to maintain all aspects of the serialized materials in one easy-to-manage way. If your organization uses the customer service module, you'll also be able to search for serial numbers you don't know and review the history for the serial numbers by looking for installation or removal data, operation affected, and latest status.

And Here's How ...

To list serial number records for your materials, run Transaction IQ08 or follow the menu path:

> LOGISTICS • CUSTOMER SERVICE • MANAGEMENT OF TECHNICAL OBJECTS • SERIAL NUMBERS • LIST EDITING • CHANGE

Like with most other SAP reports, selection parameters on the first section will help make this transaction run more efficiently, so specify as much detail as possible. When finished with selection data, click on EXECUTE or press F8. The subsequent screens will vary depending on your search results.

If your search returned a single serial number without equipment record activated, you'll see the details of CHANGE MATERIAL SERIAL NUMBER: SERNO.DETAIL, which will look like running Transaction IQ02. If your search found a single serial number with the equipment record maintained, your screen will present CHANGE EQUIPMENT (like running Transaction IE02). If your search returned multiple serial numbers, you'll see a list CHANGE MATERIAL SERIAL NUMBER: SERIAL NUMBER LIST as shown in Figure 1.

Change Material Serial Number: Serial Number List

Material	Serial no.	Plant	SLoc	Equipment	Description of technical object	SysStatus	Batch	PP	S
P-1001	RT05	1000	0001	10000987		ESTO			
P-1001	RT04	1000	0001	10000986		ESTO			
P-1001	RT03	1000	0001	10000985		ESTO			
P-1001	RT02	1000	0001	10000984		ESTO			
P-1001	RT01	1000	0001	10000983		ESTO			
P-1001	10000967	1000	0001	10003911	Pump GG Etanorm 200-1000	ESTO		01	
P-1001	10000966	1000	0001	10003910	Pump GG Etanorm 200-1000	ESTO		01	
P-1001	10000965	1000	0001	10003909	Pump GG Etanorm 200-1000	ESTO		01	
P-1001	10000961	1000	0001	10000982		ESTO			
P-1001	10000960	1000	0001	10000981		ESTO			

≫ Figure 1 *Change Material Serial Number List*

Now, maintain the selected data by choosing the line listing for your serial number. Click on the DETAILS icon or press Ctrl+Shift+F1. This will present the CHANGE EQUIPMENT: SERNO.DETAIL screen shown in Figure 2 where you can change the following fields:

▶ SERIAL NUMBER: Update current serial number by following the path from the pull-down menu EDIT • SPECIAL SERIAL NO. FUNCTIONS • CHANGE SERIAL NO.

▶ MATERIAL NUMBER: Switch material numbers by using the menu path EDIT • SPECIAL SERIAL NO. FUNCTIONS • CHANGE SERIAL NO.

▶ DESCRIPTION: Simply overtype the existing description field contents.

You can also review more details on history, status, logs, graphical hierarchy if complex equipment structures are maintained, and much more.

▶ SERIAL NUMBER HISTORY: Shows you all goods movements, sales orders, delivery documents, handling units, and where it was installed, for example. Notice that the history is color-coded. Go to the legend using the menu path SETTINGS • COLOR LEGEND to find out the meaning of each of the colors (see Figure 3).

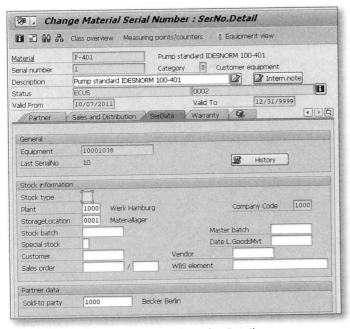

≫ *Figure 2 Change Material Serial Number Detail*

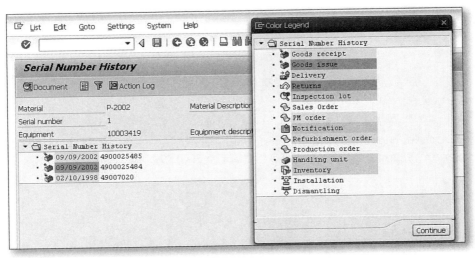

≫ *Figure 3 Serial Number History Legend*

▶ SERIAL NUMBER STATUS: Shows the current status of the serial number you're maintaining. Click on the STATUS icon to get to the CHANGE STATUS screen.

▶ SERIAL NUMBER ACTION LOG: Shows detailed log capturing who performed serial number data maintenance per individual field and when.

▶ ACTIVATE/DEACTIVATE SERIAL NUMBER: You can also choose to deactivate the serial number or re-activate one depending on your business requirements.

▶ DELETION FLAG: You can set the deletion flag if your serial number data needs to archived, for example.

▶ WARRANTY AND PARTNER: Use this tab to maintain warranty information for your customer and to capture information on your supplier warranty.

To exit the transaction and go back to the list, click on the BACK icon or press F3.

Maintaining Pricing Data with a Single Transaction

You can update a large number of pricing records for different condition types in a quick and clean manner with a single transaction.

As you know, there are several ways to perform the simple task of updating pricing records in SAP. Some methods are older than others and are less intuitive, with a crude look and feel, and allowing only certain things to be updated, while other methods are modified to make your maintenance more efficient. In this tip, we'll show you a one-stop shop for all of your pricing maintenance activities that will also allow you to stay within the same familiar interface regardless of whether you're creating or changing existing records.

 And Here's How ...

To maintain pricing records for all of your criteria, run Transaction VK32 (change condition records) or follow the menu path:

> LOGISTICS • SALES AND DISTRIBUTION • MASTER DATA • CONDITIONS • CHANGE

On the initial screen you'll see the ASSIGNMENT AREA MENU panel on the left side. The standard area menu has a pre-built set of condition selections, or you can modify this area menu to include your own specific pricing conditions. You can change this area menu by accessing the pull-down menu using the path ENVIRONMENT • ASSIGNMENT AREA MENU. The pre-delivered area menu for condition maintenance is COND_AV. This area menu can be modified to include your company-specific pricing conditions and it's freely definable. If you need to mold this feature to your needs, always create a copy and never modify the SAP objects; use Transaction SE43N to create your own area menus.

For our example, select CONDITIONS • BY MATERIAL from the area menu. On the next screen shown in Figure 1, you'll be prompted for selection data. Fill in the relevant data and then click on the EXECUTE icon or press ⌈F8⌋.

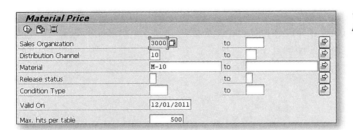

« *Figure 1 Conditions by Material Selection Screen*

If you have multiple conditions that met your selection criteria, they'll be available for changes. In our example, we can see all pricing conditions relevant for a single material ready for updates in one window. All you need to do is change your prices and click on the SAVE icon to complete the process (see Figure 2).

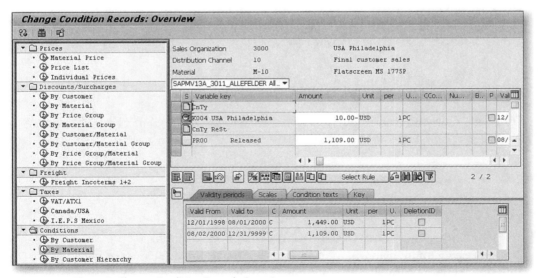

⌃ *Figure 2 Change Condition Records Overview*

Part 2

Sales Support

Things You'll Learn in this Section

Sales support in the SAP ERP system refers to all those activities related to promoting the sales of your company's products. You can use sales support to help you keep the sales personnel updated regarding the activities that are being performed by the team as it relates to contacting customers and prospects. It also gives you tools to keep track of your competition's products and helps you create sales promotions to increase sales. In this part of the book, we'll help you use the transactions we discuss in your company's sales process and stop using other systems so that your customer's information isn't spread among so many sources.

Tip 13

Assigning Sales Activities to Users

You can speed up the sales cycle during the pre-sales process by assigning activities for users to schedule in the SAP ERP system.

The SAP ERP system contains many transactions that can support the sales cycle. You can schedule activities with your customer or prospects, such as telephone calls and visits. If you've been wondering how to create sales activities to assist you in the sales process, we'll tell you how in this tip.

 And Here's How ...

Prerequisites

Before you can create activities and assign them to people, you need to make sure that sales activity types and sales activities are configured in the system. Make sure that the right security settings are configured in the following paths:

▶ SALES AND DISTRIBUTION • AUTHORIZATION MANAGEMENT

▶ SALES AND DISTRIBUTION • SALES SUPPORT • SALES ACTIVITIES

You also need to make sure that the following master data is completed:

▶ Users are created as employees in the HR component

▶ Vendor master data includes at least one contact person

Create a Sales Activity

You can create sales activities that are a type of to-do list that can be accessible to all sales employees. You can create reminders for calling or visiting a customer, sending a letter, or anything else that applies to your specific sales operations. To create sales activities, use Transaction VC01N or follow the path:

LOGISTICS • SALES AND DISTRIBUTION • SALES SUPPORT • SALES ACTIVITIES • EDIT

In the screen that appears (see Figure 1), select a customer and a contact person at your business. You can also assign an employee responsible at this time.

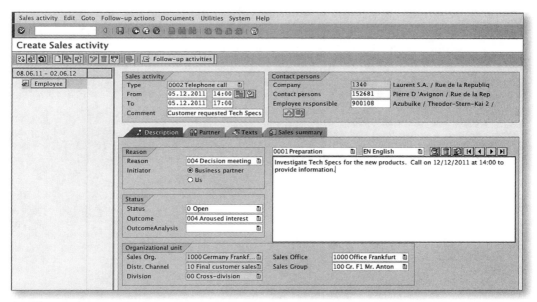

⊼ *Figure 1* *Sales Activity Screen*

At the bottom of the screen, enter the sales area information: SALES ORGANIZATION, DISTRIBUTION CHANNEL, and DIVISION. Optionally, you can also enter a SALES OFFICE and a SALES GROUP.

You can enter comments in the comment field at the top right; you can use this field to have a short reminder of why this activity was created.

In the middle section, select a reason for creating this activity from the match-code menu and who's responsible for the activity—your company or your client. You also qualify the activity by its status (opened, in process, or completed), its outcome, and an outcome analysis. Here, you can also enter texts for the different states of the activity, like preparation, report, address notes, and confidentiality notes.

There are different tabs with information about the customer. Probably the most useful is the SALES SUMMARY tab. It contains master data information, sales qualifications, credit information, and also information about the most recent orders all in one screen. This report is also available in Transaction VC/2.

If you want to create sales activities for a prospect that you haven't yet created in the SAP system as a customer, you can use a one-time customer, as shown in Figure 2. This is a customer master entry with ACCOUNT GROUP CPD or a custom entry, depending on the specific configuration of your system.

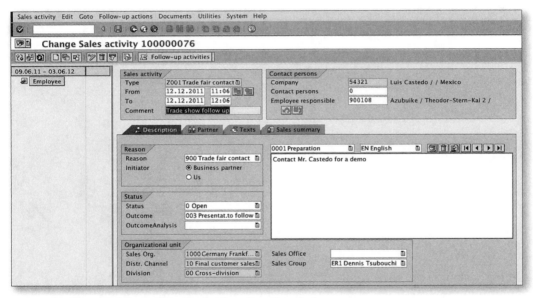

⌃ *Figure 2 Sales Activity Created for a One-Time Customer*

If you use a one-time customer, the system will prompt you for the contact information when you enter the customer number. This will allow you to record telephones and email for the contact person.

The sales activities can also be maintained in this transaction by using the menu option SALES ACTIVITY • GET. Alternatively, you can use the Sales Activity Monitor in Transaction VC05.

Tip 14

Finding Duplicate Sales Activities with the Crossmatching Report

If several people are unknowingly working on the same customer and accidentally create duplicate sales efforts, you can use the crossmatching report to find these instances.

Sometimes more than one person may approach the same customer without noticing until the customer brings it to the management's attention. To help avoid this situation, you can proactively check on sales activities that are being created on the system using the sales activities crossmatching report. This report determines partners for the specified date range that have more than one sales activity like phone calls, mailing of information, presentations, or others.

And Here's How ...

To run the crossmatching report, use Transaction VC15 or follow the path:

> LOGISTICS • SALES AND DISTRIBUTION • SALES SUPPORT • SALES PROMOTIONS • CROSSMATCHING

In the selection screen shown in Figure 1, enter the sales area combination and a date range. Alternatively, you can directly enter the customer number or the contact person that you want find sales activities for.

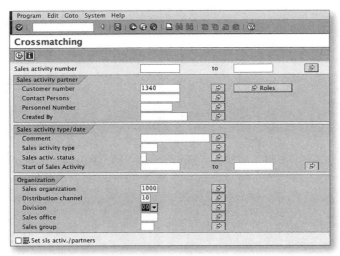

⌃ *Figure 1* Selection Criteria in the Crossmatching Report Selection Screen

Execute the report, and the result of your search criteria will be displayed in the following screen. The report is presented in a tree format and displays the customer number, name, and the number of sales activities that are open for each customer. You can expand the tree and look at the contact persons' names, the number of open sales activities, and the percentage of assignment for each contact person by clicking on the blue box icon to the left of each customer number and contact person number.

As shown in Figure 2, you can verify if they're all valid or, as in this example, there are duplicates.

⌃ *Figure 2* Scroll to the Right to Look at Relevant Information for the Activities

Double-click on the activity you want to change or delete and it will take you to the maintenance screen. From here you can update the information or completely delete the activity. You can also maintain individual sales activities in Transaction VC02.

Listing Valid Sales Deals by Date

You can easily find out how many sales deals are valid for your company at a specific point in time.

Sales deals are tools that are widely used to boost sales of a certain product or for a certain customer. However, sometimes companies lose visibility of which deals are still valid and can forget to offer them or apply them to their customers; thus reducing the effectiveness of the deals. The transaction we'll discuss in this tip will help you to access a list of all the sales deals that are valid on a certain date by sales area.

And Here's How ...

Access Transaction VB25 or follow the path:

> LOGISTICS • SALES AND DISTRIBUTION • MASTER DATA • INFORMATION SYSTEM • AGREEMENTS • LIST OF SALES DEALS

The report is very flexible because it doesn't have any mandatory fields and could help you find several things depending on your search criteria (see Figure 1).

Note the following pointers for working with this list:

▶ If you don't enter any criteria and execute the transaction, it will give you a list of all the sales deals that exist in your system. This will help locate that sales deal you used last year so you can copy it to use again.

▶ With a validity date, it will give you all the sales deals that are valid on a specific date.

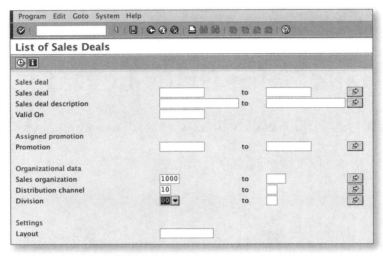

⌃ **Figure 1** *List of Sales Deals Entry Screen*

▶ With a sales area, it will give you all the sales deals that exist in your system for that combination of sales organization, distribution channel, and division.

▶ With a sales promotion number, it will list all the sales deals assigned to that sales promotion.

The list produced by executing the report, as seen in Figure 2, will show you the deal number and description. You can also look at the validity period and the assignment to sales promotions. All these deals have been created in Transaction VB21.

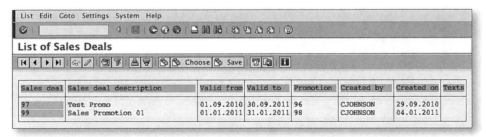

⌃ **Figure 2** *List of the Sales Deals with Validity Date and Promotion Assignment*

You can double-click on a given deal and look at the details. This will take you to the DISPLAY SALES DEAL screen (Transaction VB23), and from here you can look at every detail, including the condition records created for this deal by clicking on the CONDITIONS button.

Listing Active Promotions in the System by Sales Area

You can easily find out how many promotions are valid at a specific point in time.

The SAP ERP system allows companies to create promotions to boost the sales of a certain product line during its market launch, for example. However, tracking multiple promotions during peak sales seasons could be challenging because of the sales order volume and the number of customers placing orders. In this tip, we'll show you a report you can use to list all promotions that are valid on a certain date by sales area.

 And Here's How ...

To get to this report, access Transaction VB35 or follow the path:

> LOGISTICS • SALES AND DISTRIBUTION • MASTER DATA • INFORMATION SYSTEM • AGREEMENTS • PROMOTION LIST

The report is very flexible and can help you find several things depending on your search criteria because the search screen has no mandatory fields (see Figure 1).

Let's go over the options you to filter the list:

▶ With no fields maintained, it will give you a list of all the promotions that exist in your system. This can help you locate that promotion you used last year and copy it to use it again. Be careful using this search criteria because processing time can grow very large depending on the number of promotions you have.

▶ With a validity date, it will give you all the promotions that are valid on a specific date.

▶ With a sales area, it will give you all the promotions that exist in your system for that combination of sales organization, distribution channel, and division.

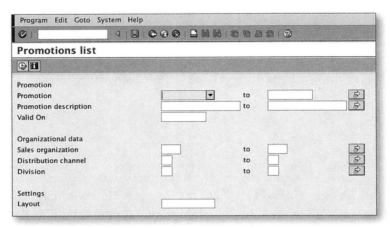

⌃ *Figure 1* *Promotions List*

The list that the report produces, shown in Figure 2, will show you the promotion, description, and validity period. All these promotions have been created in Transaction VB31.

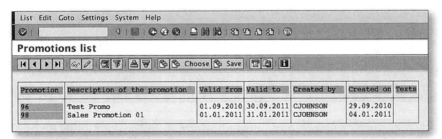

⌃ *Figure 2* *List of Promotions Including the Description and Validity Date*

By looking at this list you'll be able to track the currently valid promotions in your company. You can also look at the history of past promotions to know what's been offered to customers in a period of time.

Double-click on a given promotion and look at the details. This will take you to the DISPLAY PROMOTION screen (Transaction VB33; see Figure 3), and from here you can look at every detail.

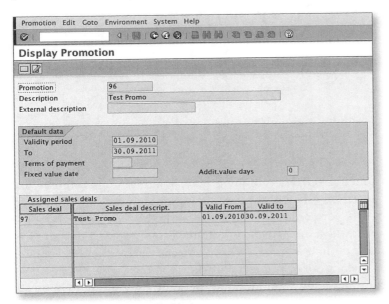

⊼ *Figure 3 Promotion Details Display*

If you double-click again on any of the assigned sales deals, it will show you the detail for that deal, taking you to Transaction VB23. You can also click on the CONDITIONS button and see the discount conditions that apply for that deal.

Tip 17

Tracking Item Proposals

You can trace what items are suggested to be sold together with a simple report and make sure they're up-to-date.

In the SAP ERP system you build lists of items that should be suggested together with a main item, which are called item proposals. A very famous example would be if you want fries with your order or a pie with your milkshake. If your system's configuration allows it, these items will be automatically proposed during sales order creation. The list of item proposals helps you keep track of how many item proposals a material belongs to or is the main item of. In this tip, we'll show you how to use this report to review item proposals periodically to keep them up-to-date with your company's objectives and prevent them from becoming obsolete.

And Here's How ...

Before you get started, make sure that you have item proposals existing in the system already (Transaction VA51). To look at the list of item proposals for a material, use Transaction VA55 or follow the path:

> LOGISTICS • SALES AND DISTRIBUTION • MASTER DATA • PRODUCTS • ITEM PROPOSAL •
> LIST BY MATERIAL

In the initial screen of this report, enter the material number of the item you're looking for. Validity periods and/or document creation dates are also helpful. One field that's very often overlooked is MY ITEM PROPOSALS. This selection field allows the users to only display those item proposals created by their own user ID.

Press the ⌈Enter⌉ key, and you'll be prompted for the sales area of the document (sales organization, distribution channel, and division). The result of running the report is a list of all the item proposals of which the material you entered is part (see Figure 1).

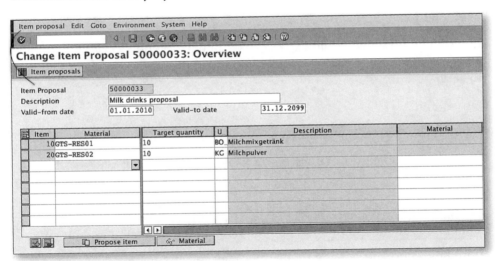

≫ **Figure 1** All Item Proposals for a Material

From this list, you can identify how many proposals use your material, check their validity dates (Figure 1), and if you double-click on any line, you can see the details and maintain the item proposal.

≫ **Figure 2** Maintaining the Item Proposal

To be able to maintain item proposals from this report, as shown in Figure 2, you need to have "change" privileges for Transaction VA52. Otherwise you'll only be able to display the list.

Listing Competitive Products in a Product Hierarchy

If your company keeps records of competitive products sold by other companies, you can create lists in the system to keep them up-to-date and track similar products between companies.

Competitive products are those materials created in the SAP ERP system using the material type WETT (competitive product). These materials correspond to materials made and sold by your competition and that you want to keep track of.

In this tip, we'll show you how to keep track of the *competitive products* that you've entered in the system so that you don't lose visibility of them and you can keep them up-to-date.

And Here's How ...

To access the report, use Transaction VCR1 or follow the path:

> LOGISTICS • SALES AND DISTRIBUTION • SALES SUPPORT • INFORMATION SYSTEM •
> COMPETITIVE PRODUCTS

With this report you can find competitive materials in a product hierarchy as well as find products sold by your company that are similar to your competition's products.

You find these products by using the three input fields in the selection screen: PRODUCT HIERARCHY, MATERIAL NUMBER, and INFORMATION STRUCTURE (see Figure 1). It's very important that you don't change the info structure number that appears on this screen unless your specific configuration requires otherwise.

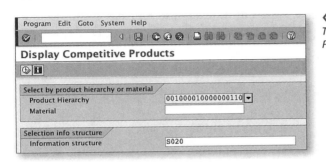

《 *Figure 1* Search Screen for Transaction Display Competitive Products

Enter a value in the product hierarchy field to get a list of all the materials that belong to that hierarchy structure. The list, shown in Figure 2, contains both OWN MATERIALS and COMPETITIVE MATERIALS, and this is indicated in one column of the report.

Here you'll either see the legend "own material" or the competitor number, which has been assigned in the basic data view of the material master. This competitor number is a customer number already existing in the system with account group 0006 Competitor.

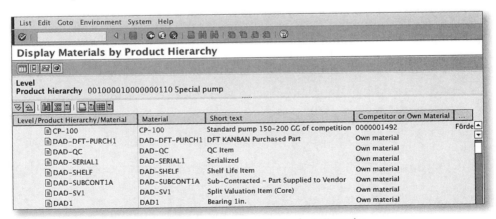

《 *Figure 2* List All Materials That Belong to a Specific Product Hierarchy

To find which materials are sold by your company that are similar to a competitor's, enter a competitive product material number. The resulting list, as shown in Figure 3, will contain all of your company's products that belong to the same product hierarchy as the competitive product you entered in the search screen.

This can help you, for example, if you find out a customer has been offered a certain material by your competitor and you want to offer an equivalent product from your company.

⩘ **Figure 3** *List of Materials That Belong to the Same Product Hierarchy as the Competitive Product*

Part 3
Sales

Things You'll Learn in this Section

Sales transactions capture all activities from initial inquiries to sales contract creation to sales order creation. You must be proactive and efficient to improve the effectiveness of your order fulfillment. While you're already familiar with sales order creation transactions, there are a lot of dynamics in the order life cycle that are overlooked and forgotten. In this part of the book, we'll walk you through a few transactions and reports that can help you to be a more efficient, proactive SD user.

Adjusting the Layout of Your Order Entry Screen

When you process a large number of sales orders, you can adjust your column layout to be more efficient.

All transaction screens in SAP are designed to satisfy almost any business scenario you can imagine. However, sometimes it's difficult to populate these screens with speed and accuracy when sliders, selection bars, and tabs get in the way. In this tip, we'll show you how to customize the columns, sequence, and position in your sales order screen to make your data entry very efficient.

✓ And Here's How ...

To enter the screen to create the sales order, use Transaction VA01 or follow the menu path:

> LOGISTICS • SALES AND DISTRIBUTION • SALES • ORDER • CREATE

When you open the order entry screen, you'll usually start on the SALES tab when you enter the item data. You can rearrange the columns' positions in the list of ALL ITEMS by clicking on the column heading and dragging it to a desired position. When arranging the columns, think about the sequence of the data entry, and position them with the most frequently used on the left side. Once you're satisfied with your new column arrangement, click on the CONFIGURE icon in the upper right corner of the display list to save your settings (see Figure 1).

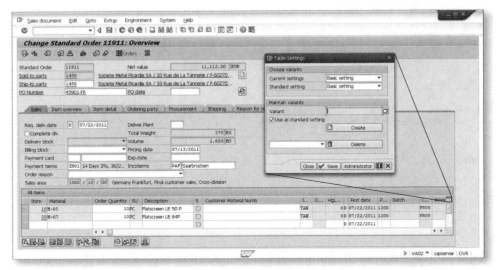

Here you can save your variant and you can also decide how you want this variant to be used. In the MAINTAIN VARIANT section (click the icon shown in Figure 1), enter a variant name, make sure the USE AS STANDARD SETTING check box is marked if you intend to use it as a default, click on the CREATE icon, and then click on the SAVE icon to complete the process.

You can review all of the sales order data tabs and the configuration settings and adjust them using the same method described above. Note the indicator USE AS STANDARD SETTINGS, which means that all users will see the same default screen variant. Typically this is protected by security to avoid such problems.

The ADMINISTRATOR button on the TABLE SETTINGS popup shown in Figure 1 allows you to access additional features that are normally limited to a small group of people who are allowed to maintain them globally (these people must have authorization object S_ADMI_FCD). Administrator functions allow you to change the current configuration of the table control by hiding columns, changing the number of fixed columns and the separator lines, and displaying field length and position (see Figure 2).

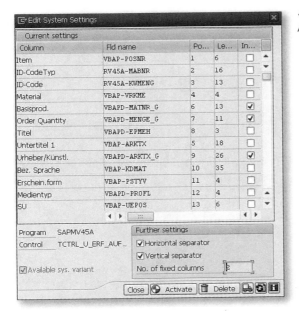

« Figure 2 *Administrator Variant Maintenance View*

You can always change your variant by selecting from the TABLE SETTINGS popup and choosing your CURRENT SETTING and STANDARD SETTINGS using the dropdowns as shown in Figure 3.

« Figure 3 *Choose Screen Variant*

You can now successfully maintain your personal preferences for sales order screen list layouts.

Processing Incomplete Sales Documents

You can use one transaction to complete data in sales documents that can't be finalized due to various checks set in the system.

Your sales documents are subject to incompletion check procedures that prevent them from being available for further processing. Missing data can cause your business a multitude of consequences from penalties to loss of business. The incompletion checks can also make searching for a particular sales document that needs completion almost impossible. In this tip, we'll show you an easy way to bypass all of these pain points.

And Here's How ...

To complete data for sales documents, start with Transaction V.00. Notice that the initial screen opens up with preselected sales document type value set to 0 – Sales Orders. To execute this transaction, you can also follow the menu path:

> INFORMATION SYSTEMS • GENERAL REPORT SELECTION • SALES AND DISTRIBUTION • SALES • WORKLISTS • INCOMPLETE SD DOCUMENTS

You can access the same information by executing Transaction V.02, which shows the sales document values pre-set to blanks. Other than that, execution steps are identical. Follow these menu path steps to start the incompletion log:

> SALES AND DISTRIBUTION • SALES • INFORMATION SYSTEM • ORDERS • INCOMPLETE ORDERS

On the initial screen of the transaction, specify the following information:

▶ INCOMPLETENESS
Check the appropriate boxes for areas of incompleteness like price determination.

▶ ORGANIZATIONAL DATA
This may also limit the number of records returned for processing, so fill in the SALES AREA data whenever possible.

▶ DOCUMENT INFORMATION
Specify the created by or choose the SD transaction, selecting the document types you want to be processed (see Figure 1 for allowed sales document types).

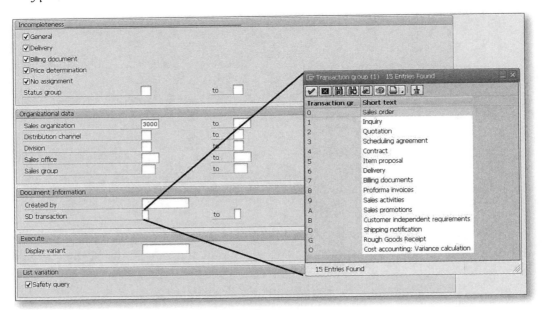

⌃ **Figure 1** *Incomplete SD Documents Selection Screen*

Once you've completed the information, click on the EXECUTE icon or press F8 to run the report. On the following screen, you'll see the list of all incomplete documents showing summary in the basic list.

You'll find there the SD document type, information about creation, incompleteness types, and total number of incomplete fields (see Figure 2).

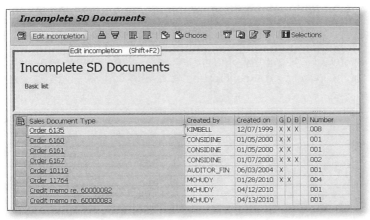

≫ *Figure 2 Incomplete SD Documents Basic List*

Select the appropriate sales order line, and click on the EDIT INCOMPLETENESS button or press Shift + F2. In our example shown in Figure 3, you'll be redirected to Transaction VA02 (Sales Order Change) incompletion screen, which will allow you to update the missing data.

Select the line of incompletion you wish to change, and click on the EDIT INCOMPLETE DATA button or press F2. You'll be sent to the actual order field that needs to be maintained. Complete the data entry and then click on the EDIT NEXT DATA button or press F2 to return to the incompletion log. Once all order data is complete, save your order by clicking on the SAVE button or press Ctrl + S to return to the incompletion report list.

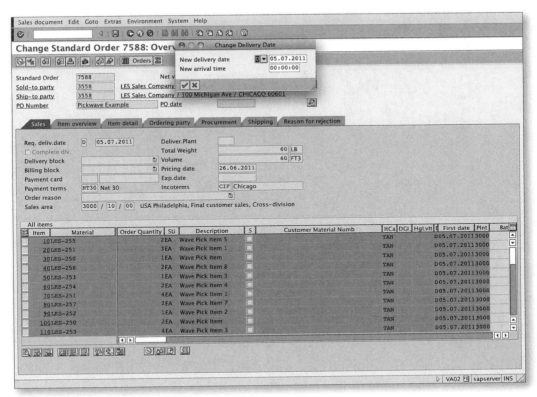

⌃ *Figure 3* Change Order Incompletion Data Screen

You've now entered all missing data reported by your sales document incompletion procedures.

Executing a Sales Order Quick Change

You can quickly and easily change sales order item data en masse when something unexpected pops up.

You know the story: It's Friday afternoon, you're ready to go home, and then you get a call from your customer telling you that their order will need to be express delivered. No problem, right? The only thing between you and your weekend is changing the delivery priority for 167 order items.

In the SAP system, the attributes of a sales order reside at the item level; changing a large order can prove to be very challenging, tedious, and time-consuming. In this tip, we'll show you how to bypass these problematic changes to sales orders for rejection, delivery date, shipping priority, billing block, delivery block, and shipping plant.

 And Here's How ...

Go to Transaction VA02 or follow the path:

> LOGISTICS • SALES AND DISTRIBUTION • SALES • ORDER • CREATE

Enter the sales order number you want to change and press Enter. In the CHANGE SALES ORDER: OVERVIEW screen, select the items you want to modify manually or select all items using the SELECT ALL button at the bottom of the screen. Once you've selected the items, click on EDIT • QUICK CHANGE OF...

Here you'll see a few different options, and each will lead you to a different sub-screen as shown in Figure 1. Note that the data you enter will apply to all of the items you select, so choose the items carefully.

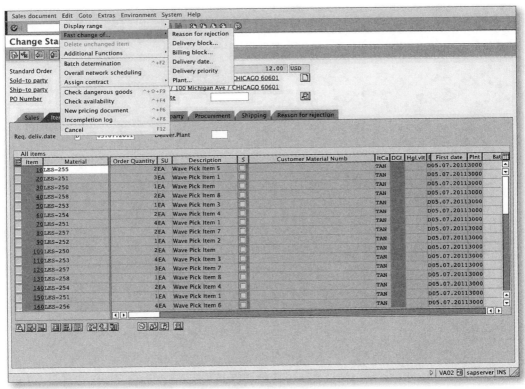

⌃ *Figure 1* Change Order Item Screen with Fast Change of... Menu

Let's discuss some of the menu options you'll come across.

▶ REASON FOR REJECTION: This option will allow you to reject or cancel several items from an order at one time. When you select this option, the system will prompt you to enter the reason code for rejecting the items.

▶ DELIVERY BLOCK...: This option will allow you to prevent some or all items from being shipped by the warehouse. A delivery block will prevent the creation of an outbound delivery order. When you select this option, as shown in Figure 2, the system will prompt you to enter the appropriate delivery block code at either the header or item level.

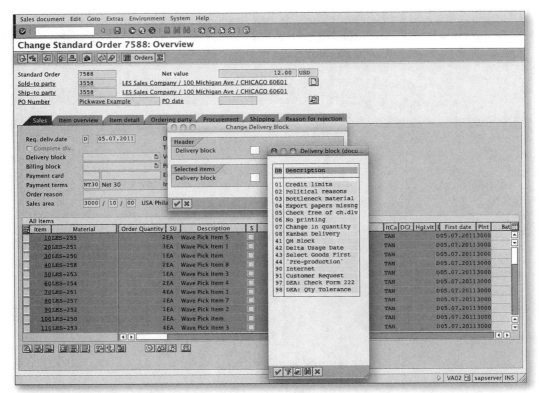

⌃ *Figure 2 Pull-Down Menu for Delivery Block Codes—Similar Menus Appear Depending on the Chosen Quick Change Option*

▶ BILLING BLOCK...: This option will allow you to prevent some or all items from being invoiced. A billing block will prevent the creation of a billing document. When you select this option, the system will prompt you to enter the appropriate billing block code at either the header or item level.

▶ DELIVERY DATE...: This option will allow you to update/change the delivery date for the selected items (see Figure 3).

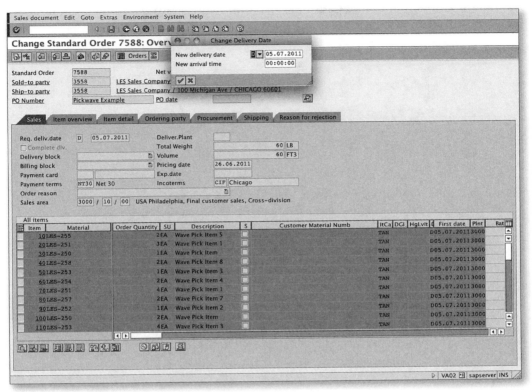

⩔   *Figure 3* *Window for Entering the New Delivery Date.*

▶ DELIVERY PRIORITY: This option will help you change the delivery priority for
the selected items. You can use this to expedite or delay a customer delivery.

▶ PLANT…: You can use this option to change the plant where the selected items
will be shipped from. This might help you accommodate changes in production
balancing or priorities.

Processing Backorder SD Documents to Manage Customer Priority

You can adjust or short shipments for one customer to supply a more important customer, or simply fill a shipment that needs to go out immediately.

Let's say you have a shortage of a material that's appearing on several sales orders. Due to that shortage, some of the orders will be subject to backorder processing. Your ATP (available-to-promise) check results change dynamically during the day and stock could become available or, simply using the pull of quantities on hand and customer master priority, you can realign commitments automatically.

Your orders with committed material quantities have dates that allow you to adjust quantities. We have a couple of ways to change your committed orders. We'll cover Transaction V_RA, which allows for data selection using sales document. You can also use Transaction CO06 (covered in Tip 23) to manipulate your commitments using the material number as selection criteria.

✓ And Here's How ...

To short shipments of items that were backordered using the sales order as selection criteria, start with Transaction V_RA or follow the menu path:

> LOGISTICS • SALES AND DISTRIBUTION • SALES • BACKORDERS • BACKORDER PROCESSING • SD DOCUMENTS

On the initial screen of the transaction (see Figure 1), specify the following:

▶ MATERIAL NUMBER (or a range you want to process): To see all backorders, simply enter material range covering all of your material numbers. In first box enter 0 and in the second box enter ZZZZZZZZZZ. See Figure 1 for initial screen details.

▶ PLANT: There's a plant range available if you're processing backorders for a specific location(s).

▶ CUSTOMER DATA: Narrow your selection further by filling in this section.

▶ ORGANIZATIONAL DATA: Use this to limit the number of records returned for processing; fill in the sales area data whenever possible.

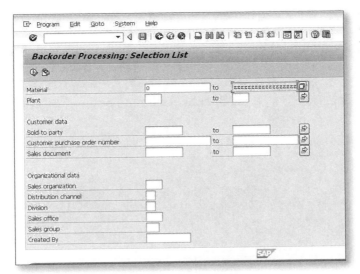

« *Figure 1 Backorder Processing Selection Screen*

After executing the screen, you'll get a list of the materials that meet your initial selection criteria. Each report line will show details including material, sales document, delivery date, order quantity, confirmed quantity, and open quantity (see Figure 2).

Drill into the individual sales documents to display details by double-clicking on the specific line. This will open the order in change mode, like running an order change transaction where you can re-run availability check or make other changes directly.

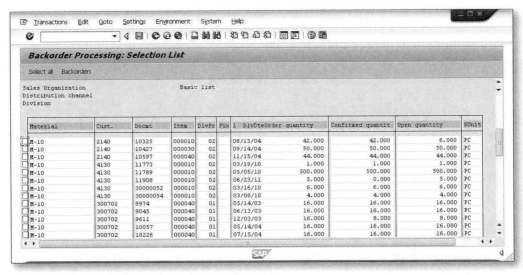

⩘ *Figure 2* Backorder Processing Selection List

Select a line for processing, and click on the BACKORDER button or press F8 (see Figure 3).

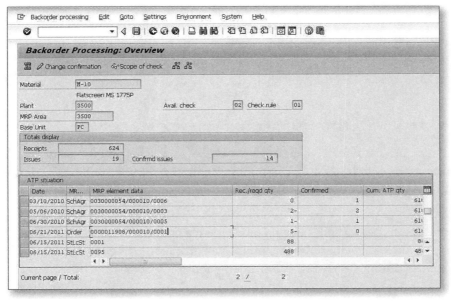

⩘ *Figure 3* Backorder Processing Overview

Just like in Transaction CO06, the overview displays all requirements, dates, MRP elements, requirement quantities, and confirmed quantities. Your sales order will be highlighted and this will be the only element that you'll be allowed to change or update. Select the element you want to update and click on the CHANGE CONFIRMATION button or press F2.

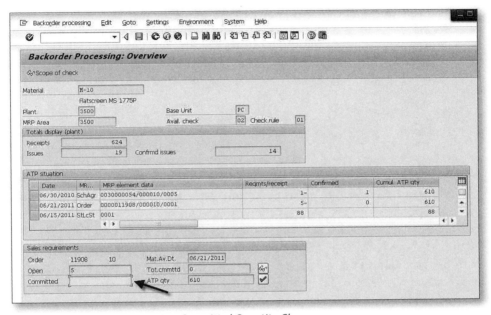

⨠ *Figure 4* *Backorder Processing Committed Quantity Change*

Once you're satisfied with the updated committed quantities, as shown in Figure 4, press Enter or click on the COPY button to return to the BACKORDER OVERVIEW screen. Save your changes. This action will save all backorders where some already-committed sales orders could be uncommitted and vice-versa, also allocating stock and causing potential future backorders. This is a very common case when large sales orders are processed in nightly batches.

Tip **23**

Processing Backorders: Changing Committed Quantities

You can quickly adjust stock commitments between orders with confirmed and unconfirmed quantities to ship to customers who have higher priorities.

If you have a bunch of sales orders for a specific material that commonly has procurement issues, it can cause numerous backorders. The goods receipts for incoming purchase orders or production orders will suddenly make the materials available. Let's say you also have sales orders for a specific material with committed quantities, but your delivery dates are far in the future and you have other orders with delivery dates coming up shortly. If you don't realign committed stock to fulfill orders with approaching delivery dates due to all the changes to your stock balances and processing priorities, you may run into a logistical nightmare.

Because standard SAP order entry is based on first come-first serve, backorder processing helps to overcome this ATP allocation problem. In this tip, we'll show you how to perform the adjustments needed in your system to maximize your profits and keep your customers happy.

And Here's How ...

To process backorders by changing committed quantities for a specific material, execute Transaction CO06 or follow the menu path:

> LOGISTICS • SALES AND DISTRIBUTION • SALES • BACKORDERS • BACKORDER PROCESSING • MATERIAL

On the initial screen, enter your selection criteria, including the following fields:

▶ MATERIAL: The material-in-stock shortages that need attention

▶ PLANT: Your delivery plant

▶ MRP AREA: An optional field that you can leave blank

▶ CHECKING RULE: Use A-SALES ORDER; this is an optional field, however

▶ SPECIAL STOCK SALES ORDER: Use this field if you deal with sales order stock; otherwise, leave it blank

▶ SPECIAL STOCKS WBS ELEMENT: Use this field if you work with project stock; otherwise, leave it blank

Once you're done with selection data entry, press Enter or click on the green check mark. This will display the BACKORDER PROCESSING OVERVIEW list (displayed in Figure 1), which shows deliveries and sales orders in chronological order starting with the oldest first. Note that customer sales orders in this report are highlighted with a light blue color and are labeled ORDER in the MRP ELEMENT column.

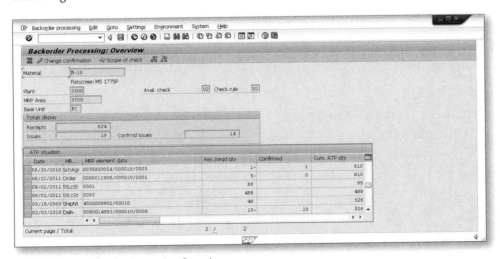

⋀ **Figure 1** Backorder Processing Overview

To adjust committed material from one customer sales order that's shown with a positive value in the CONFIRMED column, to an unconfirmed customer sales order that's shown with quantity of 0 in the CONFIRMED column, find the order you want to remove or change confirmation. Then select the listed sales order line by clicking on the selection block on the left side of the report and click on the CHANGE CONFIRMATION button.

A sub-screen will be displayed at the bottom of the report where you can enter your changed/lowered quantity or zero-out the entire quantity shown in the field COMMITTED. Click on the COPY button. This will make the committed quantity available for other orders that require immediate stock confirmation. The quantity committed section should be blank.

Next, confirm the available material to a sales order that lacks the committed quantity. To do this, execute the same steps as before, locate the order in need of material, select the line again by clicking on the selection block on the left side of the report, and click on the CHANGE CONFIRMATION button.

On the bottom of the report sub-screen, you'll see 0 as the quantity shown in the TOT.CMMTTD field (see Figure 2).

⌃ *Figure 2 Zero Committed Quantity Ready for Adjustment*

Change the committed quantity value to the desired quantity and make sure you don't exceed the REQMTS/RECEIPT QUANTITY column. Click on the COPY icon to confirm the selected order line.

With this action (similar to Tip 22), you'll save all updated backorders where some already committed sales orders could be uncommitted and vice-versa, also allocating stock and causing potential future backorders.

Note that your unconfirmed orders will need to be manually re-confirmed once stock becomes available.

Tip (24)

Running a Backorder Report for Financial Impact Summary

You can generate a backorder report summary to show you exactly how your results are impacted by backorders in dollars and cents.

If you're in sales, you need to know if your performance is affected by the logistics and procurement backlogs. There are multiple transactions and reports in SAP that allow you to perform different actions, such as rescheduling and the backorder commitment changes that we've covered in other tips in this part of the book already. None of these reports, however, show you the financial impact summary in a simple and easy-to-understand way. Let's learn how to do this.

✓ And Here's How ...

To review your backorder report, execute Transaction V.15 or follow the menu path:

> SALES AND DISTRIBUTION • SALES • INFORMATION SYSTEM • ORDERS • DISPLAY BACKORDERS

On the initial screen of the report, you can narrow down your queries by specifying data. If you repeat your entries, you can save them as variant, just like with any other SAP reports. The selection screen (shown in Figure 1) of this report includes:

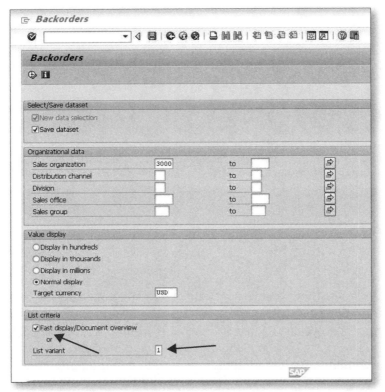

⤒ *Figure 1* Backorders Data Selection Screen

▶ SELECT/SAVE DATASET: When you select the NEW DATA SELECTION radio button, the system will execute a new query, and by choosing SAVE DATASET, the system will display results of the previous backorder display run. If you select both, you'll create a new dataset and save it for further use. The LAST DATA SELECTION date field will show you how old your last dataset is.

▶ ORGANIZATIONAL DATA: Specify the sales organization data you're running the report for. Always make your selection as narrow as possible since all backorder reports are very resource intensive.

▶ VALUE DISPLAY: Here you can choose how values are displayed and what currency is used as a base.

▶ LIST CRITERIA: Here you can choose how your report will look. By selecting FAST DISPLAY/DOCUMENT OVERVIEW, you'll get a summary header of information followed by the LIST VARIANT selected data, chosen from available options.

The available variants for this report are:

▶ MONTHLY OVERVIEW SUMMARY: Shows you the confirmed order value of backorders displayed in monthly buckets using the goods issue date to determine the month (see Figure 2).

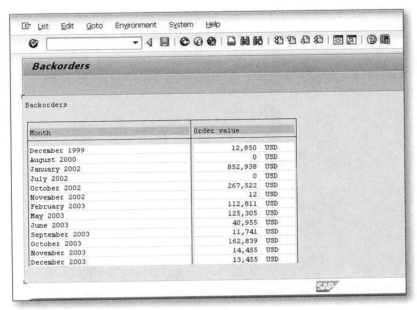

⌃ *Figure 2* Backorders Monthly Summary List

▶ CUSTOMER LIST VARIANT: Your backorders are sorted by order/customer number, showing backorder values.

▶ MATERIAL LIST VARIANT: Orders are sorted by order/material number, showing backorder values on the goods issue date (shown in Figure 3).

▶ CUSTOMER/MATERIAL LIST VARIANT: This will show you both lists; customer first and material variant second.

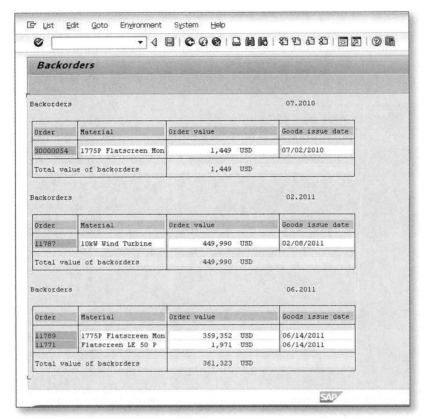

⋩ *Figure 3 Backorders Material List View*

Once your selections are made, click on the EXECUTE button or press ⌈F8⌉. You can also use your pull-down menu options and choose your start selection from there. On the next screen you'll see data presented accordingly to your orders; orders still due for shipping are displayed in this list with order values. Note that order values are determined from the confirmed quantities of the order items. The list is also sorted by goods issue date, shipping point, and ship-to party.

From this report you can open sales transactions VA02 (Order Change) or VA03 (Order Display), where you can make changes as needed.

Automating Material Reallocation and Rescheduling Based on Delivery Priority Settings

You can process your sales orders and re-run availability to recommit your inventory based on delivery priority.

When you enter sales orders into the system, stock is promised to each of the documents on a first-come, first-serve basis. This doesn't take into account that some of your customers are more important than others and the limited supply of material should be offered to them first. In this tip, we'll show you a way to automate this and execute rescheduling when either more products become available, or simply to fill priority one deliveries and ship them immediately by taking stock from a customer with a lower delivery priority setting.

✓ And Here's How ...

To access the rescheduling transaction, execute Transaction V_V2 or follow the menu path:

> LOGISTICS • SALES AND DISTRIBUTION • SALES • BACKORDERS • RESCHEDULING • EXECUTE

This automated method will use delivery priority settings proposed from a customer master or customer material info record. The system will sort the orders based on the delivery priority, reshuffling committed quantities to orders of a higher priority. (See Tip 26 for details on these influencing factors and Rescheduling Evaluation transaction details.)

You should always run this job in a background mode during the time when system resources aren't critical since this transaction can dramatically affect system performance.

To execute rescheduling in the foreground mode, fill out the following sections (see initial screen in Figure 1):

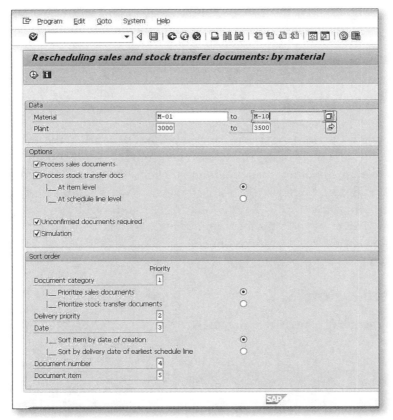

⌃ *Figure 1* Rescheduling Selection Screen

▶ DATA: Select your material or range of materials and plants in scope for rescheduling.

- OPTIONS: Select the following objects:
  - Select what kind of documents you are rescheduling; checkmark PROCESS SALES ORDERS.
  - If you want to include STOCK TRANSFER DOCUMENTS, select the radio button (shown in Figure 1).
  - Specify if the line item or a schedule line detail should be taken into consideration.
  - You'll be carrying out rescheduling for documents with at least one uncon-firmed transaction. If you select UNCONFIRMED DOCUMENTS REQUIRED, you'll increase the number of records for processing.
  - Select SIMULATION if you want to review the proposed changes. When ready, simply deselect this option before the true execution takes place and updates your documents.
- SORT ORDER: Define the priority for processing your order items. Priority 1 is highest priority and priority 5 is the lowest. If you want to exclude specific cri-teria, enter 0 in the priority field. The items and schedule lines found in the selection are sorted according to these criteria:
  - DOCUMENT CATEGORY: Either sales documents or STO's
  - DELIVERY PRIORITY: Obtained from customer master or info record
  - DATE: Creation date of the item or earliest schedule line date, document num-ber, and document item
  - DOCUMENT NUMBER: Sequential order of your documents
  - DOCUMENT ITEM: Document line item number

When you're ready to run the simulation, click on the EXECUTE button or press F8 to see the list of the proposed changes for your review (see Figure 2).

Next comes the checking rule selection. A checking rule defines the checking pro-cedure for the availability check, taking into account, for example, purchase orders, reservations, and production orders; this is all set in IMG configuration. Checking rule A is used by default as a basis for rescheduling sales orders. Use checking rule B for rush order exceptions, and for orders with individual customer stock, use checking rule AE.

A list of proposed changes will show you materials, customer account numbers, documents, order quantities, and old and new confirmed dates.

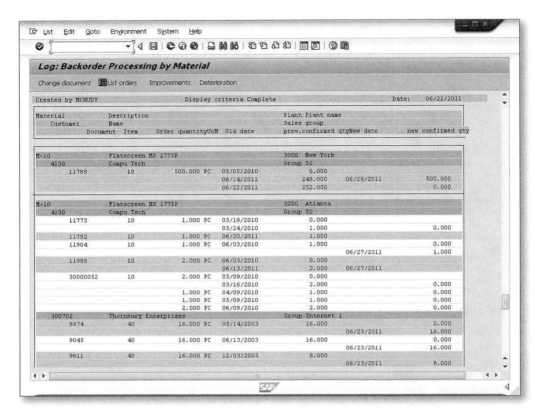

⌃ **Figure 2** *List of Proposed Rescheduling Changes*

If errors are displayed, you can review the log by using the pull-down menu (selecting EDIT • ERROR LOG) as shown in Figure 3.

⌃ **Figure 3** *Error Log Display*

By double-clicking on the listed sales orders or by clicking on the CHANGE DOCU-MENT button, you can open orders in change mode, allowing you to make modifications as needed, like running Transaction VA02.

Another useful feature included on this list is the LIST ORDERS button, which links you directly to Transaction VA05 (Order List).

You can also change the scope of the list by clicking on the IMPROVEMENTS button. Change the scope of the list again by clicking on the DETERIORATION button.

Once you review the results, return to the main selection screen, deselect the SIMULATION radio button, and click on EXECUTE or press ⌈F8⌋. You'll be prompted to accept your action.

Tip 26

Evaluating a Rescheduling Job

If some of your important customers didn't get their orders for priority processing once you rescheduled jobs, you can review the results to make sure the strategies you have in place actually execute the intended changes per plan.

As mentioned in Tip 25, you can evaluate the results of your rescheduling run. If your results weren't exactly what you expected, you should review some of the supporting master data that's considered when rescheduling is applied (such as the delivery priority that's maintained in the customer master). In this tip, we'll show you how to find and analyze the results and determine if the system prioritized the orders according to your needs.

✅ And Here's How ...

In order to review the results of your last execution of Transaction V_V2, run Transaction V_R2. Alternatively, follow the menu path:

> LOGISTICS • SALES AND DISTRIBUTION • SALES • BACKORDER • RESCHEDULING • EVALUATE

You can restrict the documents you want to analyze using the selection parameters in the initial screen.

Once you've indicated which documents you want to view, click on the EXECUTE button or press F8. You'll see a list of changes applied in the last rescheduling run (see Figure 1) showing materials, customer account numbers, documents, order quantities, and old and new confirmed dates.

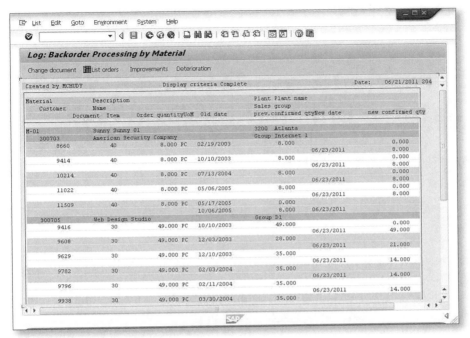

⌃ *Figure 1* Backorder Processing Results Report

Some useful functions of this list include:

▸ The ability to drill into any of the orders displayed by opening them in change mode, allowing you to make changes as needed on the fly. Double-click on the listed sales orders, click on the CHANGE DOCUMENT button, or press ⎡F2⎤.

▸ The LIST ORDERS button links you directly to Transaction VA05 (Order List).

▸ Change the scope of the list by clicking on the IMPROVEMENTS button or pressing ⎡F7⎤ and the DETERIORATION button or ⎡F8⎤.

▸ If any errors were recorded during processing, you can review the log by using the pull-down menu (select EDIT • ERROR LOG) or press ⎡Shift⎤ + ⎡F6⎤.

If you don't like the results of the changes applied, you can go back to the initial rescheduling transaction (V_V2, see Tip 25) and run the update with the original or changed selection criteria.

Processing Sales Documents That Are Blocked for Delivery

You can quickly review and unblock documents that need to be processed for delivery.

Sales orders are defined in such a way that a block can be applied to the document due to configuration settings, credit check, and many other influencing factors. These blocks will prevent them from being available for delivery. Another important fact is that a block can be applied to the header, item, or both. If you have a significant number of orders that go on the delivery block, you need to review and unblock these orders immediately to prevent a loss of revenue.

✓ And Here's How ...

To review and remove delivery block from sales documents, start with Transaction VA14L or follow the menu path:

> SALES AND DISTRIBUTION • CREDIT MANAGEMENT • SALES AND DISTRIBUTION DOCUMENTS • SALES AND DISTRIB. DOCUMENTS BLOCKED FOR DELIVERY

On the initial screen of the transaction (shown in Figure 1), specify the following fields:

▶ CUSTOMER: If you know the customer or a range of numbers, enter it here.

▶ HEADER BLOCK: Select the type of delivery header block (this report doesn't provide item-level selection options).

▶ ORGANIZATIONAL DATA: You can limit the number of records returned for processing, so fill in the SALES AREA data whenever possible.

- ▶ DOCUMENT INFORMATION: Specify the SD document number or range of numbers and specify SD document category (sales order, contract, etc.).
- ▶ SELECTION CRITERIA: Select OPEN SD DOCUMENTS or ALL SALES DOCUMENTS if you want to see all orders, including processed orders.

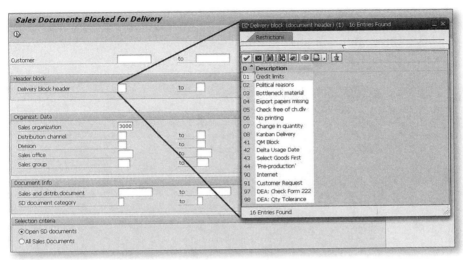

⌃ *Figure 1* SD Documents Blocked for Delivery Selection Screen

Run the report by clicking on the EXECUTE icon or pressing F8. On the following screen you'll see the list of all blocked documents in the ALV list format (Figure 2).

⌃ *Figure 2* SD Documents Blocked for Delivery Basic List

Here, you'll find the SD document number, SD document category (like sales order, contract), delivery block description and code, required delivery date, sold-to and ship-to account numbers, sales document type, and block data. Select the appropriate sales order line, and click on the EDIT SALES ORDER button or press [Ctrl]+[F10] on your keyboard.

In the example shown in Figure 3, you're basically executing Transaction VA02 (Sales Order Change). Go to the appropriate tab showing the block information where you can review the data and remove the delivery block.

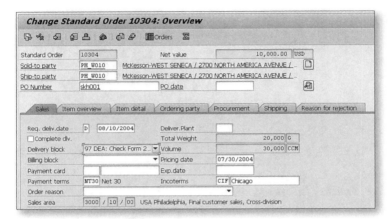

« Figure 3 Change Order Header Data Screen Delivery Block

Select the line data if you need to unblock the items as well. Once all order data is complete, save your order by clicking on the SAVE button or pressing [Ctrl]+[S] to return to the report. You've now successfully unblocked sales documents that were blocked for delivery.

Tip 28

Removing the Billing Block from Sales Documents

You can save time by reviewing documents that have been blocked for billing and removing the block.

Most SAP customers use some sort of a billing block function to prevent sales organizations from processing disputes. If your implementation followed SAP standards, most credit and debit memos will usually end up with an automatic block. This forces your organization to perform a review before releasing for payment, or a wrongfully created debit memo asking your customer to pay for something they may disagree with. However, there's a transaction that will help you to select, display, and allow you to access individual documents and remove billing blocks.

 And Here's How ...

You can review and analyze the sales documents blocked for billing by executing Transaction V23 or following the menu path:

> LOGISTICS • SALES AND DISTRIBUTION • SALES • INFORMATION SYSTEM • WORKLISTS • SALES DOCUMENTS BLOCKED FOR BILLING

On the initial screen, enter selection data that's as detailed as possible to make your report execution more efficient.

You can save your selection criteria as variants, which will make the process more efficient. Once your selection data is specified, click on EXECUTE or press [F8]. You'll see a list of documents ready for review, as shown in Figure 1.

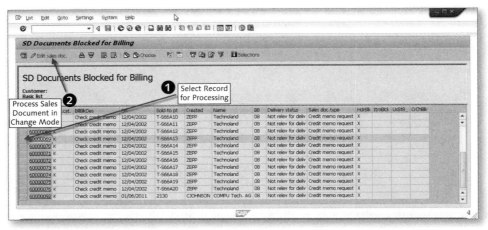

⊼   *Figure 1* SD Documents Blocked for Billing

Here you can select the sales document to be processed. Click on the selection line and then click on the EDIT SALES DOC button to access the sales document change mode (see Figure 2).

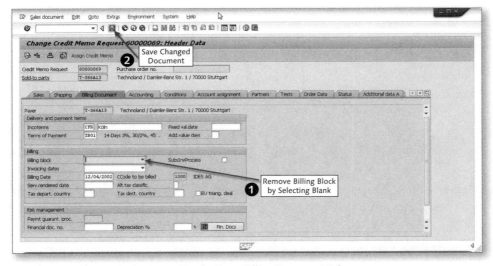

⊼   *Figure 2* Change Credit Memo Header Data Billing Document Tab

Review the sales document and make changes where necessary before you choose to release the billing block. Use the pull-down menus, which you access via the HEADER BILLING DATA tab by following the menu path GOTO • HEADER • BILLING.

Locate the BILLING section and BILLING BLOCK field. Select the DROPDOWN ARROW and remove the billing block by selecting the Blank entry from the list. Click on SAVE or press Ctrl+S on your keyboard to exit the document and return to the blocked document list.

The next time your billing run is executed, the sales document will be processed without the billing block.

Tip **29**

Eliminating Duplicate Sales Documents

You can search for sales orders with the same customer, currency, and total value, and then perform a detailed item level comparison to confirm whether duplication has occurred.

If you're wondering how you can search the system for duplicate sales orders that cost your business extra handling time, return fees, penalties, and internal issues with returns and crediting—you're not alone.

In many types of businesses, duplicate orders are a problem, especially in business-to-business relationships where electronic exchange, as well as phone order placement, is allowed. The SAP system will treat these orders as two individual orders, when really they're one and the same. Your SAP system has a tool in its arsenal to look for and eliminate these suspected orders before they ever hit the warehouse floor.

✅ And Here's How ...

To analyze and clean your system from duplicate orders, execute Transaction SDD1 or follow the menu path:

> Logistics • Sales and Distribution • Sales • Information Systems • Orders • Duplicate Documents

On the selection screen, maintain the fields as needed to make your report execution as selective as possible (see Figure 1). To continue, click on the Execute icon or press [F8].

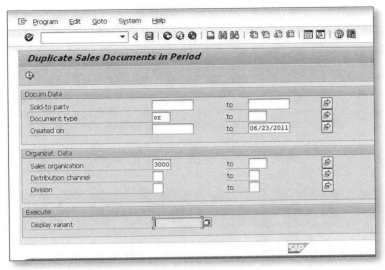

⌃ *Figure 1* Duplicate Documents Selection Screen

On the following screen you'll see a collapsed list of customer accounts that matched your selection criteria from the initial screen. There will either be a green or yellow traffic light in front of them.

▸ A green traffic light indicates that no duplicate sales documents exist for a customer account selected by your query.

▸ A yellow traffic light alerts you that one or more listed sales documents for this customer have the same currency and same total value, meaning you have a potential duplicate order to review.

To determine if customers flagged with the yellow traffic light have true duplicates, click on the EXPAND icon. The list of individual orders will be shown, and you can review the orders listed to see if they're identical or not.

Modify the Report

You can modify the look and feel of this report and filter the data to what is absolutely relevant to efficiently process your day-to-day tasks. For example, you can limit the list down to yellow and red traffic light lines only. Standard reporting tools apply here to manipulate the layouts but you can't save them as variants.

One of your criteria to keep one of the identical orders and delete another is to choose an order with already-recorded activity in the DLSt (Delivery Status) column. Partially processed deliveries with posted goods issue transaction are marked with the red traffic light or marked with the green light if the delivery document has been created, but goods issue wasn't posted yet. See Figure 2 for details.

Remember, you can only select and process two orders at a time. When you're ready, perform comparisons by clicking on the COMPARE icon, or pressing [Ctrl]+[Shift]+[F9]. Alternatively, you can right-click and choose COMPARE to start the process.

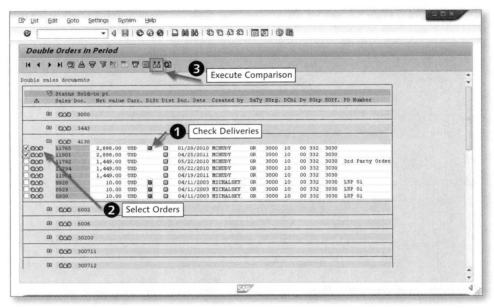

⌃ **Figure 2** Double Orders Execute Comparison

If your comparison returns red traffic lights, all of your line items are an exact match. SAP considers orders for the same customers, purchase order data, same exact items, currencies, and total values to be a match. You can then drill down to each of the duplicate orders to decide which order should be removed.

To cancel sales orders directly, double-click on the orders listed, which will execute Transaction VA02. Click on the DISPLAY ITEM DETAILS icon.

Remember that you can't reject a sales document that's been partially or fully delivered. Once on the item details, fill in the REASON FOR REJECTION field and click on the SAVE button or press [Ctrl]+[S]. This will complete your process and you'll go back to the duplicates report.

Tip 30

Including Kits in Sales Orders

You can sell products bundled into kits more efficiently by using sales bills of materials, while at the same time simplifying the process from sales order creation to picking and billing.

Many companies sell different finished products together to form a kit. A good example is a stereo system with two speakers and a CD player. Very often these items have to be entered separately in the sales order, or they create a new material for the bundle, which then generates problems in the warehouse when you try to pick the individual components.

In this tip, we'll show you how to create a sales BOM (bill of materials), how to include it in a sales order, and how it generates a delivery for the individual components.

And Here's How ...

First, create the new material for the kit or BOM by using Transaction MM01 or following the path:

> LOGISTICS • MATERIALS MANAGEMENT • MATERIAL MASTER • CREATE (GENERAL) • IMMEDIATELY

Create a finished goods (FERT) material or the equivalent that you use in your company. In the SALES VIEW 2, make sure that you select LUMF in the ITEM CATEGORY GROUP (see Figure 1). This will enable the BOM explosion in the sales order.

⌃ Figure 1 *The Value LUMF Triggers the BOM Explosion*

Next, create the BOM for the kit. This is done in Transaction CS01 or via the path:

LOGISTICS • PRODUCTION • MASTER DATA • BILLS OF MATERIAL • BILL OF MATERIAL • MATERIAL BOM • CREATE

Here, you create a list of materials that form the kit. Enter the material number for the kit you created in the previous step and the plant (Figure 2). In the BOM USAGE field, select 5 for sales BOM, and enter the date on which the BOM will start to be valid. Press [Enter] to continue.

⌃ Figure 2 *The BOM Create Screen*

In the next screen, enter all the components for the kit or BOM (Figure 3). Type the different BOM components and their quantities in each line, as shown in Figure 1. You also need to indicate that the item is a stock material by entering "L" in the

ITEM CATEGORY column. After entering all the components, save your work by pressing ⌧F11⌧, and the BOM will be created.

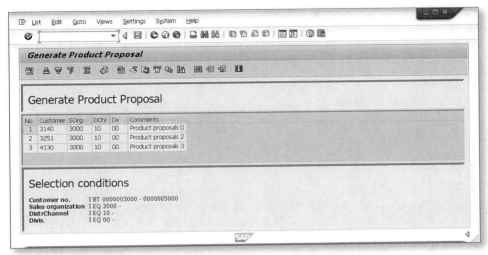

> **Figure 3** *Entering the Components and Component Quantity for Each Kit*

Next, create the sales order with Transaction VA01 or follow the path:

LOGISTICS • SALES AND DISTRIBUTION • SALES • ORDER • CREATE

Enter the order type and the sales area. Press ⌧Enter⌧ to go to the item overview screen. Enter the BOM material and supplying plant (make sure it's the same plant in which you created both the material and the BOM). Press ⌧Enter⌧ again, and the BOM will be exploded and you'll see the components appear under the BOM material creating two new items (see Figure 4).

The BOM explosion is triggered because by having LUMF as the item category group in the material master, the system determines an item category TAP. TAP is a standard-delivered item category that explodes a single-level BOM in the sales order. The pricing for the kit is made up by the individual cost of the kit elements or BOM components. The TAP item is not priced, and the total order price is the sum of all the total item values (see Figure 5).

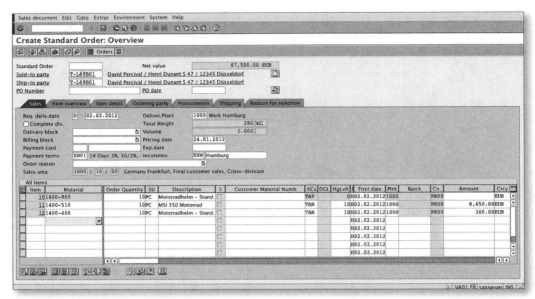

⌄ *Figure 4* The Item Category TAP

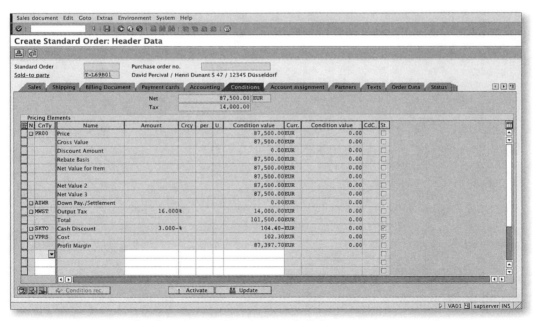

⌄ *Figure 5* Total Order Value Based on the Sum of All the BOM Components Values

Last, create an outbound delivery for the order in Transaction VL01N or follow the path:

> LOGISTICS • LOGISTICS EXECUTION • OUTBOUND PROCESS • GOODS ISSUE FOR OUTBOUND DELIVERY OUTBOUND DELIVERY • CREATE • SINGLE DOCUMENT • WITH REFERENCE TO SALES ORDER

Enter the sales order number and the delivery date for the order. Press Enter and the system will take you to the overview screen. Here you'll see that only the components are relevant for picking, instead of the BOM or kit material, as shown in Figure 6. From here you'll be able to proceed with your regular picking process. Item category TAP isn't relevant for picking or warehouse management activities.

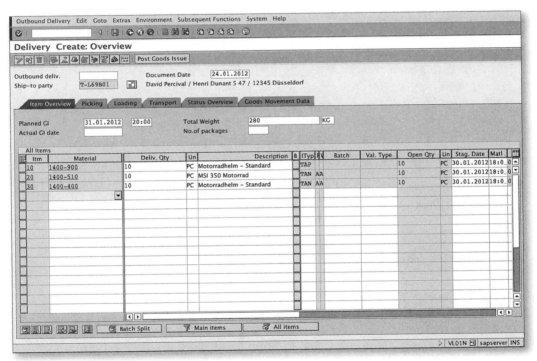

⟰ *Figure 6 The BOM Material Not Relevant for Picking*

The BOM material will appear as completely picked after all the components are completely picked.

Tip **31**

Updating a List of Sales Orders en Masse

You can easily and automatically update sales orders data like pricing, change materials, or delivery plants en masse and create a report in Microsoft Excel.

You may have come across a situation where you need to apply a change in pricing, material, or supplying plant that affects several of the sales orders. Instead of processing each order individually, you can update them and send an exported list to the shipping department to make sure they supply the right product from the correct location based on your last-minute changes.

And Here's How ...

To execute a mass update to your open sales orders and to create an Excel extract, run Transaction VA05 or follow the menu path:

> LOGISTICS • SALES AND DISTRIBUTION • SALES • INFORMATION SYSTEM • ORDERS • LIST OF SALES ORDERS

You can select orders for your list based on a variety of selection criteria. Depending on what changes you're trying to apply, tailor your selection to be as specific as possible. If you're planning to change material on the sales orders, make sure your selection applies to a subset of data needed. Don't run the report wide open.

Start by selecting your sales area data. Click on the ORGANIZATIONAL DATA button or press [Ctrl]+[F9]. Fill in the SALES ORGANIZATION, DISTRIBUTION CHANNEL, and DIVISION fields at the minimum, and click on CONTINUE or press [Enter]. If you

want to use additional fields, click on the FURTHER SEL CRITERIA button or press
$\boxed{\text{Shift}}$+$\boxed{\text{F8}}$. On the popup you can select up to three additional fields that will
be applied to your selection/filter criteria. To further limit your selection, specify
a SOLD-TO PARTY by entering the customer number or range of customers. You can
also use other partner functions instead of sold-to party, like ship-to or sales rep,
by clicking on the PARTNER FUNCTION button or by pressing $\boxed{\text{Ctrl}}$+$\boxed{\text{F9}}$.

Fill in the MATERIAL field if you're planning to replace a specific material in all
orders that need an update. PURCHASE ORDER NUMBER is an optional field that will
usually limit selection to a single sales order number. Another good way to limit
down the number of orders for your list is to maintain the DOCUMENT DATE for
selection where you can specify the date range. And finally in the section SELEC-
TION CRITERIA, choose if you want to process OPEN SALES ORDERS (recommended
if you're planning to mass update your selection), ALL ORDERS, or MY ORDERS (if
the list is to be limited to orders created by you; see Figure 1).

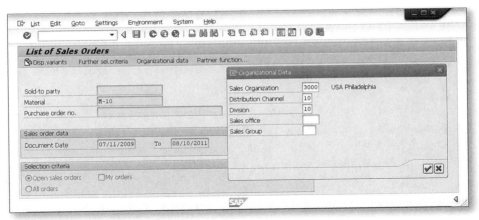

⚠ *Figure 1* *List of Sales Orders Initial Screen*

If you want to modify what information will appear on the following screens, click
on the DISPLAY VARIANT button or press $\boxed{\text{Ctrl}}$+$\boxed{\text{Shift}}$+$\boxed{\text{F8}}$. The three standard
SAP layouts provided will display:

▶ 0SAP, Requests: Order header information

▶ 1SAP, Order Item: Line item details

▶ 3SAP, Orders Schedule: Schedule line details

Execute your report by clicking on the ENTER button or pressing ⸢Enter⸥ on your keyboard. On your lists you can double-click any line of the report to display the sales order, like executing Transaction VA03. Clicking on the BACK icon or pressing ⸢F3⸥ will get you back to the report. You can also sort the list however you wish by clicking in the header of the column you want to sort, and clicking on the SORT IN ASCENDING ORDER or SORT IN DESCENDING ORDER icons. Columns can also be repositioned by click-holding the mouse button and dragging the column header to the new location.

Perform Mass Change

You can execute a mass change on the list of selected orders by first using the pull-down menu path

EDIT • MASS CHANGE • NEW PRICING

In order to apply any of the changes, you must have security permissions that allow you to execute Transaction VA02 (Order Change).

Depending on your business scenario, you can update your order(s) with the following fields:

► NEW PLANT: This will change the delivery plant for your order lines. When selected, you'll get a popup window showing you the current delivery plant and the blank new delivery plant. Populate it with a new value and confirm. Your delivery plant will be replaced in the background.

► NEW MATERIAL: Replaces current material with a substitute. Again, a popup window will be displayed showing you the current material and the blank new material field ready for a substitute material. Your orders will be updated in the background upon confirmation.

► NEW PRICING: This action will allow you to re-price your items. Upon execution the popup window displaying pricing options will be shown. You need to make a selection from the available pricing actions and confirm to apply.

► NEW CURRENCY: This will allow you to change currency.

Sometimes you won't be able to apply changes for different reasons, like a plant not allowed for a sales organization or a material number not extended for use at this sales area. Error messages captured during the mass change process will be displayed in the popup at the end of the process run. You can take steps then to fix the issues and retry the changes manually.

Exporting Sales Order List to Excel

Now you've made your changes and want to export the results to Excel so you can share it with business partners, customers, or other departments.

To export your report, click on LIST • SAVE • FILE. On the popup, choose SPREAD-SHEET, specify a file name and location for your extract file, and then click on the GENERATE button.

Tip **32**

Generating Dynamic Product Proposals for Customers

You can easily speed up the order entry process for your customers by configuring your system to automatically suggest the items they order time and time again, using their past order data.

During sales order creation, you want to use the fastest way to look at past customers' activity to automatically propose lines for new orders. You can exercise several methods for suggesting materials, such as item proposals, customer-material info records, cross selling, and document copy function using past orders. However, these aren't the most efficient ways to automatically propose items based on past activity—we'll show you what is by configuring the SAP system to propose products automatically.

✅ And Here's How ...

In order to automatically create a product proposal, you must have all supporting configuration in place:

- ▶ Customer procedure for product proposal
- ▶ Document procedure for product proposal
- ▶ Assignment of document procedure for product proposal to order types
- ▶ Origin for product proposal
- ▶ Product proposal procedure and determine access sequences
- ▶ Procedure determination for product proposal for background and online mode

Once you verify that your supporting configuration is ready, verify the customer master using Transactions XD02 or VD02. Open the SALES area data tabs where you should find the product proposal procedure assignment as shown in Figure 1.

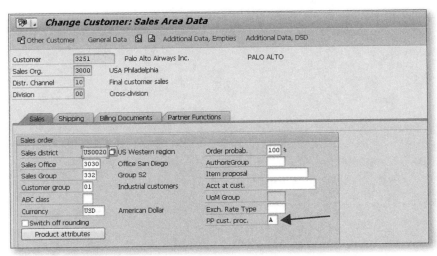

≫   *Figure 1 Customer Master Product Proposal Procedure Assignment*

Next, execute Transaction SDPV or follow the menu path:

LOGISTICS • SALES AND DISTRIBUTION • SALES • ENVIRONMENT • GENERATE PRODUCT PROPOSAL

On the initial screen, enter the customer account number or a range, and specify the sales area data (see Figure 2). Press `F8` to continue.

In our example we accessed the customer order history. Note that if you select online processing, your product proposal procedure is determined using customer and document determination procedures. However, when selecting background processing, only customer procedure is used—document determination procedure isn't available for background processing.

Once the transaction run completes, you'll see a very simple screen listing the number of product proposals, customer accounts, sales area data, and a note in the COMMENTS column telling you the number of product proposals generated (see Figure 3).

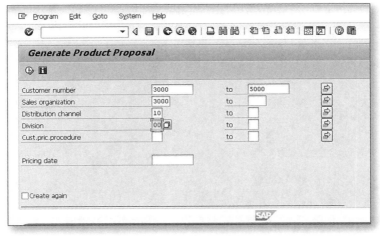

⋩ *Figure 2* *Generate Product Proposal Initial Screen*

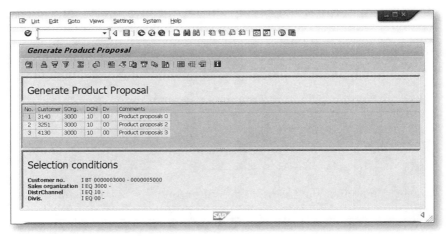

⋩ *Figure 3* *Product Proposal Completed*

Now that you've generated the product proposals, you can create a new sales order using Transaction VA01, and items will be automatically inserted as new lines. You can remove the proposed lines simply by selecting them and deleting if your customer order doesn't call for them. Remember this functionality is most useful for customers that order the same items all the time, so removal of lines should be minimal. Your order entry time and accuracy will benefit immediately. You've completed generation of product proposal.

Checking Material Availability Before Creating a Sales Order

Anytime you create a sales order or plan on using materials, you can easily check material availability so that you don't run into a stock shortage situation.

When you plan the consumption of materials in SAP, you transfer your requirements, which influence the availability check. Requirements can come from sales orders, planned consumption, and planned stock transports, for example. Many factors could influence the availability check results, such as materials that could be potentially provided by an internal production facility or external supplier. In this tip, we'll teach you how to simulate the availability check to verify that materials will be available on the date of your consumption or planned delivery. Using this report, you can identify on what day exactly you'll have stock shortages, alerting you to communicate your concerns to material planners to initiate procurement activities.

✅ And Here's How ...

To run a simulation of the availability check, run Transaction CO09 or follow the menu path:

> LOGISTICS • SALES AND DISTRIBUTION • SALES • ENVIRONMENT • AVAILABILITY OVERVIEW

On the initial screen of the transaction, specify the material, plant, and the checking rule (see Figure 1).

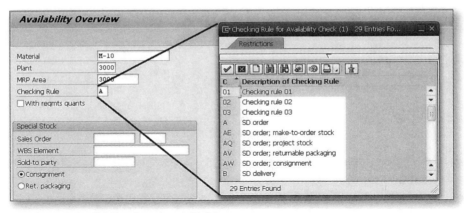

≫ **Figure 1** *Availability Overview Initial Screen*

Using the drop-down menu, select the type of checking rule you need to apply to your scenario (usually rule A: SD ORDERS, B: SD DELIVERIES, or AW: SD ORDER CONSIGNMENT) and press Enter. On the following screen, you'll see a report that shows the results of the simulated availability.

If you don't get anything on your simulation, don't be discouraged. Not all materials require an availability check (this is defined on material master and in the SALES GEN./PLANT view), which you can maintain using Transaction MM02.

You can manipulate the report and arrange displayed results to suit your needs by selecting different options by clicking on available buttons like PERIOD TOTALS (where you can display results in daily, weekly or monthly buckets), STOCK, TOTAL RECORDS, and so on. Click on the SCOPE OF CHECK button to see what types of stock (like safety stock, stock in transfer, or stock in quality inspection), what incoming stock (like materials on pending purchase orders or production orders), and what outbound transactions (like sales orders or reservations) are included in the availability check. These settings are done in configuration and cannot be changed.

Tip 34

Reviewing Expiring Open Quotations

You can display a customer's open quotations and see how they compare to the expiration date.

You have a bunch of open quotations that you've submitted to your customers, and the validity dates are approaching or are past due for subsequent actions. This is very common if you receive EDI quotation requests, which are commonly placed in the system but not always followed up or delayed. You want to find out which of them are still open without any sales activity. You need to follow up with the customers to make sure you address their concerns and see why the expected sales orders aren't placed yet.

In this tip, we'll describe the process required to display expiring quotations for a customer, which produces a list of open quotations that are compared to the expiration date you've entered.

✓ And Here's How ...

To review a customer's expiring quotations, execute Transaction SDQ1 or follow the menu path:

> LOGISTICS • SALES AND DISTRIBUTION • SALES • INFORMATION SYSTEM • QUOTATIONS • EXPIRING QUOTATIONS

On the initial screen, narrow down your selection by specifying as much detail as possible:

▶ DOCUMENT DATA

    ▶ DOCUMENT TYPE: Specify the types of sales documents in scope, like QT (Quotation), for example.

    ▶ PARTNERS: Specify the customer account number or range of accounts.

▶ ITEM DATA: Specify the material or range of material numbers.

▶ ADDITIONAL DATA

    ▶ EXPIRED BY: Quotation expiration date (remember that the current system date is proposed as a default on start of the transaction).

    ▶ CREATED BY: Name of the person who created the quotation document.

When you've filled in all the information, click on the EXECUTE button or press ⌐F8⌐; the report will show the data for your review according to your selection criteria (see Figure 1). This is a pretty basic report, covering just the minimum amount of data required for your assessment of the situation. As you can tell, standard SAP reporting tools are available, allowing you to modify the standard display of fields, filtering, sorting, and more.

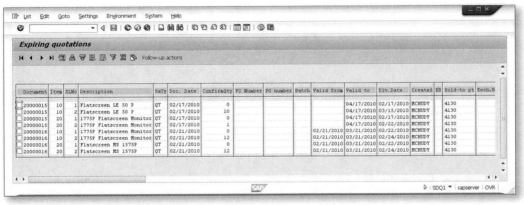

⊗ *Figure 1 Expiring Quotation Document List*

You can use these tools by accessing the ENVIRONMENT option from the pull-down menu on top of the screen. Figure 2 shows available menu options. You can select the radio button on the left of the document number and then execute on the shown document modification options. You can also achieve this by double-clicking directly on data fields in the report.

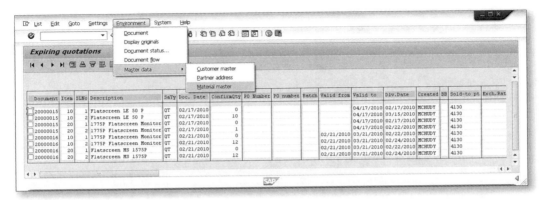

⌃ *Figure 2* Environment Menu Options

The ENVIRONMENT menu also allows you to access various master data objects related to your quotations, such as customer master, partner address, and material master.

When ready, exit the report by clicking on the EXIT button on the screen or pressing `Shift`+`F3`. To exit the transaction completely, repeat the exit steps again. You can also perform follow up actions for each of the quotations you want to update; this is like executing Transaction VA22. You can update the relevant data and follow up with the customer if needed. Upon saving the quotation change, you'll be back in your report. You've successfully reviewed the list of expiring quotations documents.

Note: You can use these transactions to list quotations that have expired or have been completed already:

► SDQ2 (Expired Quotations)
► SDQ3 (Completed Quotations)

Tip 35

Generating a List of Expiring Contracts

You can generate a list of contracts that are fast approaching the expiration dates to find out which are still open with partially processed items or don't have any subsequent activity.

Monitoring contracts is always a complex but very important activity—contracts relate to expiring rebates and other pricing conditions, in addition to the bounding agreement. Just as with quotations, contracts are considered to be open if they have line items with partially processed quantities or no processed quantities at all—basically you have some partial or no subsequent sales documents. Tight control is always needed; in this tip, we'll show you how to monitor your open contracts to achieve the best business results.

✔ And Here's How ...

To review your expiring contracts, execute Transaction SDV1 or follow the menu path:

LOGISTICS • SALES AND DISTRIBUTION • SALES • INFORMATION SYSTEM • CONTRACTS • EXPIRING CONTRACTS

Enter your selection data information (shown in Figure 1). Narrow down your criteria by specifying as much detail as possible:

▶ DOCUMENT DATA

   ▶ DOCUMENT TYPE: Specify the types of contract in scope such as SC (Service and Maintenance) and QC (Quantity Contract)

   ▶ PARTNERS: Specify the customer account number or range of accounts

▶ ITEM DATA: Enter your material or range of material numbers

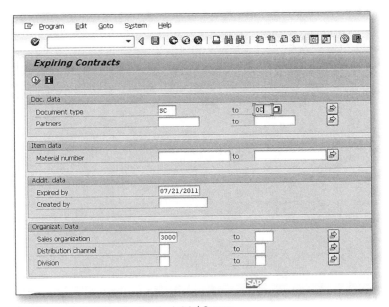

⌃ *Figure 1* *Expiring Contracts Initial Screen*

▶ ADDITIONAL DATA

   ▶ EXPIRED BY: Contract expiration date (remember that the current system date is proposed as a default on start of the transaction)

   ▶ CREATED BY: Name of the person who created the contract

▶ ORGANIZATIONAL DATA: Fill in the SALES ORGANIZATION, DISTRIBUTION CHANNEL, and DIVISION fields

To start the program, click on the EXECUTE button or press [F8]. The report will return the data for your review showing objects that met your selection criteria. This is a basic report covering just the minimum amount of data required for analysis. Standard SAP ALV functions and tools are available that allow you to hide or display fields, filter, sort, and more.

You can also access a document change by executing Transaction VA42, and get to master data objects by using the ENVIRONMENT option from the pull-down menu on top of the screen. Figure 2 shows the menu options. You can select the radio button to the left of the DOCUMENT NUMBER, and then execute on the shown document modification options, or double-click on data fields in the report directly.

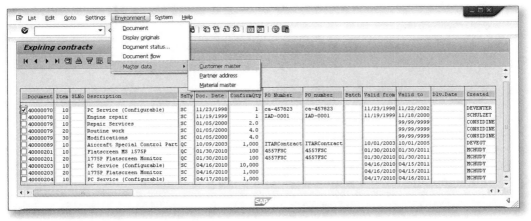

⟰ *Figure 2* *Environment Menu Options*

Use the ENVIRONMENT menu to access various master data objects like:

▸ CUSTOMER MASTER

▸ PARTNER ADDRESS

▸ MATERIAL MASTER

Exit the report by clicking on the EXIT button or pressing ⎡Shift⎤+⎡F3⎤. To exit the transaction completely, repeat the exit steps again. You've successfully reviewed the list of expiring contract documents.

For your reference, you can use the following transactions (in similar fashion as SDV1) to list contracts that have expired or have been completed already:

▸ SDV2 (Expired Contracts)

▸ SDV3 (Completed Contracts)

Tip 36

Generating Companion Sales Analysis for Future Orders

You can automatically determine items that your customers frequently buy together and use them in product proposals when taking new orders.

You've noticed that customers placing orders have a tendency to order a main item, and frequently order another item to go with it (a customer ordering a camera may also order batteries and an extra memory card to go with it). Unlike in Tip 32 where items are suggested from historical order analysis, this tip allows you to serve your customer better by offering items that logically complete each other. This is a perfect opportunity to increase sales numbers as well as customer satisfaction.

And Here's How ...

You can suggest items or products by performing analysis that will be used to automate companion product proposals. These are stored in the database table, which will be automatically used for cross-selling proposal next time you create a sales order; this mechanism is defined in configuration for product proposal. When you create a sales order and enter a material saved in the table as a result of the companion analysis, the system will automatically display a dialog box showing the paired material from the same analysis table, and when you specify the quantity, this companion material is copied to your sales order.

To execute the analysis of companion products, run Transaction SDVK or follow the menu path:

LOGISTICS • SALES AND DISTRIBUTION • SALES • ENVIRONMENT • COMPANION SALES ANALYSIS

You can populate selection criteria on the initial screen of the transaction to narrow down the data pull for analysis; at minimum, specify your sales area data (see Figure 1). Make sure your EXECUTE IDENTIFIER field is set to CROS.

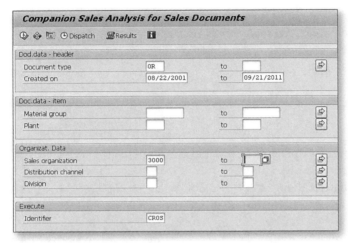

⤒ *Figure 1* Companion Sales Analysis Initial Screen

You can run this report as a background job by clicking on the DISPATCH icon or by pressing [Shift]+[F9]. To start the online version, simply click on the EXECUTE icon or press [F8]. You can review past analysis by clicking on the RESULTS icon or pressing [F5].

You can access the created record in the VCRSALE table, which provides a link to a material and document number for cross-selling analysis using Transaction SE16N. To access the analysis results again, use SE16N and check the VCRSELA_RES table. When you execute the analysis transaction, however, the online version uses the data stored in these tables and will display the analysis report, breaking it into four sections (see Figure 2).

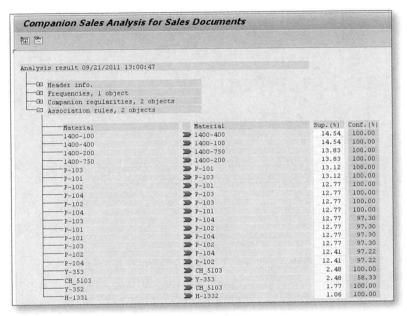

Companion Sales Analysis for Sales Documents

Analysis result 09/21/2011 13:00:47

- Header info.
- Frequencies, 1 object
- Companion regularities, 2 objects
- Association rules, 2 objects

Material	Material	Sup. (%)	Conf. (%)
1400-100	1400-400	14.54	100.00
1400-400	1400-100	14.54	100.00
1400-200	1400-750	13.83	100.00
1400-750	1400-200	13.83	100.00
P-103	P-101	13.12	100.00
P-101	P-103	13.12	100.00
P-102	P-101	12.77	100.00
P-104	P-103	12.77	100.00
P-102	P-103	12.77	100.00
P-104	P-101	12.77	100.00
P-103	P-104	12.77	97.30
P-101	P-102	12.77	97.30
P-101	P-104	12.77	97.30
P-103	P-102	12.77	97.30
P-102	P-104	12.41	97.22
P-104	P-102	12.41	97.22
Y-353	CH_5103	2.48	100.00
CH_5103	Y-353	2.48	58.33
Y-352	CH_5103	1.77	100.00
H-1331	H-1332	1.06	100.00

⌃ *Figure 2* Companion Sales Analysis Results

▶ HEADER INFO

Stores general information about the analysis, such as number of documents and materials processed.

▶ FREQUENCIES, 1 OBJECT

Shows the percentage of total sold per single material.

▶ COMPANION REGULARITIES, 2 OBJECTS

Displays percentage of total sales for a pair of companion materials.

▶ ASSOCIATION RULES, 2 OBJECTS

In this section, the SUP. (%) column displays percentage of total sales for a pair and how frequently the two items were ordered together. In the CONF.(%) column, the statistical score is captured, where 100 identifies a pair that's always ordered together (see Figure 2).

This analysis will be stored and accessed by the product proposal and cross-selling configurations, helping you to improve customer satisfaction and increase product offering and sales numbers.

Tip **37**

Preparing Data for INTRASTAT Declaration

To create the periodic declarations in SAP, you need to have posted goods receipts, invoice receipts, and billing documents completed with accounting documents.

In European Union countries, you must report imports and exports to the appropriate authorities. Goods movements between the EU members must be reported using INTRASTAT declaration, and exports and imports between EU and non-EU partners must be reported with EXTRASTAT declaration. These declarations can be submitted to authorities on paper or electronically. You don't want to have third party or manually generated processes—you want system-generated reports that can be produced within your own organizational structures, ensuring accuracy and audit trace.

✅ And Here's How ...

As long as all your supporting foreign trade master data is in place and all checks are working, this declaration creation process should be easy to execute. We'll show you how to execute INTRASTAT Receipts/Imports.

INTRASTAT Receipt/Import

Use Transaction ENGR or follow the menu path:

> LOGISTICS • SALES AND DISTRIBUTION • FOREIGN TRADE/CUSTOMS • PERIODIC DECLARATIONS • COCKPIT-PERIODIC DECLARATIONS

On the initial screen, choose the CREATE PERIODIC DECLARATIONS button under the OPERATIONS section. On the next screen, choose the country where the declaration has to be sent (select from the INTRASTAT menu on the left pane). For demonstration purposes, we'll show you the creation of an INTRASTAT declaration for Germany as a reporting country.

On the RECEIPT tab, click on the STEP 1 button. Make sure that the DESCRIPTION window shows DATA SELECTION for an entry. If you've maintained any variants for your subsequent transaction screens, you can also specify them before you execute Step 1. Alternatively, you can run Transaction MEIS (Receipt) or follow the menu path:

> LOGISTICS • SALES AND DISTRIBUTION • FOREIGN TRADE/CUSTOMS • PERIODIC DECLA-RATIONS • PERIODIC DECLARATIONS • OPERATIONAL • CREATE PERIODIC DECLARATIONS • EUROPEAN UNION • INTRASTAT • BUSINESS TRANSACTION • RECEIPT

On the initial screen shown in Figure 1, enter the data required for this report to run.

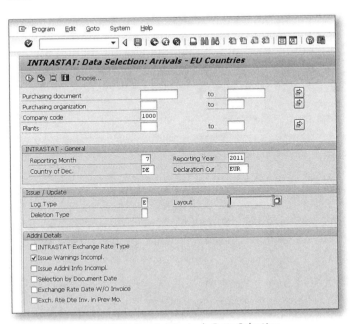

⤢ *Figure 1 INTRASTAT Receipt/Arrivals Data Selection*

Save your selection as a variant by clicking on the SAVE button and giving your variant a name. Execute the report by clicking on the EXECUTE button or pressing [F8].

On the selection log report you'll have all applicable, invoiced purchase orders ready for your review. These orders may have various degrees of incompletion, indicated by the traffic light for COMPLETION STATUS field, shown at the header section of the report.

If you see a red icon there, there's some foreign trade data missing that needs your attention. In the NAVIGATION pane on the left, choose to display the INCOMPLETION LOG. This action will change your current view to show the detail list of missing but required data to complete your INTRASTAT report, as shown in Figure 2. The action icons shown in the CORRECT column enable you to access, review, correct, or simply add any missing data. Click on the EXECUTE icon in the line you want to maintain.

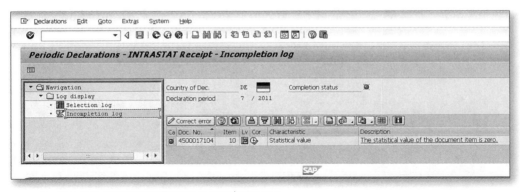

⋀ *Figure 2 INTRASTAT Receipt Incompletion Log*

If you have an error showing that vendor master has a VAT registration number missing, click on the EXECUTE button, which launches Transaction XK02. This allows you to maintain the required piece of data for report INTRASTAT to complete. Once your corrections are applied and saved, you'll be taken back to your report.

To maintain missing values, click on the EXECUTE icon to access the purchase order in question. Once in the PO change mode, access the CONDITIONS tab to maintain pricing. Specify the condition GRWR and maintain the condition values as shown in Figure 3.

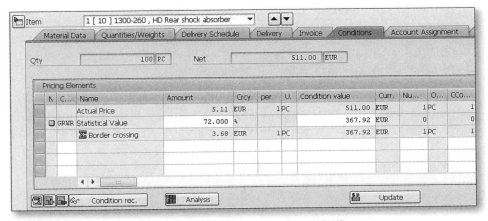

≳ Figure 3 *Correct Purchase Order Data Statistical Condition GRWR*

Save your PO to return to the body of the report. Correct any other data that may be incomplete, and go back to the starting point to choose to process exports.

Dispatch/Export

Select the DISPATCH tab on the initial screen of the PERIODIC DECLARATION selection screen, and then click on the STEP 1 button, again making sure the selection appears. If you have variants available, specify them before you execute Step 1. Alternatively, you can run Transaction VE01 or follow the menu path:

> LOGISTICS • SALES AND DISTRIBUTION • FOREIGN TRADE/CUSTOMS • PERIODIC DECLARATIONS • PERIODIC DECLARATIONS • OPERATIONAL • CREATE PERIODIC DECLARATIONS • EUROPEAN UNION • INTRASTAT • BUSINESS TRANSACTION • DISPATCH

On the initial screen, maintain the fields. Again, your selection can be saved as a variant, as discussed. Execute the report by clicking on the EXECUTE button or pressing F8. The subsequent screen will display relevant billing documents.

A red light will tell you that foreign trade data is missing in your documents. In the NAVIGATION pane on the left, choose to display the INCOMPLETION LOG. You'll get the detail list of incompletions in your billing documents.

To complete some of the billing document, cancel the billing document using Transaction VF11 (see Tip 74), and correct the data either in the predecessor document using Transaction VA02, delivery document using Transaction VL02N, or complete your data during re-creation of the billing document when executing

Transaction VF01. To maintain the missing foreign trade data, click on the EXECUTE icon. This will open up Transaction VF02. Maintain the data and save the invoice to return to the incompletion report. Process any other incomplete documents and exit the report.

If you executed your import or export using log type setting A, B, you could also execute the document creation function immediately by clicking on the CREATE FORM option in the NAVIGATION pane on the left.

We'll cover the details of issuing the form in Tip 38.

Tip 38

Creating a Paper Version of Your INTRASTAT Report

You can easily print your INTRASTAT report and submit it to the authorities.

In Tip 37, we explained the preparation steps for INTRASTAT declaration. While most of your time and energy was spent on the preparation steps, you still have to create the actual printed form that will be submitted to authorities. You can manually try to create documents outside of your SAP system using the data you've prepared, but this would be time consuming and full of potential errors. In this tip, we'll discuss the procedures that SAP offers, which will allow you to print reports and submit them to the required EU authorities.

And Here's How ...

To print a paper version of your prepared INTRASTAT report, execute Transaction ENGR (Periodic Declarations) from Tip 37, but proceed with Step 2, printing the INTRASTAT as shown in Figure 1.

Select the RECEIPT/IMPORT tab on the initial screen of the PERIODIC DECLARATION, select FORM in the description field, and then click on STEP 2. Repeat your steps for DISPATCH/EXPORT. You can also run Transaction VE02 or follow the menu path:

> LOGISTICS • SALES AND DISTRIBUTION • FOREIGN TRADE/CUSTOMS • PERIODIC DECLARATIONS • PERIODIC DECLARATIONS • OPERATIONAL • CREATE PERIODIC DECLARATIONS • EUROPEAN UNION • INTRASTAT • CREATE DOCUMENT • GERMANY

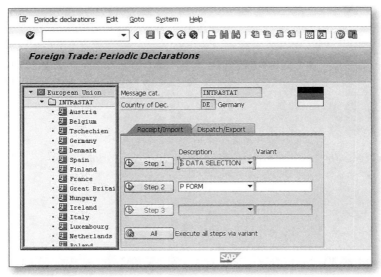

⤂ *Figure 1* *Periodic Declarations Initial Screen, Step 2*

Maintain the fields on the resulting selection screen.

Execute the report by clicking on the EXECUTE button or pressing F8. The screen shown in Figure 2 will appear. Note the NAVIGATION PANE with available printing options under the PRINT OUTPUT node. You can print the declaration form and the cover sheet.

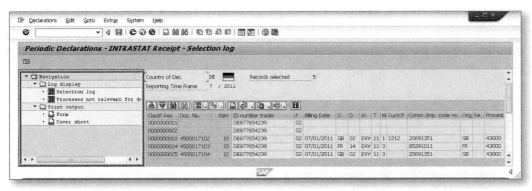

⤂ *Figure 2* *Periodic Declaration Printing Execution*

Choose the printer and collect your report. You've now created a paper version of your INTRASTAT periodic declaration.

Tip 39

Changing a Customer's Open Order Currency

You can change the order of a customer's local currency to a new currency by using a special planning workbench provided by SAP or individual transactions.

Several of your customers from the Euro expansion candidate countries have reached the date to join the European Monetary Union (EMU) and are ready to abandon their local currencies in favor of the Euro. You don't want to manually convert each of the sales documents to the new currency, and performing such conversion manually for a large number of orders would be extremely inefficient and time consuming. You need a report for open documents such as quotations, sales orders, scheduling agreements, or contracts to convert their currencies to the new currency. In this tip, we'll show you how to use a report to convert a Polish customer (a candidate country to join EMU in 2012). You'll convert all open orders from PLN (Polish Zloty) to EUR (Euros).

✓ And Here's How ...

For future EMU member countries and customers from these geographical areas, SAP provides a planning workbench (Transaction WEWU: Euro Workbench) to coordinate and maintain all conversion activities from one spot. This transaction accommodates the European conversion, and is also applicable when countries switch currency (deflate inflation) or a newly born country establishes a new currency. For the sake of this tip, we'll show you a more currency-independent process. To execute currency conversion of any kind, run Transaction EWUO or follow the menu path:

> LOGISTICS • SALES AND DISTRIBUTION • SALES • ENVIRONMENT • CURRENCY CONVERSION • SALES DOCUMENTS

Populate selection criteria on the initial screen of the transaction to narrow down the sales area data used for analysis as shown in Figure 1.

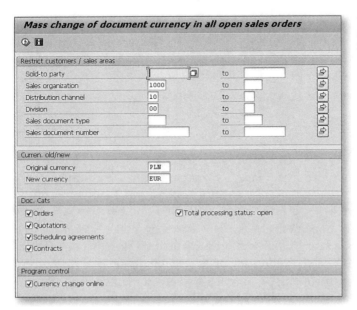

« Figure 1 Change Document Currency Selection Criteria

In the CURRENCY OLD/NEW section, specify the original document currency in the ORIGINAL CURRENCY field—the system will select orders with the same document currency as specified. If you don't use the ORIGINAL CURRENCY field, and if you enter EUR in the NEW CURRENCY field, the system will only choose documents with a currency that's participating in the EMU.

Select the CURRENCY CHANGE ONLINE flag to execute this transaction in the online dialog mode, and then click on the EXECUTE icon or press F8. If you want to run the transaction in the background, uncheck the CURRENCY CHANGE ONLINE flag; the transaction will automatically convert all documents that meet your selection criteria. Navigate back to the online mode, where the system will display a list of documents on the screen. Choose the documents you want to convert, or simply select all documents (see Figure 2).

Mass change of document currency in all open sales orders

✔ Change currency	▤ ▤	🖨 ▼

Mass change of document currency in all open sales orders

Old currency: PLN   New currency: EUR

S	Text	SOrg.	DChnl	Divis.	DocumentNo	Cust. no.	Name	Doc. type	Currncy
✔	Orders	1000	10	00	11914	6625	Browar Poznan	OR	PLN
✔	Orders	1000	10	00	11915	6625	Browar Poznan	OR	PLN

⌃ **Figure 2** *Change Order Currency Order Selection*

Take note of a few important restrictions before you run this program:

▸ If you run the conversion for partially billed orders, you cannot change the currency again, or change it back to the original currency.

▸ If the sales document has billing documents, they must be forwarded to Financial Accounting.

▸ Once you've changed the currency, billing documents that were billed in the original currency can no longer be cancelled.

When you're ready to convert your documents, click on the CHANGE CURRENCY button or press [F5]. All selected documents will be converted from the old to new currency. The new currency will be displayed in the report showing EUR (see Figure 3). Make sure to follow up this process with customer master currency conversion (refer to Tip 40 for more details). Bear in mind that when changing currency, the total amount of each order may vary due to the exchange rate at the time.

Mass change of document currency in all open sales orders

Old currency: PLN   New currency: EUR

S	Text	SOrg.	DChnl	Divis.	DocumentNo	Cust. no.	Name	Doc. type	Currncy
✔	Orders	1000	10	00	11914	6625	Browar Poznan	OR	EUR
✔	Orders	1000	10	00	11915	6625	Browar Poznan	OR	EUR

⌃ **Figure 3** *Completed Conversion Showing New Currency*

Tip **40**

Changing the Master Currency for Several Customers en Masse

You can update the default local currency for several customers to a new currency en masse via several different transactions.

When you convert customers' open orders currency to Euros (see Tip 39), you also need to run a report for the customer master to convert their currencies to a new currency. In Tip 39, we showed you how to convert all orders for a Polish customer from PLN (Polish Zloty) to EUR. Again, this transaction is specific to Euro conversion; however, it is also applicable to other situations including new countries or new currencies. To prevent future orders from being created with the customer's old currency, you also need to convert the default currency on the customer master.

✓ And Here's How ...

You can execute any Euro conversion transaction using Transaction WEWU (Euro Workbench). For this tip, we'll show you a more currency-independent process that allows conversion between currencies other than Euro. Run Transaction VDDI or follow the menu path:

> LOGISTICS • SALES AND DISTRIBUTION • SALES • ENVIRONMENT • CURRENCY CONVERSION • CUSTOMER MASTER

On the initial screen of the transaction, fill in as much data as possible such as the customer account number or a range and sales area data.

Specify the original document currency in the CURRENCY OLD/NEW section. In the ORIGINAL CURRENCY field (old currency), the system will select records with the same default currency. If you don't use the ORIGINAL CURRENCY field, and if you enter EUR in the NEW CURRENCY field, this will be a new currency, and the system will only choose accounts with a currency that's participating in EMU.

In the PROGRAM CONTROL section, you'll notice that the DEACTIVATE CHANGE DOCUMENTS flag is set as a default; this prevents the change documents capturing the history of the customer master changes from being created. Next, check the TEST RUN box if you want to review the proposed changes before applying them, and then click on the EXECUTE icon or press ⌨F8⌨ on your keyboard. The system will display a list of accounts you want to convert. Simply select all and click on the CHANGE button or press ⌨Shift⌨+⌨F1⌨ (see Figure 1).

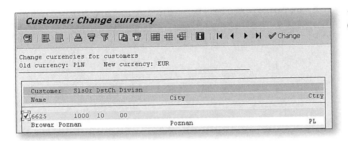

《 Figure 1 *Change Currency Customer Selection*

All selected customer master accounts will be converted from the old to the new currency. The conversion results will be displayed in the report as shown in Figure 2, showing the old and new currency, as well as the number of records processed.

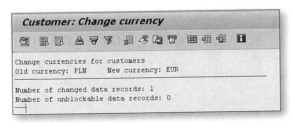

《 Figure 2 *Change Currency Conversion Results*

Part 4

Shipping

Things You'll Learn in this Section

Shipping is one of the most important activities within the sales cycle. It's where we take the product from the warehouse, pick it, pack it, and load it into a truck to be sent to your customers. If your shipping processes aren't efficient enough and you're wondering how to improve them, here we'll share a collection of tips that can help you improve the performance of these activities, including grouping deliveries for picking, executing wave picks, working with pick HUs, and more.

Creating and Scheduling the Delivery Due List as a Background Job

You can schedule a periodic background job for the delivery due list to establish a processing routine and to avoid strain on the system resources by running the job at night.

The standard SAP system provides a series of VL10 transactions that allow you to execute delivery due lists in the foreground. You can also run these as jobs in the background, but only one at a time. However, say you want to facilitate logistics planning and avoid long periods on delivery execution and manage very complex deliveries with ease. To do just that while saving time and allowing for maximum efficiency, we'll show you how to schedule the delivery due list to be executed automatically every day at your system's least critical operating time.

✅ And Here's How ...

Define your background job for delivery due list using Transaction VL10BATCH, or follow the menu path:

> LOGISTICS • LOGISTICS EXECUTION • OUTBOUND PROCESS • GOODS ISSUE FOR OUTBOUND DELIVERY • OUTBOUND DELIVERY • CREATE • COLLECTIVE PROCESSING OF DOCUMENTS DUE FOR DELIVERY • PLAN BACKGROUND PROCESSING

You'll see a list of available variants needed to execute the transaction on the selection screen. If none are listed, you need to define your own variant. You can change the existing variants listed by clicking on the CHANGE icon or by pressing F7 . To create, click on the CREATE button or press F7 + Shift (see Figure 1).

« **Figure 1** *Create Delivery Batch Job Variant*

You'll get a popup window asking you to enter a name for your variant and continue by clicking on the CREATE icon or pressing ⌈Enter⌋. You'll get another popup widow where you have to choose the subscreens for which you want to maintain data (see Figure 2).

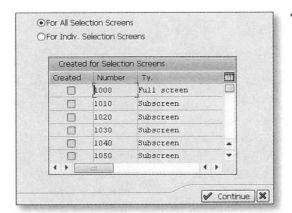

« **Figure 2** *Subscreen Selection*

Always choose the FOR ALL SELECTION SCREENS radio button, since the subscreens will be automatically enabled or disabled depending on the user role selected. Let's review what you can maintain on each of the listed subscreens:

▶ 1000 – FULL SCREEN: Shows selected scenario-specific data tabs (like GENERAL DATA, SALES ORDER, MATERIAL, PARTNERS, and USER ROLE). The data for the variant is limited, however, to the shipping point, delivery creation date, and calculation rules. Don't maintain data on the tabs; it won't be saved. Maintain it on individual subscreens.

▶ 1010 – GENERAL DATA: Enter data like delivery priority, route, ship-to party, and sales area.

▶ 1020 – SALES ORDERS: Helps restrict sales order data being pulled into the delivery due list.

- ▶ 1030 – ADDITIONAL CRITERIA – STOCK TRANSPORTS: Restricts the number of purchasing documents like stock transport orders found and relevant for delivery processing.

- ▶ 1040 – MATERIAL: Helps to limit selection of both stock transport orders and sales orders relevant for delivery.

- ▶ 1050 – PARTNERS: Further restricts the data selection by partner function and partner code.

- ▶ 1060 – USER ROLE: Defines the behavior of the entire transaction, governs which tabs are available, and how data is displayed and processed (see Figure 3). Always navigate to this screen first using the NEXT SCREEN icon or by pressing [F8]. For our example, we chose role 0001 – SALES ORDERS, FAST DISPLAY. All of the delivery processing lists share one common denominator called scenario and profile definition. The role is linked to scenario, driving what fields are allowed or disallowed for maintenance and manipulation. All delivery work list settings are normally controlled in the IMG and aren't available to the users unless specifically allowed by the administrator.

« *Figure 3* User Role Screen Detail

- ▶ 1070 – UNCHECKED DELIVERIES RELEVANT DATA: If your business scenario crosses systems where preceding documents come from a different system (like APO, or other instances of SAP) you can differentiate your selection between unchecked deliveries and checked deliveries.

Maintain data on the selected subscreens. Click on the BACK button or press [F3] to continue. You'll be prompted to save values for your variant and confirm by clicking on the YES button. On the next screen (VARIANT ATTRIBUTES), enter the meaning data, a description for your variant, and then click on the SAVE button. To exit the variant maintenance portion of this transaction, again click on the BACK icon or press [F3].

Once you're back on the initial screen you can make a selection to run your job immediately, which will be executed once and right when you click on the START IMMEDIATELY button or press [F5]. If, however, you're scheduling the periodic job, click on the SCHEDULE icon or press [F6]. On the next screen, define the job parameters like start date and time. We're showing the start time as one minute past midnight, and the period values, are specified as a daily job (see Figure 4). Once you define the start parameters, click on the CREATE icon. You'll see a message on the bottom left portion of the screen informing you that the job has been scheduled.

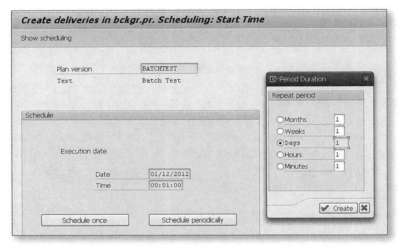

⌃ *Figure 4* *Maintaining Background Job Start Time*

To leave this screen, click on the BACK icon or press ⌷F3⌷. With your job defined, you can now access the status by clicking on the DISPLAY SCHEDULING icon or using the pull-down menu GoTo • DISPLAY JOBS. See Figure 5 showing the latest job status information.

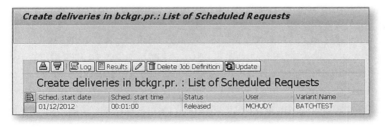

« *Figure 5* *Display Scheduling List*

Press ⌷F3⌷ to go back to the initial screen. Your background job will start automatically. You can access log data, review results, change job parameters, delete the job definition, or simply update the screen with the latest status by clicking on the UPDATE button.

Creating a Delivery Group for Better Delivery Processes

You can organize and manage picking activities in the warehouse much more easily by creating delivery groups.

A delivery group has many applications; one of the most obvious is picking materials for a number of deliveries all belonging to the same *customer* or all having the same *route*. By creating a delivery group, the warehouse can then process these deliveries collectively. With collective processing, the warehouse can collect all the items for all the orders belonging to the same customer, or all the deliveries in the same shipping route. This can help load and dispatch trucks more efficiently.

✓ And Here's How ...

The groups you create in this transaction can be used to process the follow-up actions for a delivery: picking, picking confirmation, transportation planning, and goods issue. All these follow-up functions can be executed from Transaction VL06O (Outbound Delivery Monitor) where you can enter this group number as part of your selection criteria. To create a delivery group, use Transaction VG01 or follow the menu path:

> LOGISTICS • SALES AND DISTRIBUTION • SHIPPING • GROUPS OF OUTBOUND DELIVERIES • CREATE

The screen shown in Figure 1 will prompt you to enter a group type. For our example, enter K for picking group and press Enter.

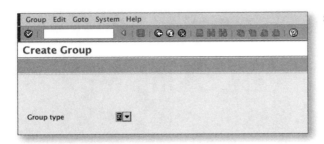

↟ Figure 1 *Create Group Screen*

In the next screen shown in Figure 2, enter the list of deliveries for each delivery you have access to via the standard search match codes by pressing ⌜F4⌝ or by clicking on the MATCH CODE pull-down to the right of the DELIVERY field.

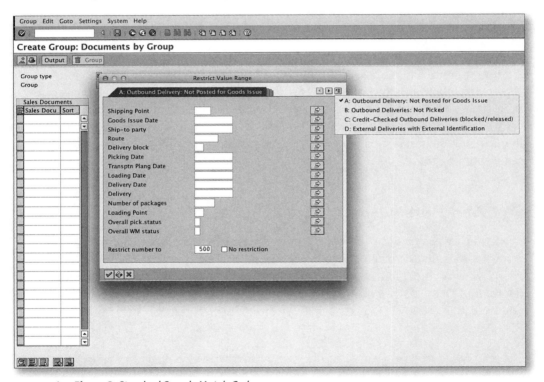

↟ Figure 2 *Standard Search Match Codes*

After you enter the list of deliveries, you can also enter a sort sequence and the system will rearrange the list once you press ⌜Enter⌝ (see Figure 3).

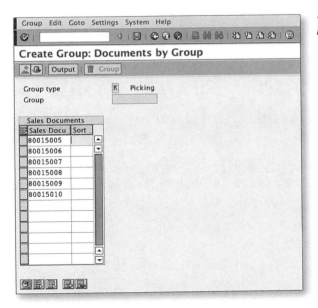

≪ Figure 3 Collectively Process List of Deliveries

Save the group and you'll see a group number, which you'll use later for collective creation of transfer orders in Transaction LT42 if your system is configured for two-step-picking, or directly in VL06O if it's not.

✅ **Group number 5974 saved**   **≪ Figure 4** Saved Group is Uniquely Identified by a Number

By creating delivery groups you are now able to collectively process follow-up functions with a unique identifier. You won't need to have a list of deliveries to process in Excel or any other tool outside of the SAP system.

Tip 43

Adding Additional Search Fields in the Outbound Delivery Monitor

You can customize your SAP system by adding more search fields in the Outbound Delivery Monitor to quickly and easily find the information that's most important for your business.

Can't find that delivery or list of deliveries that you're looking for in the Outbound Delivery Monitor? Do you wish you could enter the specific delivery group you want to process? Or do you only want to look at deliveries that were created by you or on a certain date? In this tip, we'll show you how to add more search fields to enhance your search abilities.

And Here's How ...

The Outbound Delivery Monitor helps you display and process several deliveries at one time. It's a very flexible and effective tool that allows you to perform collective selection and processing of documents. You can select deliveries according to their processing status, allowing you to work on deliveries due for the following:

▶ Picking
▶ Picked and ready for confirmation
▶ Confirmed and ready for loading
▶ Confirmed and ready for transportation planning
▶ Deliveries ready for goods issue

For each of these different statuses, you can list deliveries for collective processing using a number of selection fields. Depending on the status of the deliveries,

152

there's a different section of the Outbound Delivery Monitor, and for each of these sections, the selection criteria is preset.

To go to the Outbound Delivery Monitor, use Transaction VL06O or follow the path:

> LOGISTICS • LOGISTICS EXECUTION • OUTBOUND PROCESS • GOODS ISSUE FOR OUTBOUND DELIVERY • OUTBOUND DELIVERY • LISTS AND LOGS • OUTBOUND DELIVERY MONITOR

In every selection screen, there's a *button bar*, and in that bar, there's a button that suggests "expanding." The button is called ALL SELECTIONS (Shift+F7), and when you click on it, it expands your search criteria, presenting more fields (▣). To go back to the standard search criteria, the button changes into SELECTIONS CHOSEN (▣; Shift+F8).

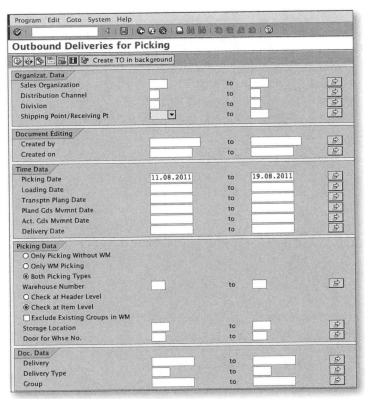

⌃ *Figure 1 Search Screen for Deliveries Due for Picking after Expanding the Search Fields*

Let's look at an example: in the section for deliveries due for picking, the standard search criteria includes 11 sections with 15 search fields. After clicking on the ALL SELECTIONS button, there are 14 sections with 54 fields plus checkboxes and radio buttons (see Figure 1). Among the most notable fields that will be available on your screen are:

- ► CREATED BY
- ► CREATED ON
- ► DELIVERY
- ► DELIVERY TYPE
- ► MATERIAL

You need to click on the ALL SELECTIONS button every time you use the delivery monitor if you want to enter selection data in the hidden selection fields.

You can save selection variants that include values entered in the hidden fields by entering your search criteria and clicking on the SAVE button or pressing [Ctrl]+[S]. The next time you run the report and select the variant you saved, your values will be there, but you won't be able to see them until you again click on the ALL SELECTIONS button or press [Shift]+[F7].

Creating a Transfer Order for a Group of Deliveries

By creating transfer orders for a group, you can direct the warehouse to start picking faster than if you created each transfer order individually.

The SAP system allows you to create transfer orders for multiple deliveries simultaneously instead of having to create them one by one, which will save you time and effort. When you create transfer orders for the deliveries in a group, you're grouping operations with the same movement type for the warehouse, you're able to better plan the stock movements, and you have a better method of monitoring the stock removal.

And Here's How ...

If you manually created a delivery group in Transaction VG01 and now want to create transfer orders for that group of deliveries, use Transaction VL06P or follow the path:

> LOGISTICS • SALES AND DISTRIBUTION • OUTBOUND DELIVERY • PICKING • CREATE TRANSFER ORDER • VIA OUTBOUND DELIVERY MONITOR

In the main selection screen, enter the shipping point number, the group number, and click on EXECUTE or press F8.

You should now see the list of all the deliveries that are part of the group. Select them all and push the [□ TO for Group] button (see Figure 1).

This will take you to Transaction LT42[1] to create the transfer orders for each of the deliveries; at the same time, the SAP system takes the warehouse number information from the delivery and creates a link between the delivery group and the warehouse number. This link can't be created manually. If you execute LT42 directly, you'll get an error saying that the delivery group number you entered doesn't exist in that warehouse.

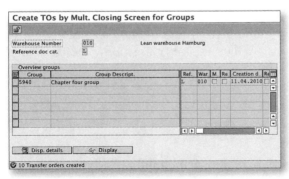

≫   *Figure 1 Select All Deliveries to Create Transfer Orders*

In the selection screen for Transaction LT42, you'll see options to run the transaction either in the foreground or the background. SAP recommends that this transaction always run in the background, which also saves you a few steps.

After the TOs are created, you'll see a screen that displays the groups that were processed (here we only have one; see Figure 2). You won't see a confirmation screen unless you run the transaction in the foreground.

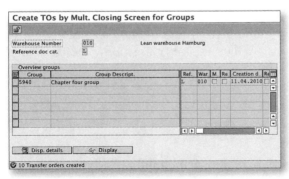

≫   *Figure 2 The Processed Groups List*

---

1   Transaction LT42 also allows you the option of two-step picking, which allows you to consolidate picking of materials that are included in several different deliveries to optimize the moving of stock from the racks.

After processing, the result is displayed (see Figure 3). You can see the individual TO numbers by selecting the group and clicking on the DISPLAY DETAILS button.

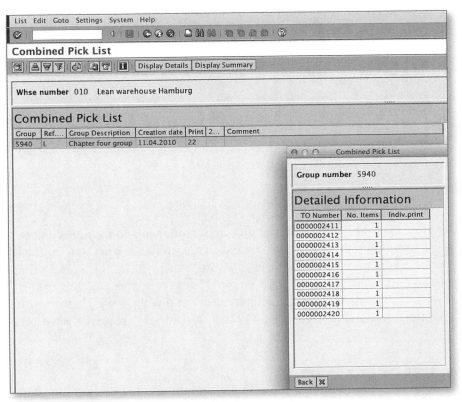

⤒ *Figure 3 Pick List Result*

Tip **45**

Creating a Picking Wave According to Delivery Time

Creating picking waves by delivery time can help you implement several daily picking waves in the warehouse in a very organized way.

Picking waves are used to consolidate picking requirements to maximize the output at the warehouse. They can be created in two ways: manually by utilizing Transaction VL06O (Outbound Delivery Monitor), or by using the delivery time. The system documentation isn't very clear on what to configure and how to create the wave picks when you're using delivery time; in this tip, we'll give you some configuration hints and instructions on how to successfully create the waves.

And Here's How ...

Prerequisite Customizing Steps

Before you create picking waves using time slots, you need to make sure the following are configured via SPRO • LOGISTICS EXECUTION • SHIPPING • PICKING • WAVE PICKS:

- ▶ NUMBER RANGES FOR WAVE PICKS: Define and assign the number ranges for picking waves
- ▶ DEFINE GROUP TYPES FOR WAVE PICKS: SAP default
- ▶ DEFINE NUMBER RANGE FOR GROUP: Assign number ranges for groups of deliveries
- ▶ CALCULATE WORKLOAD: Define the duration of warehouse activities and form a warehouse workload with them

▶ CONTROL UPDATE OF WORKLOAD DATA: Define determination procedures for updating the data into the SIS info structures using the statistical relevance of customers, materials, and sales documents within a sales area

▶ MAINTAIN TIME OF COMPARISON FOR FORMING WAVE PICKS: Determine which time in the delivery will be used as a base for selection

▶ MAINTAIN WAVE PICKS PROFILE: Determine as many profiles as you need for your warehouse, which determine capacity behavior and control parameters

▶ MAINTAIN TIME SLOTS: Units of time for creating picking waves — by warehouse shift, hourly, or any other periodic measure used

▶ MAINTAIN TIMESLOT GROUP FOR WAVE PICK: Time slot groups used to relate time slots

If you want the pick/pack times to be determined automatically by the system, enter work times in the shipping point configuration. These times can be set by default, or based on the times entered in routes as shown in Figure 1.

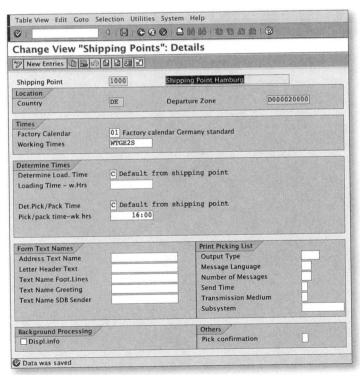

⌃ *Figure 1* Set Up Work Times for the Shipping Point

Create Picking Waves

To create picking waves according to delivery time, use Transaction VL35 or follow the path:

> LOGISTICS • LOGISTICS EXECUTION • OUTBOUND PROCESS • GOODS ISSUE FOR OUTBOUND DELIVERY • PICKING • WAVE PICKS • CREATE • ACCORDING TO DELIVERY TIME

When you reach the selection screen, maintain the following at the minimum as shown in Figure 2:

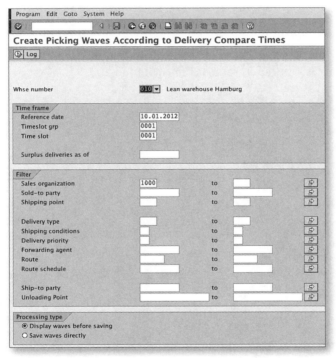

⌃ **Figure 2** Selection Screen to Select Deliveries for Picking Wave

- ▶ The reference date, which is related to the time you selected in Customizing as the time for comparison
- ▶ The time slot group
- ▶ The time slot
- ▶ The shipping point or sales organization

The route is a value that's very helpful in some organizations, but it depends on your individual needs.

Select a processing type. Here you can look at the search results before saving the wave or having the system save it in the background.

With your selection criteria completed, execute the transaction by pressing F8 . The search result screen shown in Figure 3 will show you the detailed information about the delivery group that is about to be created, and you can look at the deliveries that were selected by expanding the group. The resulting list of deliveries are selected based on the planned processing times. Depending on your selection in the TIME USED FOR COMPARISON set in Customizing, this could be either the picking time, loading time, or goods issue time.

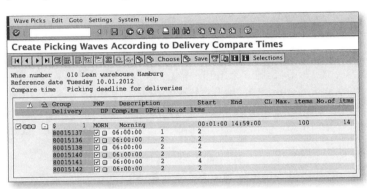

≫ *Figure 3 The Delivery Group or Wave That Will Be Created*

At this point you can deselect any deliveries you don't want to process at the time, or just save the picking wave. After saving you'll see the group number in the status line.

If you have problems during configuration and your deliveries aren't being selected, it might be because they aren't being added to the SIS info structure S159. One great tool to troubleshoot your configuration of the determination procedure for update is the log for workload data update. You can find it under Transaction VLLP or in the path:

> LOGISTICS • LOGISTICS EXECUTION • OUTBOUND PROCESS • PICKING • WAVE PICKS •
> LOGS • UPDATE

Working with the Picking Wave Monitor

By using the Picking Wave Monitor, you can follow up on the status of all the picking waves.

The Picking Wave Monitor allows you to look at the picking waves and their statuses. The report gives you an up-to-the-minute status for all the delivery groups that are in process. However, sometimes it's hard to understand what information is displayed and how the status is being derived for a group based on the status of the individual deliveries. In this tip, we'll clarify the information that comes from the Picking Wave Monitor.

And Here's How ...

To run the Picking Wave Monitor, access Transaction VL37 or follow the path:

> LOGISTICS • LOGISTICS EXECUTION • OUTBOUND PROCESS • PICKING • WAVE PICKS • MONITOR

The monitor allows you to select picking waves by time slot group, time slot, directly by group number, or by creation date or creating user. Because of these selection fields, you can only monitor waves created based on delivery time and not manual waves created in Transaction VL06O.

As you display the report, you're able to see the following statuses for each picking wave:

▶ OVERALL WAREHOUSE MANAGEMENT

▶ OVERALL PACKING

▶ TRANSPORTATION PLANNING

▶ TOTAL GOODS MOVEMENT

▶ BILLING

You can see the total number of deliveries in the wave, and you can look at the detail of these statuses for each delivery.

In the selection screen shown in Figure 1, enter your selection criteria including at least the warehouse number. You can also find picking waves by time slots or by creation date. If you know the delivery group numbers, you could directly enter them too, or you could run it without maintaining any other criteria to find all waves within the warehouse.

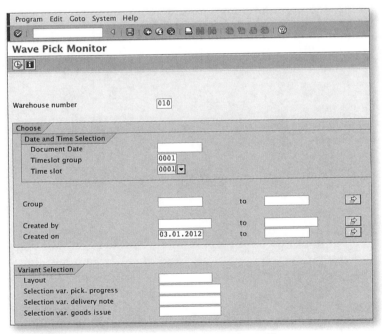

⌃ *Figure 1* *List of Waves Created Based on Delivery Time*

Execute the report by pressing F8, and the system will present the status of the picking waves using a two-level list. In the top level, it presents the wave or delivery group, and in the bottom level, it displays the deliveries that form that group.

In order to aggregate the delivery statuses to have a wave status, the system takes the following premises:

- A blank status does not aggregate.
- If all deliveries have the same status, then that status is taken as the aggregated value.
- When all the deliveries have a status B or C, then the aggregated status is B.
- If at least one delivery has an A status, then the aggregated status in A.

The monitor is displayed in two levels. On the top level is the group/wave information, and you can expand or collapse each group to look at the deliveries in the lower level. You can double-click on any delivery to display the detailed information about it. The detail will appear in a pop-up window, as shown in Figure 2, and will contain the different delivery statuses along with its explanation text.

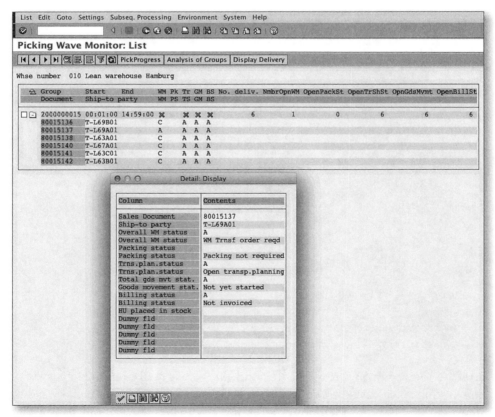

⏫ *Figure 2* Two-Level Display with Aggregated and Individual Statuses

If you want to look at the delivery itself, select the delivery and click on the button DISPLAY DELIVERY or press `Ctrl`+`F1`.

The statuses change as the work progresses; you can look at the summary of all groups by clicking on the ANALYSIS OF GROUPS button or pressing `Ctrl`+`Shift`+`F5`, as shown in Figure 3.

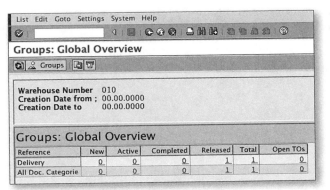

« *Figure 3* *Consolidated View of All the Picking Waves*

Warehouse personnel will benefit from using this report because it'll help them have a look at what's happening in the picking floor, which will in turn allow them to allocate resources to activities that require more attention.

Tip 47

Troubleshooting Wave Pick Issues with the Use of Logs

If your deliveries aren't being considered for wave pick creation, you can review the log we describe in this tip to find out why.

There are many cases in which problems occur when trying to create picking waves. However, there's a system log that's very useful for troubleshooting purposes when your deliveries aren't considered for creation of picking waves, especially because of configuration problems as we discussed in Tip 46. In this tip, we'll show you how to access the log and how to get valuable information from it that will help you pinpoint the right piece of configuration or data that you need to fix.

✓ And Here's How ...

The name of Transaction VLLP in the menu is a little misleading (Rough Workload Estimate)—it doesn't make changes to the picking wave or update it in any way. It's really a log, and it'll show you the result of updating or attempting to update the SIS info structure S159, which VL35 reads to consider the deliveries that are candidates for wave picking creation according to time slots.

To access this log, use Transaction VLLP or follow the path:

> LOGISTICS • LOGISTICS EXECUTION • OUTBOUND PROCESS • GOODS ISSUE FOR OUTBOUND DELIVERY • PICKING • WAVE PICKS • LOGS • UPDATE

The log shown in Figure 1 gives you the option of selecting which document categories to display in the Rough Workload Estimate log. You can choose between ALL, SALES ORDERS, PURCHASE ORDERS, or DELIVERIES.

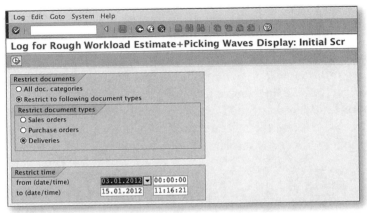

⋩ **Figure 1** *Select the Document Categories to Be Displayed*

You also need to enter date ranges. Be sure to enter the range that covers the delivery dates on the delivery orders you want to display; otherwise the log will be too long.

Execute the log by pressing ⌈F8⌉, and you'll see a list of entries that include all the operations for each document with the date, time, and user who executed them (see Figure 2).

⋩ **Figure 2** *Detailed Information about Times, Transactions, and Update Status*

You can look for errors and display them to understand why a certain document is having problems by looking at the values of the fields that are being used for update determination.

To display the detailed information for an entry in the log, expand the line using the little triangle to the left of the line you want to look at. In the lower level line, you'll see a description for what happened; this is normally very brief and usually not very clear. Double-click on the message and the detailed information will appear at the bottom of the screen, as shown in Figure 3.

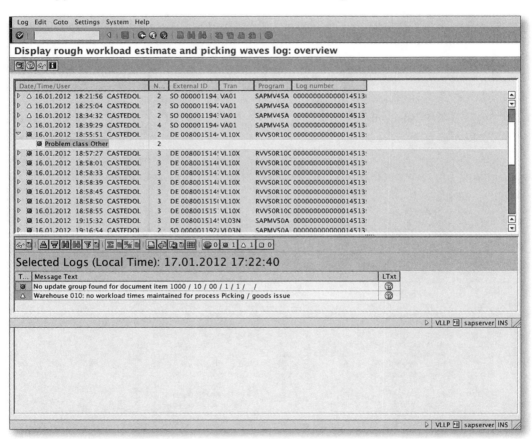

⌃ *Figure 3 Expand the Log Lines for More Detail at the Bottom*

Each of the detailed lines has a question mark at the very right of the line. If you click on it, you'll get a detailed description of the problem. This includes fields listed in the message. As shown in Figure 4, this delivery isn't being added to the SIS info structure S159 because there's no configuration in the system to update it with the combination of:

- Sales organization: 1000
- Distribution channel: 10
- Division: 00
- Status group customer: 1
- Status group material: 1
- Status group header: blank
- Status group item: blank

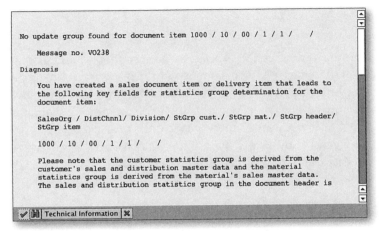

No update group found for document item 1000 / 10 / 00 / 1 / 1 /   /

    Message no. VO238

Diagnosis

    You have created a sales document item or delivery item that leads to
    the following key fields for statistics group determination for the
    document item:

    SalesOrg / DistChnnl/ Division/ StGrp cust./ StGrp mat./ StGrp header/
    StGrp item

    1000 / 10 / 00 / 1 / 1 /   /

    Please note that the customer statistics group is derived from the
    customer's sales and distribution master data and the material
    statistics group is derived from the material's sales master data.
    The sales and distribution statistics group in the document header is

Technical Information

⌃ *Figure 4 Detailed Explanation of What Happened*

In this case, you need to update either the configuration as described in Tip 46, or change the values for statistic groups in the material master using Transaction MM02.

Listing Transfer Orders by Wave Pick

After creating transfer orders for a wave pick, you can use a report to display them to better allocate your available resources.

Wave picks are just the beginning of the process in the warehouse, and as you create transfer orders (TOs) to execute the picking, you have more and more documents to follow up on. In this tip, we'll show you how to display a list that shows the transfer orders for a picking wave. If you're using two-step picking, which is regular in wave picking, you can display the transfer orders for each step separately. This way you'll always know which step of the process each picking wave is, allowing you to allocate the right resources to the right task.

✅ And Here's How ...

To list transfer orders by wave pick, access Transaction LT25A or follow the menu path:

> LOGISTICS • LOGISTICS EXECUTION • OUTBOUND PROCESS • GOODS ISSUE FOR OUTBOUND DELIVERY • PICKING • DISPLAY TRANSFER ORDER • BY WAVE PICK

When running this report, you can choose which TOs to list:

- ▶ DIRECT PICKING: For delivery items that aren't relevant for two-step picking
- ▶ PICK: Consolidated transfer orders that have the objective of retrieving totalized quantities by material from the racks to a sorting area

▶ ALLOCATION: Transfer orders to pick the individual quantities for each delivery item from the sorting area into the goods issue area

From the selection screen shown in Figure 1, select the warehouse number and the group or picking wave you want to display. Select the confirmation status for the TOs to be listed according to the two-step process, and also whether you want to display direct, pick, allocation TOs, or select them all since they're not exclusive.

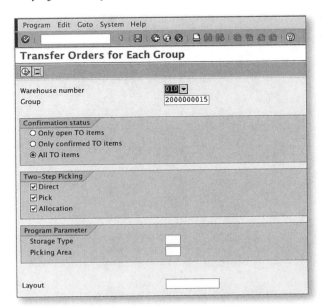

« *Figure 1 Initial Selection Screen*

Execute the report by pressing F8 , and you'll see the list of TOs (see Figure 2). By default, they're listed by TO number but you can use any of the fields to change the sorting. You can also change the layout settings and save them; you could select these layout variants from the selection screen, or make them the default layout format as you save them.

Double-click on any TO number to display the details. You can also choose the TO and confirm the picking by clicking on the CONFIRM IN BACKGROUND BUTTON or by pressing Ctrl + Shift + F9 .

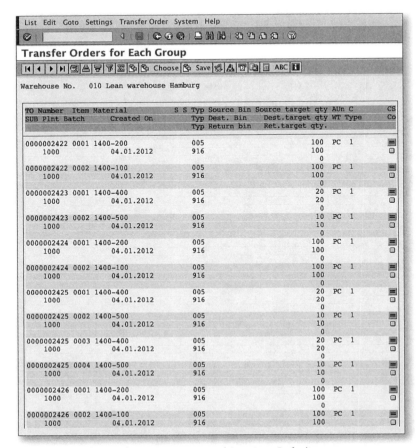

⌃ Figure 2 *Change the Report Layout and Save It as Default*

There's no way to confirm more than one TO at a time. If you need to do that, you can use Transaction LT25N or follow the path:

> LOGISTICS • LOGISTICS EXECUTION • OUTBOUND PROCESS • GOODS ISSUE FOR OUTBOUND DELIVERY • PICKING • CONFIRM TRANSFER ORDER • LT25N - COLLECTIVE PROCESSING

Here, you can confirm the remaining opened TOs for the group.

Tip 49

Moving Unfinished Deliveries to a Different Picking Wave

If a picking wave isn't finished within the originally planned time frame, you can change the unfinished deliveries to another picking wave.

Missing pieces, credit issues, and other problems can prevent a picking wave from making it all the way through the warehouse process, from picking, to packing, goods issue, and billing. In these cases, there's a chance that those deliveries will be forgotten, due to the way many companies create the batch job variants that run some of these steps in the background. We'll help you prevent this issue by moving the problem deliveries from one picking wave to the most current one.

And Here's How ...

To remove deliveries from a picking wave or move a delivery to a different picking wave, access Transaction VL36 or follow the path:

> LOGISTICS • LOGISTICS EXECUTION • OUTBOUND PROCESS • GOODS ISSUE FOR OUTBOUND DELIVERY • PICKING • WAVE PICKS • CHANGE

In the resulting selection screen shown in Figure 1, enter the reference date, time slot group, and time slot, or you can directly enter the group number or numbers you want to work with.

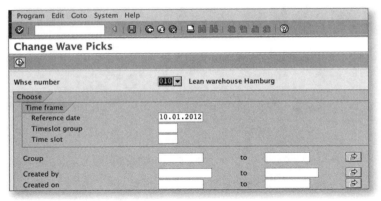

⩘ *Figure 1* Search Criteria in the Selection Screen

Once you've maintained the fields, click EXECUTE or press F8, and you'll see the resulting report shown in Figure 2. The report is a two-level list—the top level describes the picking wave, and in the lower level you'll see a list of the deliveries in each wave.

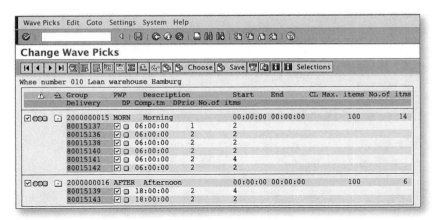

⩘ *Figure 2* Results in Two Levels

From this list, you can delete deliveries by deselecting the checkboxes in the corresponding wave and saving the list or moving deliveries from one wave to another.

To move a delivery from one group to another, press Shift, click on the delivery you want to move, and then click on the destination group. The delivery will be moved into the destination group automatically.

Changing or Deleting a Delivery Group

You can easily make changes to a delivery group if you discover that there are problems with some of the deliveries during picking.

Delivery groups can be created very easily in the Outbound Delivery Monitor, or directly in Transaction VG01. However, it's often necessary to make changes to them, and then you can waste a good deal of time trying to figure out how to do that. In this tip, we'll show you the most efficient way of changing or deleting delivery groups.

And Here's How ...

To add, remove, or change the deliveries in a group use Transaction VG02 or follow the path:

> LOGISTICS • LOGISTICS EXECUTION • OUTBOUND PROCESS • OUTBOUND DELIVERY • GROUP OF OUTBOUND DELIVERIES • CHANGE

When you get to the transaction screen, you can either enter your group number directly in the GROUP field, or use the SEARCH GROUP section to find it.

If you use the search group, enter the group type (which is very important), the user that created the group, and the date on which the group was created if you know it. As a result, you'll get a screen with the list of groups that meet your search criteria (see Figure 1).

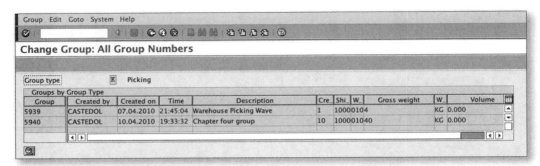

⩔ *Figure 1* *Delivery Groups Matching the Search Criteria*

Double-click on the group you want to modify, which will take you to the CHANGE screen. Here, you'll be presented with the group information and the list of all the deliveries that form the group.

Now you can add more deliveries by entering them at the bottom of the list, or delete one or several deliveries by selecting them using the SELECT button at the left of each delivery and clicking on the REMOVE DOCUMENT FROM GROUP button at the bottom of the screen (see Figure 2). You can also delete the whole group by clicking on the DELETE button or pressing Shift + F2 .

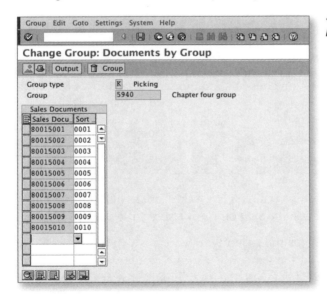

《 *Figure 2* *Add or Remove Deliveries*

Tip 51

Listing Incomplete Outbound Deliveries

If your system is configured to check incompleteness in deliveries, you can quickly use a report to list all the incomplete deliveries.

Incomplete procedures are very common in most companies using the SAP ERP system; they're used to prevent orders from completing certain steps of the sales process if they don't have all the correct information. For example, you could have an incompleteness procedure that checks for incorrect terms or the total weight of the delivery, and won't allow the goods issue to be posted until these fields have been completed.

Unfortunately, we normally find out about incomplete documents when something fails and you can't complete one of the delivery's follow-up functions. In this tip, we'll tell you how to find the incomplete sales documents so you can complete the process without interruptions.

And Here's How ...

To get to the Incomplete Outbound Deliveries report, use Transaction V_UC or follow the path:

> LOGISTICS • LOGISTICS EXECUTION • OUTBOUND PROCESS • GOODS ISSUE FOR OUTBOUND DELIVERY • OUTBOUND DELIVERY • LISTS AND LOGS • INCOMPLETE OUTBOUND DELIVERIES

When you chose this option in the menu or execute the transaction, you'll be taken to a selection screen, shown in Figure 1. Here you have several options for listing the incomplete deliveries.

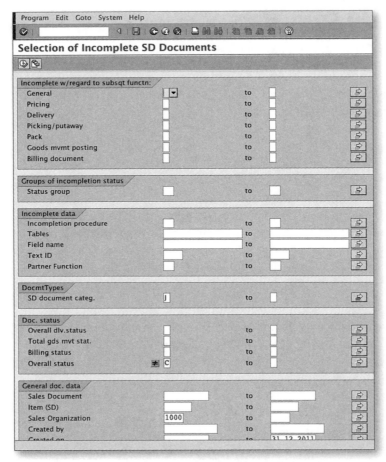

⋟ *Figure 1* Select the Follow-Up Documents for Which the Delivery is Incomplete

First, indicate the blocked documents for which the delivery is incomplete, or enter a status group. Enter a sales organization, and you can optionally enter the document's status, create date ranges, or person who created the deliveries. The latter isn't always a good strategy since, in so many companies, deliveries are created by batch jobs that run in the background, which assign the batch user to all these deliveries.

When you execute the report, the matching incomplete deliveries will be listed, as shown in Figure 2. If the incompleteness is at item level, it will indicate the item number within the delivery; otherwise these statuses refer to header incompleteness. On the right side you can look at the follow-up documents that won't be able to post until the delivery is completed.

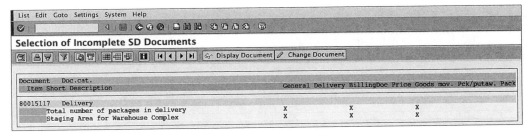

⌃ *Figure 2* *The Incomplete SD Documents Report List*

Tip 52

Displaying Changes to a Delivery

You can find out when the status of a delivery changed and who executed that particular step to comply with certain audits.

Delivery orders are documents that change constantly. They include so many fields that are updated by so many operations that sometimes you need to go back and take a look at when a certain step took place and who executed it. Fortunately, the SAP system is probably the most audit-friendly system; it takes note of who did what and when. In this tip, you'll learn how to find and display this information.

And Here's How ...

To take a look at how a delivery order has been modified during its lifecycle, use Transaction VL22 or follow the path:

> LOGISTICS • SALES AND DISTRIBUTION • SHIPPING • OUTBOUND DELIVERY • LIST AND LOGS • CHANGES

In the selection screen, enter the delivery order number (see Figure 1). If you also enter an item number, the system will show you the change log specific to that item skipping the header change log. The screen presents additional search fields, such as USER or the very useful DATE. You can also choose between displaying the OVERVIEW or DETAIL VIEW in the DISPLAY RANGE section.

The SORT section allows you to choose between sorting by DELIVERY ITEM or BY TIME OF CHANGE. Once you've filled in all criteria, click on the EXECUTE button or press F8 .

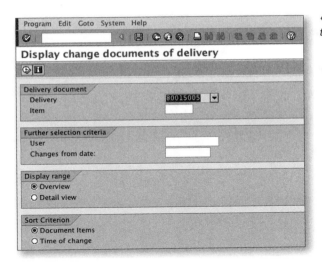

« Figure 1 Selection Screen for the Change Log

The resulting report will show you the change log, which lists the history of all actions that have been executed on the delivery. The log shows the date of the change and the name of the user who performed the change (see Figure 2). From here, you can switch between the OVERVIEW and DETAIL screens by clicking on the OVERVIEW <-> DETAILS button or pressing [F5], so you don't need to exit the report and run it with a different display range option.

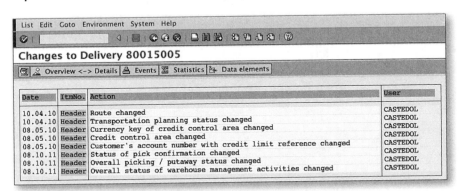

≪ Figure 2 The Change Log Lists the Actions Executed on the Delivery

The detailed screen shown in Figure 3 shows you exactly which fields changed, including the values before and after the action was executed.

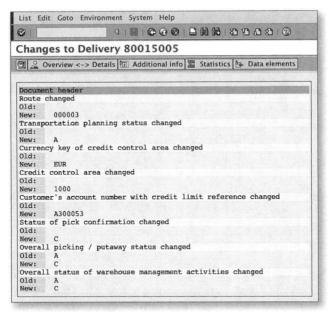

List Edit Goto Environment System Help

Changes to Delivery 80015005

Overview <-> Details | Additional info | Statistics | Data elements

```
Document header
Route changed
Old:
New:    000003
Transportation planning status changed
Old:
New:    A
Currency key of credit control area changed
Old:
New:    EUR
Credit control area changed
Old:
New:    1000
Customer's account number with credit limit reference changed
Old:
New:    A300053
Status of pick confirmation changed
Old:
New:    C
Overall picking / putaway status changed
Old:    A
New:    C
Overall status of warehouse management activities changed
Old:    A
New:    C
```

⌃ **Figure 3** *Detailed Screen Showing Before and After Values for Each Field*

This log can help you find out why a delivery doesn't appear on a follow-up action work list, like transportation planning or goods issue. Sometimes it helps you find processing mistakes, which could result in merchandise not being shipped to a customer because the system tells you the delivery has been completely processed and the physical activities haven't been executed.

Tip 53

Automatically Replenishing Fixed Bins in the Warehouse

If your sales operations include picking small quantities from fixed bins, you can set up the system to replenish these storage bins automatically.

When you use the Warehouse Management solution in the SAP ERP system as part of your distribution chain solution and you've set up a fixed bin area for picking small quantities, you can use standard functionality to have this area replenished automatically so you don't run out of stock in the middle of the picking activities.

And Here's How ...

Prerequisites

To be able to use automatic fixed bin replenishment, make sure the following have been set up beforehand by following these steps:

▸ Access Customizing via the path:

> LOGISTICS EXECUTION • WAREHOUSE MANAGEMENT • ACTIVITIES • TRANSFERS • DEFINE STOCK TRANSFERS AND REPLENISHMENT CONTROL

▸ In Customizing, make sure that WM movement type 319 has no destination storage type and that it's set up for automatic TO creation. In the DEFINE REPLENISHMENT CONTROL FOR STORAGE TYPE section, assign movement type 319 to the storage type you want to replenish automatically in the MOVEMENT TYPE FOR REPLENISHMENT column.

▶ In the material master, use Transaction MM01 to extend the materials you want to replenish automatically to the correct storage type. When you extend a material to the storage type level, the system will show you new fields in the WAREHOUSE MANAGEMENT 2 view (see Figure 1).

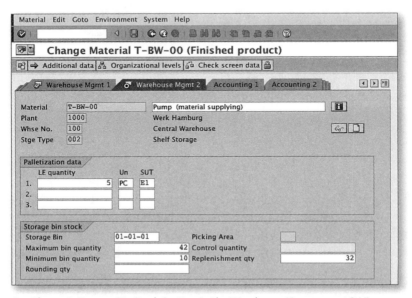

⚠ *Figure 1* Storage Bin Stock Section in the Warehouse Management 2 View

▶ When you select a storage type in the selection of organizational levels, you'll be able to enter the following data in the STORAGE BIN STOCK section:

  ▶ The fixed bin to which the material is to be replenished.

  ▶ The maximum stock this bin can hold in the base unit of measure.

  ▶ The minimum stock allowed in the bin in the base unit of measure; this quantity will be used to trigger the replenishment.

  ▶ The replenishment quantity is what will be moved to the fixed bin. When you fill this quantity, be careful so that after the replenishment is done, the stock in the bin doesn't go over the maximum bin stock.

Set Up Automatic Replenishment

Once all the prerequisites are met, access Transaction LP21 or follow the path:

LOGISTICS • LOGISTICS EXECUTION • INTERNAL WAREHOUSE PROCESSES • STOCK TRANSFERS • PLANNING OF REPLENISHMENTS • ACCORDING TO BIN SITUATION

In the selection screen shown in Figure 2, fill in the PLANT, STORAGE LOCATION, WAREHOUSE NUMBER, and STORAGE TYPE fields for what needs to be replenished. If required, also enter a requirement number.

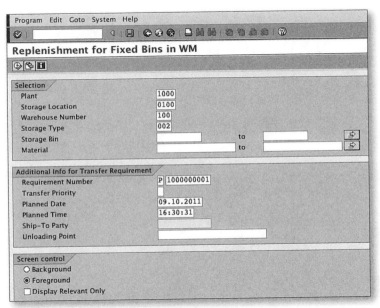

⌃ *Figure 2 Create Replenishment Transfer Requirements Automatically*

Click on EXECUTE or press ⌑F8⌑. In the next screen (see Figure 3), you'll see a list of the materials that are set up for automatic replenishment, including the current bin stock and the quantity to be replenished. Select the materials that you want to replenish and click SAVE.

⋩ **Figure 3** List of Materials Set Up for Automatic Replenishment

Transaction LP21 will create transfer requirements that you can then convert to transfer orders using Transaction LB10 (TRs for Storage Type).

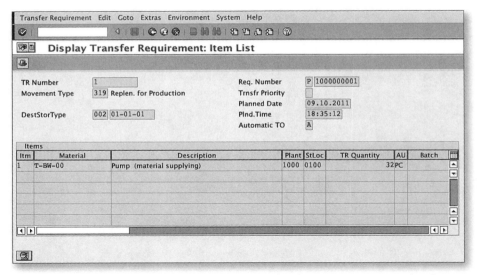

⋩ **Figure 4** Transfer Requirements Created for the Replenishment Quantity Entered in the Material Master

As an option, you can run this transaction in the background so that the process is completely automatic. Depending on the policies of your warehouse, you can run Report RLAUTA10 to create the transfer orders automatically, or you can do it manually as they're assigned to the warehouse personnel.

Tip 54

Replenishing Materials Based On Outbound Deliveries

You can configure automatic replenishment for those materials that need to be picked for outbound deliveries.

As we discussed in Tip 53, you can configure your system for automatic replenishment of fixed bins based on the stock levels of the materials that are set up for those bins. If you don't want to have open boxes/containers of materials in the small quantities/fixed bins section of your warehouse, you can base the replenishment on use. This way, you only replenish those materials that have an opened outbound delivery. This is also done in the WM module of the SAP ERP system.

✓ And Here's How ...

Before you get started, make sure you have a material that has replenishment information in the STORAGE BIN STOCK section of the WAREHOUSE MANAGEMENT 2 view of the material master, and the stock level of the material in the fix bin is either zero or it's below the replenishment levels (see Tip 53). Also, make sure you've opened outbound deliveries for the material.

To replenish the bins for those materials that have opened deliveries, access Transaction LP22 or follow the menu path:

LOGISTICS • LOGISTICS EXECUTION • INTERNAL WHSE PROCESSES • STOCK TRANSFER • PLANNING OF REPLENISHMENT • BASED UPON OUTBOUND DELIVERIES TO BE SELECTED

This action will look up opened deliveries with materials that are picked from fixed bins and will determine if those bins need to be replenished in their stock level. The result of running this transaction will display transfer requirements for those matching materials based on the data entered in the material master.

On the initial screen of the transaction, fill in the PLANT, STORAGE LOCATION, WARE-HOUSE NUMBER, and STORAGE TYPE fields for which you want to look up opened deliveries. Depending on your system configuration, the resulting transfer requirement might need a requirement number; if so, you'll also need to enter it.

You can also enter further filter information by filling in the PLANNED DATE AND TIME, SHIPPING POINT, DELIVERY GROUP, PICKING DATE, and GOODS ISSUE DATE.

Once you've entered your selection criteria, click EXECUTE or press F8. You'll see a log screen (Figure 1) telling you how many deliveries were found and how many transfer requirements were created.

« *Figure 1* Log for the Transaction Run

Tip 55

Replenishing Warehouse Materials with the Random Storage Method

If a warehouse doesn't use the fixed bin concept to store materials, you can configure the SAP system with a random storage strategy.

There are many warehouses that either don't have a large enough quantity of bins that they're able to assign one bin for each material that they pick in small quantities, or don't like the fixed bin concept at all. Whatever the reasons, if your company doesn't want to use the fixed bin method, the SAP system offers an alternative to replenishing materials into a storage type with a random storage put-away strategy.

✓ And Here's How ...

To start the replenishment of materials into a storage type with random put-away strategy, use Transaction LP24 or follow the path:

> LOGISTICS • LOGISTICS EXECUTION • INTERNAL WHSE PROCESSES • STOCK TRANSFER • PLANNING OF REPLENISHMENT • FOR WAREHOUSE WITH RANDOM STORAGE

The system will look at those materials that have a specific storage type view in the material master, as described in Tip 53, but in this case, you don't need to have a fix bin entered in the material master.

The transaction will prompt you for the PLANT, STORAGE LOCATION, WAREHOUSE NUMBER, and STORAGE TYPE that you want to replenish (see Figure 1). Enter a requirement number, and you have the options of displaying the list of materials/bins that will be replenished, or running in the background without showing the results.

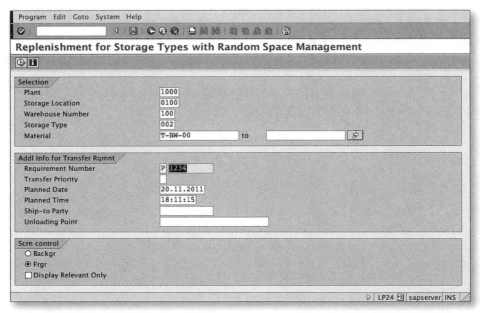

⌃   *Figure 1* Selection Criteria for the Replenishment of Warehouses with Random Storage Strategy

If you choose to run the transaction in the foreground, the result is a list of the bins/materials that need to be replenished into the storage type (see Figure 2). From here you can choose those materials that you do want to replenish and click on SAVE. Note that the quantity to be replenished is also listed.

The only downside to this transaction is that it doesn't take into account opened deliveries to determine the need to replenish as in Tip 54. Every material that indicates that the storage type stock is below the minimum stock from the material master will be replenished.

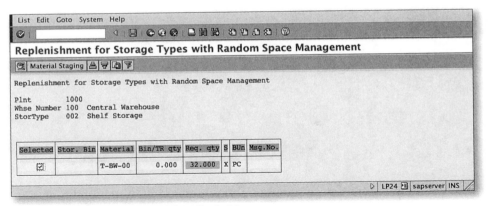

⌃ *Figure 2* *Choose Bins/Materials to Replenish*

If you choose to run in the background, the result will only be the number of transfer requirements and items that were created.

Once the transfer requirements are created, you can go ahead and process them in Transaction LB10. Figure 3 shows the list of transfer requirements.

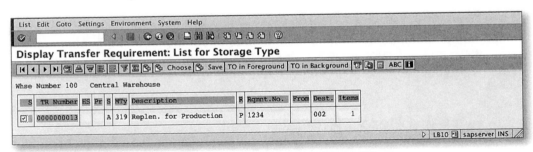

⌃ *Figure 3* *Transaction LB10—Select Transfer Requirements and Create TOs*

You can display the detailed information for the transfer requirement by double-clicking on the list.

Tip 56

Cancelling Picking for Outbound Delivery and Returning Materials to Stock

When picking for outbound deliveries is cancelled, you can configure your SAP system to return goods to the warehouse.

Changes in priorities, credit issues, order cancellation, and many other reasons can cause the picking for an outbound delivery to be cancelled. When this happens, you need an easy way to return the goods to stock. SAP provides you with a standard transaction to do just that, that at the same time logs every activity into the outbound delivery's document flow.

✓ And Here's How ...

To cancel picking for an outbound delivery, use Transaction LT0G or follow the menu path:

> LOGISTICS • LOGISTICS EXECUTION • OUTBOUND PROCESS • GOODS ISSUE FOR OUTBOUND DELIVERY • PICKING • CANCEL TRANSFER ORDER • RETURN TRANSFER FOR OUTBOUND DELIVERY

This transaction looks for outbound deliveries for which the picking status is complete within a warehouse number, and that the goods issue hasn't been posted or has been cancelled.

Enter selection criteria in the first screen shown in Figure 1, always based on a warehouse number. You can enter a list of deliveries for which you want to cancel picking or just let the system find all the delivery items for which picking is complete. You can also select the delivery or the TO item view if you want.

⋀ *Figure 1* *Search Criteria for Outbound Deliveries to Be Returned to Stock*

Once you execute the transaction, you'll see a report listing all the delivery items that have been confirmed for picking (see Figure 2). Some of these items might be locked and the system will present a little lock instead of a selection box on the leftmost edge of the line. Some items cannot be cancelled; for example, lean warehouse items.

⋀ *Figure 2* *List of Deliveries or TO Items with Picking Complete*

For the remaining items, select those you want to reverse. You have three options for action:

▶ PUT AWAY IN BACKGROUND: The system will create a new transfer order to put away the material according to the put-away strategy in the material master.

▶ PUT AWAY IN FOREGROUND: Put the items into any storage type/bin location combination you decide.

▶ RETURN TO STOCK: Stock should be put back in the storage type/bin location that it was originally picked from.

After selecting the right option for you, the system will either highlight the selected lines in green for success or red with a lightning bolt on the selection box when there's a problem.

If you have any problems, click on the LOG button to see what caused the issue. The resulting transfer order is listed in the delivery's document flow (see Figure 3).

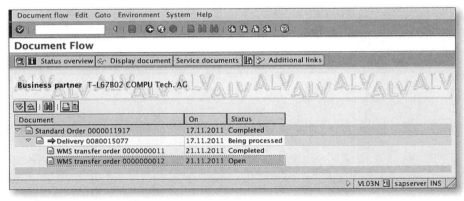

⌃ *Figure 3* Document Flow

The resulting transactions after a successful run will be new transfer orders that will take the product from the 916 - GI area of the warehouse to a destination bin in the warehouse, as shown in Figure 4, depending on the button you clicked to process.

These new transfer orders are part of the delivery's document flow (see Figure 4), which you can display through Transaction VL03N. From here you can display the transfer order by selecting it and clicking on the DISPLAY DOCUMENT button. The new TO will take the goods from the goods issue area back to a location in the warehouse.

Display Transfer Order: Single Item

Other Data... | Confirmation... | ◀ | ▶

TO Number: 12   1   Pump (material supplying)
                            Material   T-BW-00
☐ Confirmation   Plant/Stor.loc. 1000   0100
Stor. Unit Type   E1   Batch
Certificate No.
Item to subsys. ☐   Stock Category
                            Special Stock
Delivery   80015077 10   Weight   14,000.000   KG
                            Volume   0.000
                            Plnd time TOitm 0.000
                            2-step picking ☐

Movement data
Typ   Stor. Bin   Target quantity   AUn
From
916   0080015077 50   PC
Quant 11

Destinat.
001   03-02-01   50   PC
Quant 12

Back

LT21 sapserver INS

⌃ *Figure 4 New TO*

Tip **57**

Maintaining Pick Handling Unit Assignment

If your warehouse maintains a pool of handling units (HUs) created ahead of time to pack picking items, there's a transaction you can use to assign the HU to the transfer order.

In the warehouse, you pick delivery items using the box that will be shipped to the customer, but you may run into problems later when you try to pack the delivery because there's no fast way to identify the box and its contents. To solve this issue, the SAP system allows you to create handling units that aren't assigned to any document; these HUs are created with a physical status of "planned."

This tip will tell you how to assign these "planned" handling units to transfer orders to execute the picking for deliveries, executing the picking and the packing at the same time.

And Here's How ...

Prerequisites

To successfully work with this tip, the following must have already been done in your system:

▶ Your warehouse process includes picking items directly in the containers that will be shipped out.

▶ You can only assign handling units to transfer orders created in a fully implemented WM warehouse. It won't work for lean warehouse implementations.

▶ You've created packaging materials and you've assigned them to packaging material groups.

▶ You've created "planned" HUs in Transaction HU02 using the appropriate packaging material.

▶ To continue with the follow-up functions, you need to proceed to a packing station (Transaction HUPAST) for which you have a packing-for-delivery profile defined.

Assign HU

To assign an HU to a transfer order, use Transaction LH01 or follow the menu path:

LOGISTICS • LOGISTICS EXECUTION • OUTBOUND PROCESS • GOODS ISSUE FOR OUTBOUND DELIVERY • PICKING • ASSIGN PICK HU TO TRANSFER ORDER • MAINTAIN PICK HU ASSIGNMENT

In the selection screen, enter the warehouse number and the TO number to which you want to assign the HU.

Press [Enter], and the transaction will take you to an assignment screen shown in Figure 1. Here you can enter multiple HUs and assign them to the TO. You can maintain the total number of HUs needed, and the system will automatically update the HUs TO assignment number in the table.

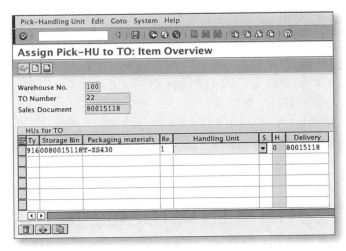

« *Figure 1 Maintaining the Handling Unit Number in the Assign Pick-HU Table*

This table is very helpful when you need to print packing labels that have to tell the total number of boxes and the corresponding number for each box within the total number (e.g. box 1 of 10). To assign a HU to the list, type the HU number or select it from the available HUs using the MATCH-CODE button as shown in Figure 2.

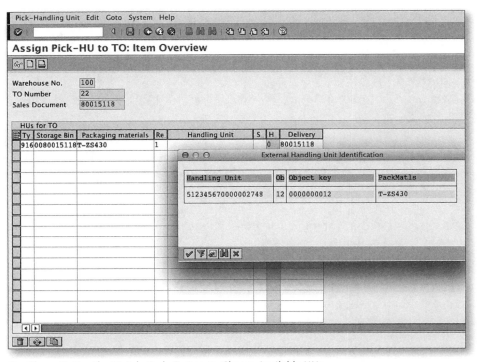

⋩ *Figure 2 Use the Match-Code Button to Choose Available HUs*

This assignment could be done even more easily if you count with bar code readers attached to your warehouse work stations. Alternatively, you could also implement this functionality on hand-held terminals to simplify the tasks.

After saving the assignment, you'll see a message confirming the action. At this point, the items in the delivery aren't packed, but the relation between TO and HU has been established in the system.

When you confirm the TO, the HU assignment appears in the PACK data. You can display it by clicking on the PACK button in Transaction LT21. After confirming the TO, the status of the HU changes to "physically exists" and "in warehouse." The HU is assigned to the delivery, but the items haven't been packed into it.

Tip 58

Displaying Pick Handling Unit Assignments

You can easily display and confirm handling units with a single transaction if you've already assigned them to a transfer order.

If you run into a problem during picking confirmation or packing for a delivery, you can display the pick HU assigned to the TO. This way, you'll know that perhaps you've assigned five HUs to a TO but you have only three at hand. This would prevent you from confirming the transfer order or from executing the packing of the delivery. If you've assigned HUs to a transfer order as described in Tip 57, then you can display them using this transaction.

✓ And Here's How ...

To display the HU assignment, use Transaction LH03 or follow the path:

> LOGISTICS • LOGISTICS EXECUTION • OUTBOUND PROCESS • GOODS ISSUE FOR OUTBOUND DELIVERY • PICKING • ASSIGN PICK HU TO TRANSFER ORDER • DISPLAY PICK HU ASSIGNMENT

In the selection screen, enter the warehouse number and the TO number. When you press [Enter], the transaction will take you to the list of handling units assigned to this TO.

The resulting list in Figure 1 shows you how many total HUs are assigned to the TO, the individual HU assignment number within the TO, and the HU numbers.

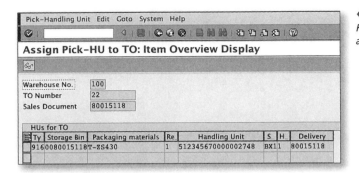

« Figure 1 *List of Handling Units Assigned to a Transfer Order*

This list will help you identify all the HUs assigned to the TO; this way you'll know how many physical containers you need to find, and you can verify that the containers are the correct ones by matching the HU number to the label on the box.

When you display this list after TO confirmation and packing, as in Figure 2, the HU number disappears from the list. This way you know which HUs have been confirmed and packed.

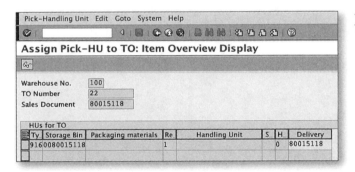

« Figure 2 *Confirming the TO and Packing the HU*

Tip **59**

Using the Packing Station for Deliveries

You can use packing stations to help you pack the contents of deliveries, print labels, and box content documents.

Packing stations are provided by the SAP system to link the physical execution of packing with the system's status of goods. This action is performed outside the outbound delivery change transactions.

You can also choose between generating the handling units at the packing table and printing the labels at that moment, or use HUs that have already been assigned to the picking TOs by means of Transaction LH01.

Working with packing stations in the SAP system can be difficult. In this tip, we'll show you the basic steps to help you understand how to use it.

✓ And Here's How ...

Before you start with this tip, make sure the following things are done in your system:

▶ You've configured packing stations and packing station profiles in Customizing under LOGISTICS EXECUTION • SHIPPING • PACKING. When you configure packing station profiles, you select if the packing station will pack with reference to a delivery number or not. This means that you could either pack the contents of a delivery, or pack an HU inside another HU.

▶ You've defined packaging materials and assigned them to packaging material groups.

▶ Optionally, you've already created and assigned HUs to picking TOs.

To pack a delivery using packing stations, use Transaction HUPAST (see Figure 1) or follow the path:

> LOGISTICS • LOGISTICS EXECUTION • OUTBOUND PROCESS • GOODS ISSUE FOR OUTBOUND DELIVERY • PACK • PACKING STATION

《 Figure 1 *Choose the Correct Packing Station*

Select the PACKING STATION from the initial screen shown in Figure 1 and press [Enter]. In the following screen shown in Figure 2, enter the delivery number that you want to pack. This could be scanned from a document or a label. Press [Enter], and the system will bring up all the handling units that are assigned to this delivery. If none exist, you can enter a packaging material in the HANDLING UNIT field, and the system will create a new HU. If you have defined it so, a HU label will be printed as you generate new handling units.

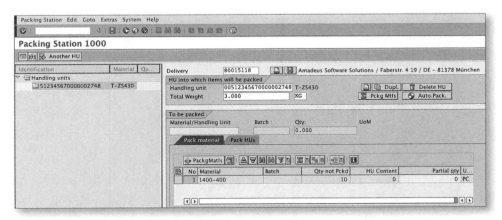

⌃ Figure 2 *Choose the Delivery You Want to Pack*

Once at least one HU exists for the delivery, you can choose it by clicking on the HU number in the tree list at the left of the screen. On the bottom part of the main window, you'll see a list of all the materials that are part of the delivery. You'll also see columns indicating the packed and not yet packed quantities.

To pack piece by piece, enter the material number, a quantity, and press ⌈Enter⌉ (see Figure 3). This will update the packed and unpacked quantities. This is very easy to execute when your materials have been individually labeled with the material number or EAN number and you can scan the bar code to capture this field.

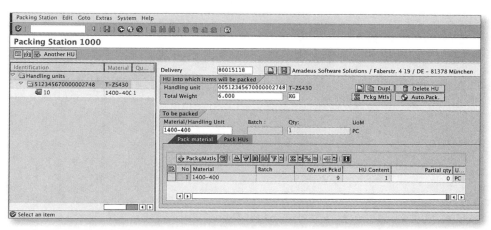

⌃ *Figure 3 Pack Individual Pieces of a Material by Entering a Quantity of One*

Once all the items in the delivery have been packed to the correct HUs, save your work to complete the packing (see Figure 4).

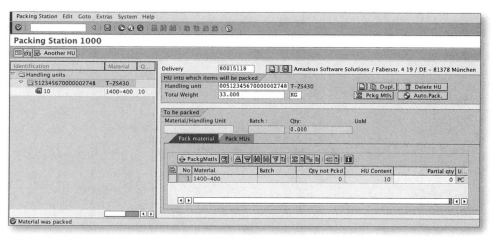

⌃ *Figure 4 Quantity Shows Zero When All Materials Are Packed*

Optionally, you can print the delivery outputs from here by clicking on the printer icon next to the delivery number.

Splitting Outbound Deliveries to Manage Logistics

You can split your delivery if you find out that it's too big to fit into a truck or you can't ship everything the same day.

There are times when you either over-plan an outbound delivery, thinking that all the material you need to ship to a customer will fit into a certain truck, or the truck you needed wasn't available and a smaller one was sent to your warehouse. It could also be that your customer called in to ask you to retain some items for a later delivery date.

In those cases, you can select the items that will actually make it into the truck that day and split the delivery.

 And Here's How ...

Use Transaction VLSP or follow the path:

> LOGISTICS • LOGISTICS EXECUTION • OUTBOUND PROCESS • OUTBOUND DELIVERY •
> CHANGE • SUBSEQUENT OUTBOUND DELIVERY SPLIT

Enter search criteria in the resulting screen to find a list of deliveries (see Figure 1), or directly enter the one delivery number that you want to split. In practice, this is the most common scenario. With your selection criteria complete, click on EXECUTE.

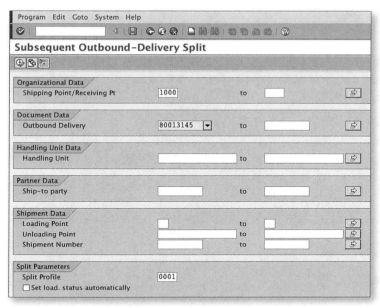

⌃ *Figure 1* Outbound Delivery Split Search Criteria

From the resulting list of deliveries that match your search criteria, you'll be able to select those that you want to process. Each delivery will have a selection box at the leftmost side of each line, and you'll see that it has an entry field for the split quantity. Here you'll enter the quantity you want to take out of the delivery and it'll be put into a brand new delivery order (Figure 2).

⌃ *Figure 2* The Split Quantity Field

After entering the split quantity, click on the SIMULATE SPLIT button to create a new entry on the screen for the delivery that will be created. This new delivery is an exact copy of your original one, with the same sales order reference, partners, dates, etc. The only difference will be the quantity for the material you select (see Figure 3).

If your delivery has several items and you want to move some of these into a new delivery by splitting, enter the whole quantity for each of those items. In this case, your original delivery will have a reduced number of items and a new delivery will be created with the remaining line items.

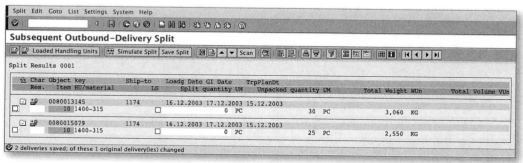

⌃ *Figure 3 A New Delivery Number Assigned to the Line*

Once you're satisfied with the results of the simulation, click on SAVE, and at that point a new delivery number will be assigned.

In the case that your outbound delivery is packed into handling units, then the HU numbers will be displayed and you need to select the full HU to be moved into a new delivery order (see Figure 4).

Char Object key	Ship-to	Loadg Date	GI Date	TrpPlanDt				
Res. Item HU/material	LS	Split quantity	UM	Unpacked quantity	UM	Total Weight WUn	Total Volume VUn
0080015074	1500	21.07.2011	02.12.2011	21.07.2011				
510005670000002732						270.010 KG	0.750 M3
510005670000002718						270.010 KG	0.750 M3
10 P-101			0 PC	0 PC		0 KG	0 M3

⌃ *Figure 4 HU Numbers That You Want to Move into a New Delivery*

Processing Collective Goods Issue via the Outbound Delivery Monitor

You can save time by processing a large number of deliveries at once using the Outbound Delivery Monitor, including posting goods issue.

Warehouses with large operations require a way to collectively post the goods issue for a list of deliveries, which saves time and effort compared to posting the goods movement individually in each delivery.

We've already talked about the Outbound Delivery Monitor in Tip 43. In this tip, you'll find more detail about the monitor's ability to process collective goods issue.

And Here's How ...

To get to the GOODS ISSUE section of the Outbound Delivery Monitor, use Transaction VL06G or follow the path:

> LOGISTICS • LOGISTICS EXECUTION • OUTBOUND PROCESS • GOODS ISSUE FOR OUT-
> BOUND DELIVERY • POST GOODS ISSUE • COLLECTIVE PROCESSING VIA OUTBOUND
> DELIVERY MONITOR

The initial screen shown in Figure 1 gives you many choices for entering a wide open or very specific search criteria. You might want to look at all the outbound deliveries that are ready for PGI in one or a set of shipping points. You can also enter a delivery group number or just a list of delivery numbers directly.

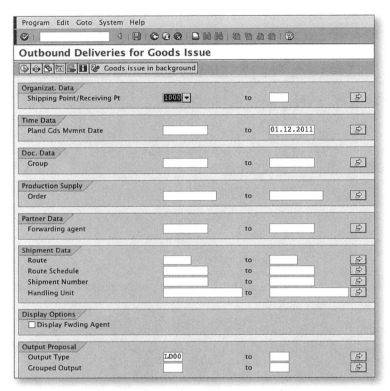

⨺   *Figure 1* Outbound Deliveries for Goods Issue Initial Screen

Once you've entered your search criteria, click on the EXECUTE button. The resulting list shown in Figure 2 will include all of the outbound deliveries that matched your parameters. To display the header info or the item info, click on the ITEM VIEW button. To get back to the HEADER INFO, click on the HEADER VIEW button.

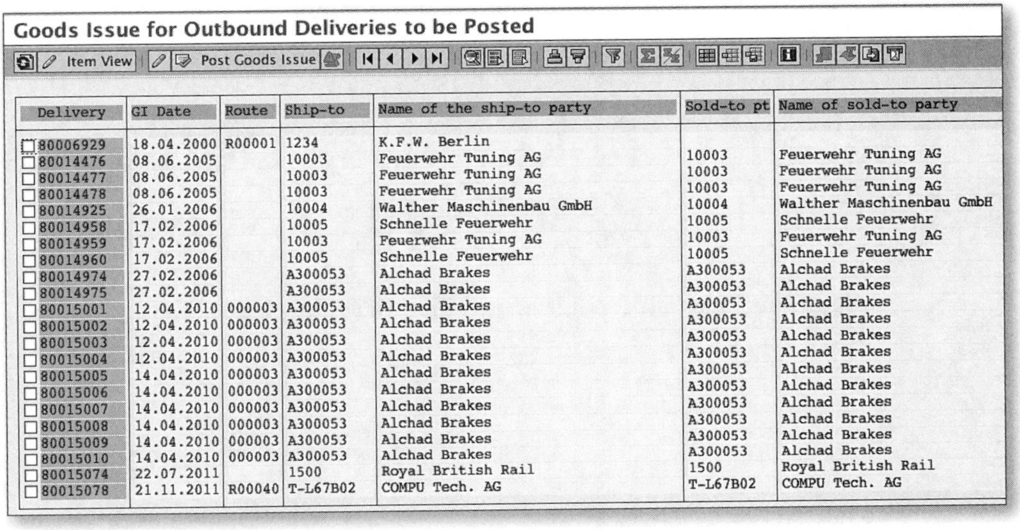

Goods Issue for Outbound Deliveries to be Posted

Item View | Post Goods Issue

Delivery	GI Date	Route	Ship-to	Name of the ship-to party	Sold-to pt	Name of sold-to party
80006929	18.04.2000	R00001	1234	K.F.W. Berlin		
80014476	08.06.2005		10003	Feuerwehr Tuning AG	10003	Feuerwehr Tuning AG
80014477	08.06.2005		10003	Feuerwehr Tuning AG	10003	Feuerwehr Tuning AG
80014478	08.06.2005		10003	Feuerwehr Tuning AG	10003	Feuerwehr Tuning AG
80014925	26.01.2006		10004	Walther Maschinenbau GmbH	10004	Walther Maschinenbau GmbH
80014958	17.02.2006		10005	Schnelle Feuerwehr	10005	Schnelle Feuerwehr
80014959	17.02.2006		10003	Feuerwehr Tuning AG	10003	Feuerwehr Tuning AG
80014960	17.02.2006		10005	Schnelle Feuerwehr	10005	Schnelle Feuerwehr
80014974	27.02.2006		A300053	Alchad Brakes	A300053	Alchad Brakes
80014975	27.02.2006		A300053	Alchad Brakes	A300053	Alchad Brakes
80015001	12.04.2010	000003	A300053	Alchad Brakes	A300053	Alchad Brakes
80015002	12.04.2010	000003	A300053	Alchad Brakes	A300053	Alchad Brakes
80015003	12.04.2010	000003	A300053	Alchad Brakes	A300053	Alchad Brakes
80015004	12.04.2010	000003	A300053	Alchad Brakes	A300053	Alchad Brakes
80015005	14.04.2010	000003	A300053	Alchad Brakes	A300053	Alchad Brakes
80015006	14.04.2010	000003	A300053	Alchad Brakes	A300053	Alchad Brakes
80015007	14.04.2010	000003	A300053	Alchad Brakes	A300053	Alchad Brakes
80015008	14.04.2010	000003	A300053	Alchad Brakes	A300053	Alchad Brakes
80015009	14.04.2010	000003	A300053	Alchad Brakes	A300053	Alchad Brakes
80015010	14.04.2010	000003	A300053	Alchad Brakes	A300053	Alchad Brakes
80015074	22.07.2011		1500	Royal British Rail	1500	Royal British Rail
80015078	21.11.2011	R00040	T-L67B02	COMPU Tech. AG	T-L67B02	COMPU Tech. AG

Figure 2 List of Deliveries Matching the Search Criteria in the Header View

From here you can either select all the deliveries by using the SELECT ALL button or pressing [F5], or select only a few by using the checkboxes on the leftmost column. Once you've selected the right deliveries, click on the POST GOODS ISSUE button or press [F8].

After processing, the lines on the screen will be highlighted in green for the successfully PGI deliveries and red for the ones with problems. The problems are reported on the error log. To display the error log, you can click on the ERROR LOG button to the right of the PGI button.

Tip 62

Cancelling or Reversing Outbound Deliveries after Goods Issue

You can cancel outbound deliveries, even after you've posted the goods issue.

When you receive indication at the warehouse to stop the shipment of goods and cancel the delivery orders, sometimes it's after the goods have been picked and goods issue has been posted. Other times you just need the material for a client with higher priority. If this cancellation is not done properly, it can lead to incomplete documents and inconsistencies. In this tip we will show you that the SAP system offers a standard way to cancel or reverse the PGI.

And Here's How ...

As a prerequisite to use this tip, you must have an outbound delivery with goods issue posted, but no billing executed.

To reverse the goods issue for a delivery order, use Transaction VL09 or follow the path:

> LOGISTICS • LOGISTICS EXECUTION • OUTBOUND PROCESS • GOODS ISSUE FOR OUTBOUND DELIVERY • POST GOODS ISSUE • CANCELATION/REVERSAL

The selection criteria for this transaction will look for all the deliveries with completed goods issue. If you don't enter very specific values, you run the risk of selecting more deliveries than you need and creating a problem for yourself. As shown in Figure 1, it's better if you directly enter the shipping point and the delivery number or numbers and EXECUTE the transaction.

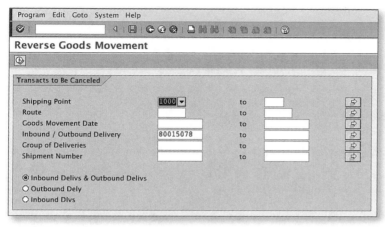

 Figure 1 Selection in Transaction VL09

The resulting list will include only the deliveries that you're absolutely sure that you want to cancel the goods issue for. In Figure 2, the next step is to select the deliveries using the button at the leftmost of each line. You can also click on the SELECT ALL button. Once the deliveries are selected, click on the REVERSE button or press F8.

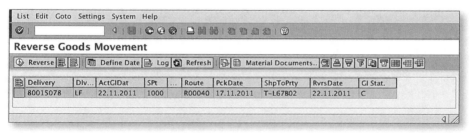

 Figure 2 Select the Deliveries to Cancel

You'll see a confirmation screen pop-up; if you confirm, you'll see another pop-up window come up with the results of each posting as shown in Figure 3.

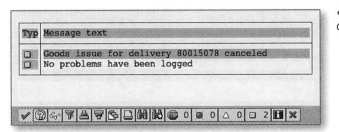

« Figure 3 Log for Each Cancelled Delivery

If you display our delivery again, you can see the cancellation posting in the document flow. From the screen shown in Figure 4, you could continue and cancel the picking and if needed, cancel the delivery.

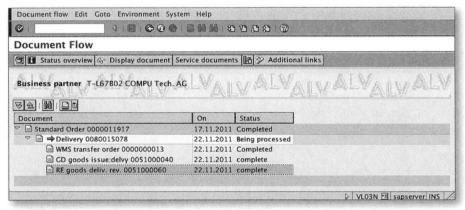

⟰ Figure 4 Updated Document Flow for the Delivery after Cancelling

Tip 63

Processing Deliveries Using the Warehouse Activity Monitor

You can configure the warehouse activity monitor to show warehouse objects and deliveries, so you're better able to review and process critical deliveries.

Usually picking is initiated using outbound delivery monitor functions. A warehouse manager will want to review and process picking for deliveries using the warehouse activity monitor, which also allows you to review all other pending WM transactions on one screen where all critical objects are listed. You should use this transaction because it allows you to review incomplete transactions as well as print, display, and complete or cancel transfer orders, transfer requirements, and posting changes.

✓ And Here's How ...

To run a report for partially processed and ready-for-processing deliveries, execute Transaction LL01 or follow the menu path:[2]

> LOGISTICS • LOGISTICS EXECUTION • INFORMATION SYSTEM • WAREHOUSE • WAREHOUSE ACTIVITY MONITOR

On the initial screen, specify a warehouse number and enter a variant for the data selection (this is usually predefined by the implementation team). You can preset the variant as a default by maintaining the user parameter LVA in Transaction SU3 and specifying the variant name as a parameter value (see Figure 1).

---

2   Prerequisites for this transaction include defining critical objects and time intervals in the IMG.

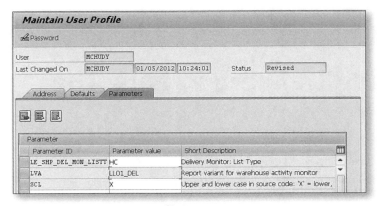

⩘ *Figure 1* Maintain User Profile Parameters

Click on the EXECUTE icon or press F8 to continue. If you haven't already maintained a variant, another selection screen will appear where you can fine-tune selection for all critical objects. To continue, simply click on the EXECUTE icon again. On the next screen, you'll see the main body of the report, listing all selected critical objects grouped by object type listing the number of transactions that met your criteria and defined in configuration time bracket (see Figure 2).

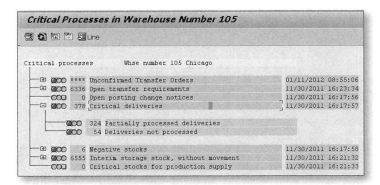

⩘ *Figure 2* Critical Processes List

An object becomes critical and will be captured on this report if it's in an unprocessed or partially processed state for longer than the defined time limit; for example, unprocessed deliveries will become critical after two hours from the time they were created. To display critical deliveries ready for processing, locate the node CRITICAL DELIVERIES. To open the subcategories that further divide the deliveries onto PARTIALLY PROCESSED DELIVERIES and DELIVERIES NOT PROCESSED, click on the FOLDER icon on the left. You'll also get the number of deliveries listed for each category. Next, double-click on the sub-category line or click once and click on the DETAILED DISPLAY icon. Your screen will show delivery document numbers ready for processing (see Figure 3).

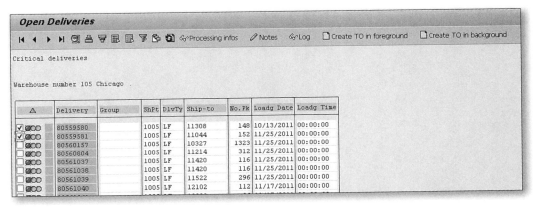

Open Deliveries

	Delivery	Group	ShPt	DlvTy	Ship-to	No.Pk	Loadg Date	Loadg Time
☑	80559580		1005	LF	11308	148	10/13/2011	00:00:00
☑	80559581		1005	LF	11044	152	11/25/2011	00:00:00
☐	80560157		1005	LF	10327	1323	11/25/2011	00:00:00
☐	80560804		1005	LF	11214	312	11/25/2011	00:00:00
☐	80561037		1005	LF	11420	116	11/25/2011	00:00:00
☐	80561038		1005	LF	11420	116	11/25/2011	00:00:00
☐	80561039		1005	LF	11522	296	11/25/2011	00:00:00
☐	80561040		1005	LF	12102	112	11/17/2011	00:00:00

Critical deliveries

Warehouse number 105 Chicago .

Figure 3 *Open Deliveries List*

To execute picking for any of the listed documents, select the delivery you want to process and click on one of the following buttons:

▶ CREATE TO IN FOREGROUND: You'll get the transfer order creation screen of Transaction LT03 (Create TO for Delivery). Complete the process by clicking on the SAVE icon.

▶ CREATE TO IN BACKGROUND: You'll create transfers in the background, which is similar to running Transaction VL06P. Upon completion, the selected deliveries traffic light color will change to either yellow, for past-due deliveries; or green, for deliveries picked on time.

▶ You can also display the delivery document itself by clicking on the CHOOSE icon; this is like running Transaction VL03N (Display Delivery Document).

Note that with this transaction you can't create picking waves or groups that will allow processing of several deliveries together. This has to be done using Transaction VL06P or using pick waves functions.

Part 5

Transportation

Things You'll Learn in this Section

The transportation functionality is a natural extension of the shipping process and completes the logistics chain. You apply transportation planning and execution to both inbound and outbound processes, making sure your shipments arrive on time. Let's say that your shipping volumes can no longer be processed manually, whether due to business growth or system upgrades. The transactions we'll cover in this part of the book will help you to understand and make progress in automating and mass processing transportation transactions. You'll also gain efficiency by learning to use transactions listed in this chapter that will let you focus on areas that really need your attention.

Running a Transportation Planning List and Applying Mass Changes

You can quickly provide information on multiple shipments' status and apply mass changes to selected data fields that need an update or maintenance.

Information availability is crucial and this scenario can happen quite often. Your forwarding agent for several shipments needs to be changed, and updating the data for individual shipments takes a lot of time. With the service provider, there's a possibility that the route has to be updated as well, making the manual change even more tedious. You need a one-stop transaction that allows you to monitor the status of your shipments. In this tip, you'll learn how to access individual shipment details and make mass changes to key data such as shipment route and forwarding agent.

✅ And Here's How ...

To execute the shipment planning report and mass maintain the required data, run Transaction VT11 or follow the path:

> LOGISTICS • LOGISTICS EXECUTION • TRANSPORTATION • TRANSPORTATION PLANNING • LISTS AND LOGS • TRANSP. PLANNING LIST

On the initial screen, enter as much data as possible. The selection data is grouped by type and you have the following options:

- ▸ PROCESSING: Includes service agent, route, and shipping type
- ▸ IDENTIFICATIONS: Lists container and vehicle ID data
- ▸ CURRENT TENDER STATUS: Includes the status, reason codes, time stamps, and validity data
- ▸ STATUS AND DEADLINES: Includes the dates and timestamps you can use for selecting either planned or actual deadline data
- ▸ GENERAL DATA: Allows for selection by shipment, shipment type, and transportation planning point
- ▸ SHIPMENT STAGE: POINT OF DEPARTURE: Multitude of criteria including departure points, loading points, and plant
- ▸ SHIPMENT STAGE: DESTINATION: Destination point, shipping point at the destination, loading point, plant, and customer at the destination
- ▸ ADMINISTRATIVE DATA: Includes user name and creation and change dates
- ▸ WITH REFERENCE TO: You have a choice of objects related to the shipment document such as purchase orders, deliveries, and other shipments
- ▸ MEANS OF TRANSPORT: Specify the type, handling units, and drivers
- ▸ HANDLING UNIT: Limit the selection by specifying the packaging material type and external ID of the HU
- ▸ ADDITIONAL DATA: Supplemental fields that are freely definable
- ▸ DANGEROUS GOODS: Select blocking indicators and choose if dangerous goods are part of your criteria

Once you've maintained these fields, click on the EXECUTE button or press F8 to continue. On the next screen, you'll get a list of shipments that met your selection criteria (see Figure 1).

To maintain individual shipment data, select the line you want and click on the CHANGE SHIPMENT icon or press Shift + F7 . This is similar to running Transaction VT02N. In order to mass change data for multiple shipments at once, select the documents you need to update and click on the MASS CHANGE icon or press Ctrl + Shift + F3 .

Now, indicate what changes you want to make to your selected shipments. Scroll through all the data tabs shown and specify the new values in the REFERENCE template line, the first line of the table displayed. You can also type the data into the individual fields instead of using the template if some of the update values are different for each of the documents. Then select the shipments this change is applicable to and click on the REFERENCE button or press ⌨F8 to transfer template data to the selected documents (see Figure 2). If you didn't use the template method and you've manually maintained the data for individual shipments, just click on the SAVE icon or press ⌨Ctrl+⌨F1.

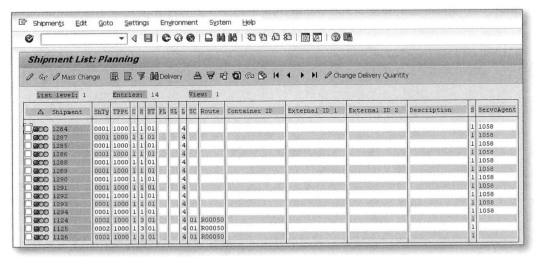

⌃ **Figure 1** Shipment List Planning

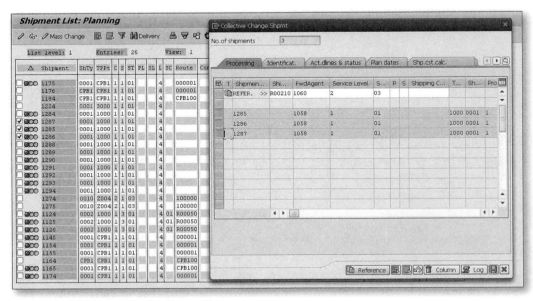

⌃ **Figure 2** Collective Change Shipment

If your update ended up with warning or error messages, you can review these by clicking on the LOG icon. This will bring up another screen where you can review messages and investigate the cause (see Figure 3).

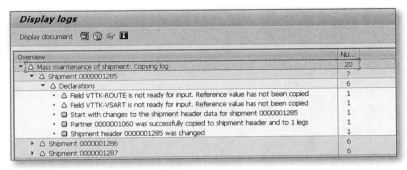

≫ **Figure 3** Display Processing Logs

From the main screen shown in Figure 1, you can also execute additional reports by navigating to the ENVIRONMENT option on your pull-down menu and selecting SHIPMENT LISTS. Here you can start additional reports such as:

▶ UTILIZATION: Starts Transaction VT14

▶ CAPACITY: Starts Transaction VT15

▶ CHECK-IN: Starts Transaction VT16

▶ SHIPMENT COMPLETION: Starts Transaction VT12

▶ COLLECTIVE PROCESSING OF FREIGHT COSTS: Starts Transaction VI04

If you choose any one of these options, you'll close the Transaction VT11 report and there's no coming back to it, so make your selection wisely. All unsaved data will be lost.

Tip 65

Automating the Creation of Shipments

If your business volume has increased dramatically, you can abandon the manual shipment processing and automate shipment creation.

If your business process includes shipment documents, when your company has progressive growth, you need to automate as many functions as possible so that you're able to concentrate on things that really need your attention. In this tip, we'll focus on how to automate how your company creates shipments via collective processing.

We'll assume that you have fairly well-defined transportation management master data like routes, route determination, and forwarding agents as a base to make the next steps into collective processing. You also want to have options to run these jobs in the foreground or background. (The background mode will be covered in Tip 66.)

 And Here's How ...

To set up collective processing (or in other words, set up a job that will create multiple shipments based on the criteria set in the variants), run Transaction VT04 or follow the path:

> LOGISTICS • LOGISTICS EXECUTION • TRANSPORTATION • TRANSPORTATION PLANNING • CREATE • COLLECTIVE PROCESSING

On the selection screen, select the variants that drive the creation of shipment documents. If your variants are already created, you can use the dropdown for each of the listed fields and choose from the available selection. If none are available, create your own variants to continue.

The screen shown in Figure 1 is divided into few sections that include:

▶ DEFAULT SETTINGS: Specify whether you want to create inbound or outbound shipments.

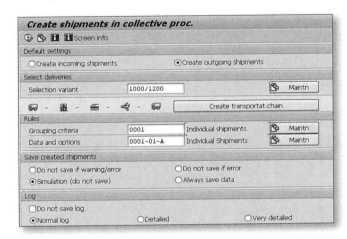

《 *Figure 1* *Create Shipments in Collective Processing Initial Screen*

▶ SELECT DELIVERIES (mandatory field): Choose existing variants or create a new variant. This will specify the criteria to select the deliveries that will be subject for analysis. You can display or modify variants by clicking on MAINTAIN to the right of the input field.

▶ RULES: In this section, you can maintain selection variants (see Figure 2):

    ▶ GROUPING CRITERIA (optional field): If left blank, all selected deliveries will be allocated to one shipment. Group deliveries into a shipment that uses the same shipping point, route, postal code of the destination address, or maximum weight, for example.

    ▶ DATA AND OPTIONS (required field): Specify additional data like transportation planning point, service agent, shipment type, and route. You can also define if you want to execute leg determination.

▶ CREATE TRANSPORTATION CHAINS: If you want to create an entire transportation chain at once in this collective processing run, click on this button and choose or create new variants for GROUPING CRITERIA and DATA AND OPTIONS. This selection, however, will be relevant for grouping of deliveries in main leg, preliminary, and subsequent leg shipments.

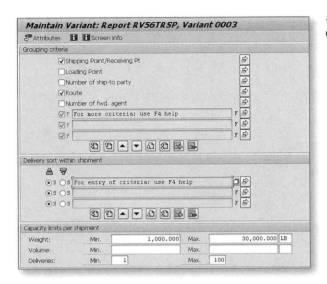

« *Figure 2* *Maintain Grouping Criteria Variant*

▶ SAVE CREATED SHIPMENTS: Here you can choose to ignore errors and warnings and create shipment documents regardless, or choose not to (this could be due to route, forwarding agent determination, or weight or volume restriction errors). You can also run simulations that will allow you to review the proposed test runs before firming the results.

▶ LOG: Choose if you want to save the processing log data and at what level of detail.

When you're done selecting or maintaining all your variants, you can save the data on the main screen as another main program variant by clicking on the SAVE icon or pressing Ctrl+S on your keyboard. These settings can be later reused for setting this selection as a background job; see Tip 66 for details. Click on the EXECUTE button or press F8 to start the process of shipment creation. Upon completion, a new screen will pop up showing the log data (see Figure 3) indicating the number of delivery documents that met your selection criteria defined in the previous steps and the number of shipments created.

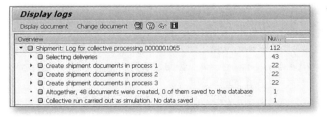

« *Figure 3* *Display Log Data*

Tip 66

Running Collective Processing of Shipments in the Background

You can schedule periodic jobs for shipment creation and run them in the background to avoid strain on your system's resources.

In Tip 65, we discussed how to create shipments collectively in the foreground. However, if you have an increased volume of transactions and processing time required, collectively processing shipments in the foreground can be a huge drain on your system. You can avoid this issue by executing these as a job in the background mode and schedule it periodically to use your system resources efficiently. This way you're removing a constant manual execution from the daily tasks of transportation management personnel so they can focus only on the results of the background job run.

✓ And Here's How ...

To start the collective processing of shipments in the background, run Transaction VT07 or follow the path:

LOGISTICS • LOGISTICS EXECUTION • TRANSPORTATION • TRANSPORTATION PLANNING • CREATE • COLLECTIVE PROCESSING IN BACKGROUND

On the selection screen (see Figure 1), you'll see a list of available variants needed to execute the transaction. These variants are basically the presets defined on the selection screen of Transaction VT04 covered in Tip 65.

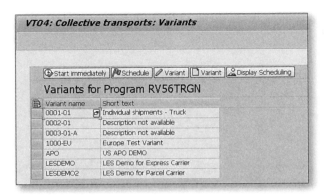

« Figure 1 Collective Processing in Background Selection Screen

You can change the existing variants listed if data has changed since the variant was originally created by selecting the variant and then clicking on the CHANGE VARI-ANT icon or by pressing F7 . On the next screen you'll have options to maintain the values, as shown in Figure 2.

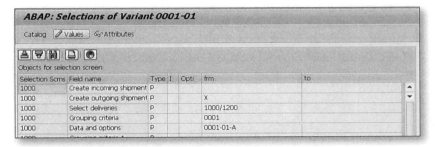

⌃ Figure 2 Change Variant Selection Screen

Click on the CHANGE VALUES icon to see the initial screen for Transaction VT04 (covered in Tip 65) where the selection data can be updated. Apply changes as needed, save your data, and return to the initial screen.

You can now make a selection to run your job immediately, which will be executed when you click on the START IMMEDIATELY button or when you press F5 . For this tip, however, you're scheduling the periodic job, so click on the SCHEDULE icon or press F6 . On the next screen, define the job parameters such as start date and time and period values (see Figure 3). Once you define the parameters that meet your criteria, click on the CREATE icon. You'll see a message on the bottom left portion of the screen informing you that the job has been scheduled.

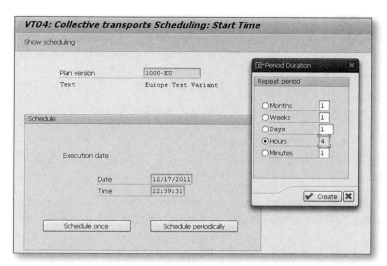

≪ Figure 3
*Scheduling of Batch
Job*

To leave this screen, click on the BACK icon or press ⌊F3⌋. With your job defined, you can now access the status by clicking on the DISPLAY SCHEDULING icon. You can also get there by using the pull-down menu GoTo • DISPLAY JOBS. You can access log data, review results, change job parameters, delete the job definition, or simply update the screen with the latest status (see Figure 4).

≪ Figure 4 Display
Scheduling List

When done, press ⌊F3⌋ to go back to the initial screen.

Tip 67

Reviewing Transportation Job Logs for Collective Shipment Processing

If you're using collective or background jobs, you can use a one-stop transaction to review results of periodic background jobs and jobs executed in dialog mode for shipment creation.

In previous tips we've discussed how to create shipments collectively in the foreground (using Transaction VT04) and in the background (using Transaction VT07). By introducing collective and background jobs for shipment creation covered in Tips 65 and 66, you also eliminated the immediate access to transaction results since these are no longer using dialog mode. In this tip, we'll show you an alternative way to review logs, look for failed transactions, and evaluate created shipments with incomplete data that will prevent you from getting your shipments on the road.

 And Here's How ...

Start Transaction VT05 or follow the path:

> LOGISTICS • LOGISTICS EXECUTION • TRANSPORTATION • TRANSPORTATION PLANNING • LISTS AND LOGS • LOGS

On the initial screen, specify your selection criteria for the jobs you're retrieving in the COLLECTIVE RUN section that includes collective run number, user, date, time, and operating mode (like batch—logs generated by Transaction VT07, or dialog processing—generated using Transaction VT04).

In the Log Class section, select the type of logs for your report choosing all logs, errors only, or errors and warnings. When you've correctly maintained this information, click on the Execute icon or press [F8] to continue. On the subsequent screen you'll see a list of collective runs for your review. In the first column you'll find the Status indicator (traffic lights; see Figure 1) notifying you about errors and warnings.

	Status	Coll.run	Date	Time	User	Transaction code	M	P	Expiry date	K	S
	⬤◯◯	1050	05/27/2009	16:56:48	MCHUDY		B	2	12/31/9999		
	◯◯◻	1060	12/15/2011	16:07:14	MCHUDY	VT04	D	4	12/31/9999		
	◯◯◯	1061	12/15/2011	16:09:25	MCHUDY	VT04	D	3	12/31/9999		
	◯◯◯	1062	12/15/2011	16:10:16	MCHUDY	VT04	D	3	12/31/9999		
	⬤◯◯	1063	12/15/2011	16:20:06	MCHUDY	VT04	D	2	12/31/9999		
	⬤◯◯	1064	12/15/2011	16:21:07	MCHUDY	VT04	D	2	12/31/9999		
	◯◯◻	1065	12/15/2011	16:26:45	MCHUDY	VT04	D	4	12/31/9999		
	⬤◯◯	1066	12/15/2011	16:31:00	MCHUDY	VT04	D	2	12/31/9999		
	⬤◯◯	1068	12/15/2011	17:25:14	MCHUDY	VT04	D	2	12/31/9999		
	⬤◯◯	1070	12/19/2011	08:29:14	MCHUDY		B	2	12/31/9999		

Figure 1 Logs Selection List

▶ **Red**: Errors were captured during the shipment creation process. This doesn't mean that shipment didn't get created; it simply indicates that some of the required tasks (like finding deliveries, excessive weight, or posting goods issue to delivery, for example) failed.

▶ **Yellow**: Warnings have been issued. This happens when some of the optional data wasn't populated, or data wasn't available in the delivery documents and wasn't copied over to the shipment (like service agent or route information).

▶ **Green**: No issues were reported.

If you want to see a detailed log message, simply drill into the listed collective run by clicking on the collective run number. Review listed messages and drill into the nodes that need your attention and potential corrections.

Once you get to the node with listed document numbers (like shipment or delivery), click on the line and access the display (like running Transaction VL03N for delivery or Transaction VT03N for shipments) or change mode (like running

Transaction VL02N for delivery or Transaction VT02N for shipments) by using the buttons in the top part of the screen (see Figure 2).

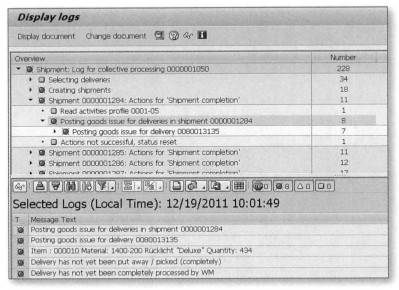

Display logs

Display document   Change document   🔲 ⑦ ⟨⟩ ⚐

Overview	Number
▼ 🔘 Shipment: Log for collective processing 0000001050	228
▶ ☐ Selecting deliveries	34
▶ 🔘 Creating shipments	18
▼ 🔘 Shipment 0000001284: Actions for 'Shipment completion'	11
• ☐ Read activities profile 0001-05	1
▼ 🔘 Posting goods issue for deliveries in shipment 0000001284	8
▶ 🔘 Posting goods issue for delivery 0080013135	7
• ☐ Actions not successful, status reset	1
▶ 🔘 Shipment 0000001285: Actions for 'Shipment completion'	11
▶ 🔘 Shipment 0000001286: Actions for 'Shipment completion'	12
▶ 🔘 Shipment 0000001287: Actions for 'Shipment completion'	17

Selected Logs (Local Time): 12/19/2011 10:01:49

T...	Message Text
🔘	Posting goods issue for deliveries in shipment 0000001284
🔘	Posting goods issue for delivery 0080013135
🔘	Item : 000010 Material: 1400-200 Rücklicht "Deluxe" Quantity: 434
🔘	Delivery has not yet been put away / picked (completely)
🔘	Delivery has not yet been completely processed by WM

⌃ **Figure 2** Display Logs Details

You can review the document directly and make necessary changes at once from here without closing your log review. To go back to the previous screen, click on the BACK button or press F3. To close the transaction immediately, click on the CANCEL icon or press F12.

Printing Shipping Documents with a Mass-Output Procedure

You can print all relevant shipping documents using one transaction including packing slips, pro forma invoices, and bills of lading.

Your carrier appointments are approaching or are already overdue and yet the documentation isn't being produced quickly enough. Instead of using individual output processing transactions, you can expedite the process of printing shipping documents in seconds using a one-stop screen that will allow you to print all relevant documents, whether they're delivery or shipment document related. This will allow you to produce all necessary paperwork in one spot instead of collecting them from different transactions or processes.

✓ And Here's How ...

In order to centralize your output processing, make sure all relevant output conditions and output determination procedures are in place. To perform the mass output procedure, use Transaction VT70 or follow the menu path:

> LOGISTICS • LOGISTICS EXECUTION • TRANSPORTATION • EXECUTION • PRINT

On the initial screen, you can manually select your data, call a variant using the GET VARIANT icon, or press [Shift]+[F5]. After doing this, a variant dialog window will pop up where you make your selection by clicking on the desired variant name and clicking on the CHOOSE icon or pressing [F2] to confirm (see Figure 1).

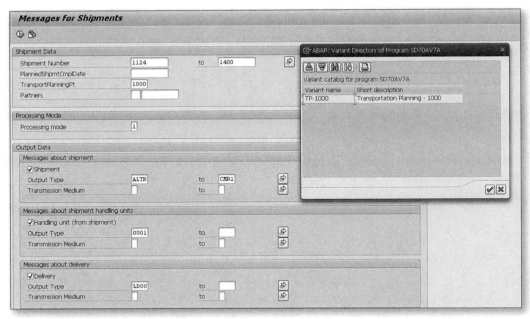

⌃ **Figure 1** *Messages for Shipments Initial Screen*

Review each of the data selection sections that will allow you to enter the following:

- ► SHIPMENT DATA: Allows you to specify either individual or a range of shipment documents, planned completion date, transportation planning point, and partner data.

- ► PROCESSING MODE: Here you specify if you'll be processing the output for the first time, issuing it again, or just reprocessing error requests.

- ► OUTPUT DATA: Specify what document types, what output conditions, and what type of message transmission medium (fax, print, or EDI) will be used. You can process output for shipment, delivery, shipment handling units, delivery handling units, and invoices.

- ► PRINTER CONTROL: Print profile will allow you to redetermined printers, and you can further automate the profile assignment by specifying the parameter ID PPT and the name of the profile you've defined in user own data (running Transaction SU3).

In our example, we've selected output for shipments BOL, delivery notes, and pro forma invoices. Click on the EXECUTE icon or press [F8] when ready with your selection data. Your documents ready for output processing will be listed on the next screen (see Figure 2).

Messages for Shipments

Shipment	Object cat.	OBJECT ID	Item	Out.	Output description	Med	Role	Name	Name 1	City
1124	Shipment ;			ALTR	Shipment:General Doc	1	SP	Forwarding agent	Nordspeed GmbH	Hamburg
1124	BillingDoc;	0090037597		RD00	Invoice	1	WE	Ship-to party	LCH Markt	Hamburg
1124	Delivery ;	0080013645		LD00	Delivery note	1	WE	Ship-to party	LCH Markt	Hamburg

⌃ *Figure 2* Messages for Shipments Details

Click on the PRINT PREVIEW icon or press Shift + F4 to preview the documents (see Figure 3).

Print Preview of LP01 Page 00001 of 00001

Archive   Print and Archive

Firma	**Delivery note**
Crocodile Enterprise	
12 Braodway	
Springfield 07081	Shipping information

	Delivery note number/date	80015111 / 12/15/2011
	Customer number	CMS0000001

Conditions   Weight - Volume

Shipping   Standard
Delivery   CFR Cost and Freight

Shipping details

Item	Material	Quantity	Weight
	Description		
000010	M-12	0 PC	0 KG
	MAG DX 15F/Fe		
	Order 11667 / 01/12/2006		
	Purchase order number_K/item 345345		
000020	M-12	0 PC	0 KG
	MAG DX 15F/Fe		
	Order 11668 / 01/13/2006		

⌃ *Figure 3* Print Preview Delivery Note

When ready, simply select the checkboxes for the documents you want to print, click on the SELECT ALL icon and click EXECUTE, or press F8 to continue. Once all documents have been printed successfully, the lines will be highlighted in green. You can repeat the steps for another set of selection criteria by returning to the initial screen using F3 or the BACK icon.

Collectively Processing Shipment Cost Documents

Once you've introduced the procedure of processing shipment cost documents, you can mass create them for several shipments at a time.

Your business process includes shipment documents and you've started tracking your freight spend using shipment cost documents. With numbers of shipments growing, the number of shipment cost documents increases in parallel. You need to automate this process, which we'll teach you how to do with this tip in the foreground. You should already have all supporting master data in place, including pricing and three-dimensional scales. (The scheduled mode will be covered in Tip 70.)

✓ And Here's How ...

To start collective processing of shipment cost documents, run Transaction VI04 or follow the path:

> LOGISTICS • LOGISTICS EXECUTION • TRANSPORTATION • SHIPMENT COSTS • CREATE • COLLECTIVE PROCESSING

On the initial screen, enter as much data as possible. You can also enable additional fields by clicking on the ALL SELECTIONS button or pressing [Shift]+[F7] to toggle back and forth. The selection data is almost identical to what we've covered in Tip 64 for Transaction VT11 and it's also grouped by type:

▶ PROCESSING: Includes service agent, route, and shipping type

▶ IDENTIFICATIONS: Lists container and vehicle ID data

▶ CURRENT TENDER STATUS: Includes the status, reason codes, time stamps, and validity data

▶ STATUS AND DEADLINES: Includes the dates and timestamps you can use for selecting either planned or actual deadline data

▶ GENERAL DATA: Allows for selection by shipment, shipment type, and transportation planning point

▶ SHIPMENT STAGE: POINT OF DEPARTURE: Multitude of criteria including departure points, loading points, and plant

▶ SHIPMENT STAGE: DESTINATION: Destination point, shipping point at the destination, loading point, plant, and customer at the destination

▶ ADMINISTRATIVE DATA: Includes user name, creation, and change dates

▶ WITH REFERENCE TO: You have a choice of objects related to the shipment document like purchase orders, deliveries, and other shipments

▶ MEANS OF TRANSPORT: Use for specifying the type, handling units, and drivers

▶ HANDLING UNIT: Limit the selection by specifying the packaging material type and external ID of the HU

▶ ADDITIONAL DATA: Supplemental fields that are freely definable

▶ DANGEROUS GOODS: Select blocking indicators and choose if dangerous goods are part of your criteria

Once you've maintained this information, press F8 to execute the transaction and continue. On the next screen, you'll see a list of shipments that met your selection criteria and are subject for shipment cost document processing (see Figure 1).

❯ **Figure 1** Shipment List Selection List

You can maintain individual shipment data from this screen; to do this, select the line and click on the CHANGE SHIPMENT icon or press Shift + F7 . This is similar to running Transaction VT02N. You can also access a shipment in display mode by clicking on the DISPLAY SHIPMENT icon or by pressing Shift + F6 ; this is the equivalent of executing Transaction VT03N.

If you need to access a shipment that has a specific delivery document assigned to it, filter your selection by clicking on the FIND DELIVERY icon or pressing F8 . On the resulting delivery search screen (see Figure 2), enter your search criteria and click on the EXECUTE icon or press F8 . The system will retrieve a single line listing the shipment the delivery is assigned to. This is useful when you need to expedite processing of shipment cost documents.

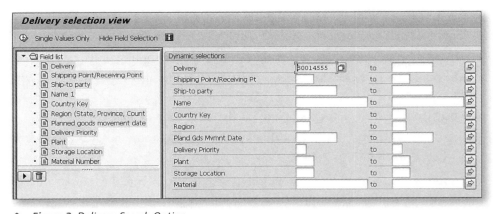

⌃ **Figure 2** Delivery Search Option

Next, select the line or lines you want to process and click on the CHOOSE button or press Ctrl + F12 to continue. Once the system has processed your collective run, you'll get a message informing you to review your results in the log, which you can access by clicking on the LOG icon or by pressing Ctrl + F10 (see Figure 3). Review the log messages, and if you need to access any of the documents listed, click on the line and click on the DISPLAY DOCUMENT icon.

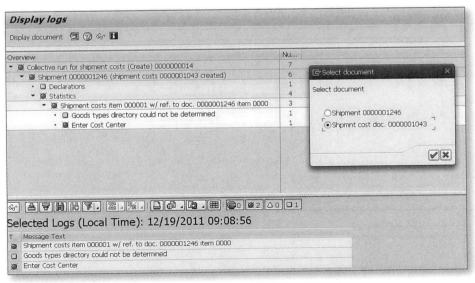

If you have multiple documents listed on the line, a popup window will display, prompting you to choose a specific document. Make a choice and press Enter to continue. In the example shown in Figure 3 we're going to display shipment costs, similar to running Transaction VI03. Press F3 to return to the list of shipments. On the main screen, you can execute additional reports by navigating to the ENVIRONMENT option on your pull-down menu and selecting SHIPMENT LISTS. Here you can access and start reports for:

▶ UTILIZATION: Starts Transaction VT14

▶ CAPACITY: Starts Transaction VT15

▶ CHECK-IN: Starts Transaction VT16

▶ SHIPMENT COMPLETION: Starts Transaction VT12

▶ COLLECTIVE PROCESSING OF FREIGHT COSTS: Starts Transaction VI04, looping back to the initial selection screen

If you choose any one of these options, you'll close the Transaction VI04 report and there's no coming back to it, so make your selection wisely. All unsaved data will be lost.

Creating Shipment Cost Documents in the Background

You can schedule periodic jobs for shipment cost documents in the background via collective processing to improve your system's performance.

In Tip 69, we explained how to execute shipment costs collectively in the foreground. The increased volume of shipments and necessary shipment cost documents requires you to execute these jobs in the background at set intervals to use your system resources efficiently. In this tip, we'll show you how to set this up.

✓ And Here's How ...

To set up collective processing in the background, run Transaction VI06 or follow the path:

LOGISTICS • LOGISTICS EXECUTION • TRANSPORTATION • SHIPMENT COSTS • CREATE • COLLECTIVE PROCESSING IN BACKGROUND

On the selection screen shown in Figure 1, you'll see a list of available variants required to execute the transaction. Variants are mandatory for this transaction to execute. You have a choice of using the existing variants, modifying the selection criteria they contain, or creating brand new variants.

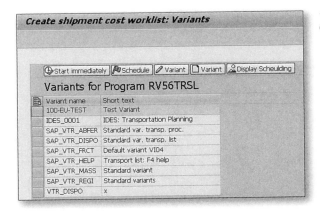

« Figure 1 *Create Shipment Costs Variant Selection Screen*

You can change the existing variants listed by clicking on the [✐ Variant] icon or by pressing [F7]. On the next screen shown in Figure 2, you'll have options to maintain the values.

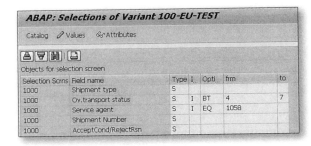

« Figure 2 *Change Variant Selection Screen*

Click on the CHANGE VALUES icon to see the initial screen of Transaction VI04. Apply your changes and save your data; the system will send you back to the initial screen of Transaction VI06.

Here you can also choose to create a new variant by clicking on the [□ Variant] icon or pressing [Shift]+[F7]. You'll see a popup window asking you to create a name for your variant; name your variant and click on the CREATE icon or press [Enter]. The following screen will look like the selection screen of Transaction VI04 from Tip 69. Maintain your selection and save your variant data.

Navigate back to the initial screen of Transaction VI06. You have an option to run your job immediately, which will be executed once and right when you click on the START IMMEDIATELY button or press [F5]. In our example, we're scheduling the periodic job using the SCHEDULE icon or [F6] on your keyboard. On the subsequent screen you'll define the job parameters, like start date and time and period values (see Figure 3).

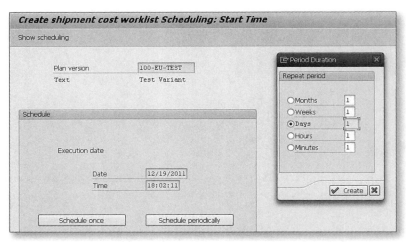

☆ **Figure 3** *Creating Batch Job for Shipment Costs*

Once you've maintained this information, click on the CREATE icon and you'll see a message on the bottom left portion of the screen informing you that your background job has been scheduled. To leave this screen, click on the BACK icon or press F3.

Check the status of the job by selecting the DISPLAY SCHEDULING icon or by using the pull-down menu GoTo • DISPLAY JOBS or by pressing Shift + F6. You can access log data, review results, change job parameters, delete the job definition, or simply update the screen with the latest status (see Figure 4).

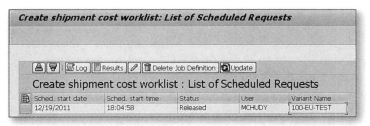

≪ **Figure 4** *Display Scheduling Details*

When done, press F3 to go back to the initial screen or click on the BACK icon.

Reviewing and Transferring Shipment Costs to Financial Accounting with a Single Report

You can review all relevant shipment costs that need completion at once and transfer them to FI.

Incomplete shipment cost documents can cause payment delays to your carriers, as well as potential service delays. You need a report that can pull information related to the shipment cost to quickly identify incomplete shipment costs and transfer them to settlement, which you do by forwarding them to FI accounting. In this tip, we'll also show you how to transfer selected documents and create purchase orders and/or create subsequent service entry sheets.

✅ And Here's How ...

Execute Transaction VI12 or follow the menu path:

> LOGISTICS • LOGISTICS EXECUTION • TRANSPORTATION • SHIPMENT COSTS • LISTS AND LOGS • SETTLEMENT LIST

On the initial screen shown in Figure 1, you'll have a lot of options to narrow down data selection to applicable documents.

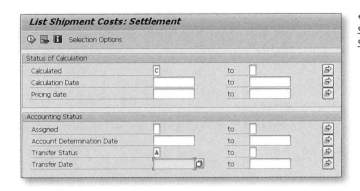

« *Figure 1* Initial List Shipment Costs Selection Screen

Selection data is grouped by sections:

▶ SHIPMENT COST HEADER: Includes shipment cost number and type.

▶ PARTNERS: Transportation service agent and invoicing party accounts.

▶ STATUS OF CALCULATIONS: Only fully calculated items are transferrable to settlement.

▶ ACCOUNTING STATUS: This is a key field to select items that haven't been transferred to settlement. Select A for transfer status, as shown in Figure 1. To transfer shipment cost items to FI, account assignment must be completed. If you want to list shipment costs that have been transferred successfully, select C.

▶ SETTLEMENT DATA: Includes company code, settlement date, item category, and account assignment category, for example.

▶ IDENTIFICATION: If you need to process shipment costs related to a specific container ID or vehicle, maintain your data here.

▶ SERVICE PROCUREMENT: By specifying purchasing data here, you can query for shipment cost documents related to a PO or purchasing organization elements and plants.

▶ WITH REFERENCE TO: Allows you to specify predecessor documents related to the shipment costs.

▶ ADMINISTRATIVE DATA: Gives you options to list selected data by user and creation date.

▶ OPTIONS: Allows the report to present header data only or both header and item as a default.

When you've maintained the appropriate information for your purposes, click on the Execute icon or press [F8] on your keyboard. The next screen will bring up the data that matches your selection criteria (see Figure 2).

≫ *Figure 2* List Shipment Costs Details

In order to complete transferring of shipment costs and to automatically create accruals, you need purchase orders to be determined and you must complete transfer of data to FI. To proceed with the transfer, double-click on the line item listed on the report or click on the Change Shipment Cost Object icon. This will open the shipment cost line detail screen, similar to running Transaction VI02. Navigate to the Settlement tab. Select the Transfer indicator box and the purchase order determination will be executed automatically (see Figure 3). Click on the Service Procurement tab and you should have the purchase order number listed in the Purchasing Document field.

≫ *Figure 3* Settlement Processing Transfer to FI

Click on the Save icon or press [Ctrl]+[S] to continue. Once you've saved the shipment cost document, the system will create a service entry sheet for the purchase order and accounting documents that will post to accruals and other relevant accounting documents. Repeat the same process to complete all items listed on your report.

Tip 72

Reviewing and Analyzing Shipment Cost Job Logs

You can review results of periodic background jobs and jobs executed in dialog mode for shipment cost documents in a single screen.

In previous tips we've covered creation of shipment costs collectively using Transaction VI04 (Tip 69) and in the background using Transaction VI06 (Tip 70) All of these transactions may end up with issues that are stored in log tables. We'll introduce you to a new transaction that will help you monitor problems, incompletions that occurred while creating shipment cost documents, and apply immediate corrections to avoid payment delays and transportation service disruptions.

✓ And Here's How ...

To review your collective run job logs for shipment cost documents, use Transaction VI16 or follow the path:

> LOGISTICS • LOGISTICS EXECUTION • TRANSPORTATION • SHIPMENT COSTS • LISTS AND LOGS • LOGS

On the initial screen, maintain your selection for WORKLIST; specify if you want to review the logs for create shipment costs or change shipment costs run (see Figure 1).

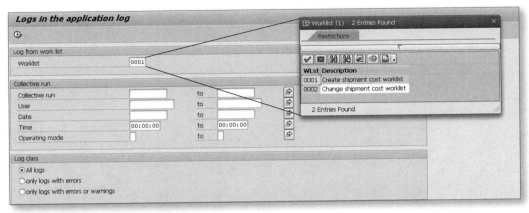

⌃ **Figure 1** Shipment Costs Logs Selection Screen

Next, choose data in the COLLECTIVE RUN section that includes collective run number, user, date, time, and operating mode (batch mode [logs generated by Transaction VI06] or dialog mode [generated using Transaction VI04]). In the LOG CLASS section, select type of logs for your report choosing all logs, errors only, or errors and warnings. To run your report, click on the EXECUTE icon or press [F8]. On the subsequent screen, you'll see a list of collective runs for your review (see Figure 2).

⌃ **Figure 2** List of Collective Run Logs

The first column shows traffic light icons that indicate errors and warnings where:

▶ **Red:** Errors were captured during the shipment creation process. This doesn't mean that shipment costs didn't get created.

▶ **Yellow:** Warnings have been issued.

▶ **Green:** No issues were reported.

To see the detailed log message, simply drill into the listed items by clicking on the collective run number. Review messages and click on the nodes that need your attention for more information that may give you hints for potential corrections. When you click on the node with listed document numbers (like shipment cost document or shipment), click on the line and then access the display (like running Transaction VI03 for shipment cost or Transaction VT03N for shipments) or change mode (like running Transaction VI02 for shipment cost or Transaction VT02N for shipments) by using the buttons in the top part of the screen (see Figure 3).

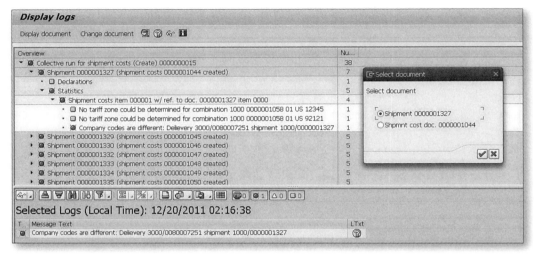

⌃ *Figure 3* Display Logs Details

You can review the document directly and maintain data without closing your log transaction. To go back to the previous screen, click on the BACK button or press F3 .

Tip 73

Maintaining New and Existing Route Data

You can easily maintain routes, stages, and connection points in one place when you add new customers.

Let's say that you're adding new customers; in order to get their deliveries processed, you need to maintain transportation master data. Because of this, you may be impacting already existing routes as well. Updating this data individually takes time and knowledge of a few transactions. In this tip, we'll show you how to create or update transportation routes that need connection points and stages all in one transaction.

And Here's How ...

Use Transaction 0VTC[1] or follow the menu path:

> LOGISTICS EXECUTION • MASTER DATA • TRANSPORTATION • ROUTES • DEFINE ROUTES •
> DEFINE ROUTES AND STAGES

On the initial screen, you'll get a list of already existing routes if you're already using transportation functionality and route determination. Your initial list could have simple routes (no stages) and complex stages listed.

---

1 Note that in some environments this transaction is considered part of configuration. If you need to make this transaction available for use in production system as a standard master data maintenance transaction, contact your basis administrator.

To maintain existing routes or create new routes starting with a definition of connection points, go to the left side of the screen and maintain folders for data type in the DIALOG STRUCTURE. Locate the TRANSPORTATION CONNECTION POINTS folder and click to display details; the list of existing connection points will be shown on the main part of the screen. You can use up to 10 characters to define your connection points.

Enter a text description for each point. Select the point you want to update and click on the DETAILS icon or press Ctrl + Shift + F2 . To add a new point, click on NEW ENTRIES or press F5 . On the resulting screen, maintain all required information (see Figure 1).

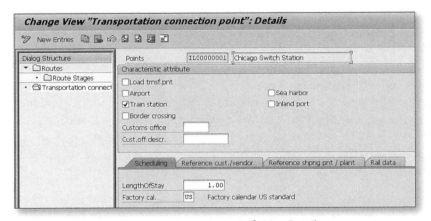

⌃ *Figure 1* Transportation Connection Point Definition Details

You have a choice of defining your point as one the following:

▶ LOAD TRANSFER POINT (specify if goods are moved from one means of transport to another like from truck to ship, for example)
▶ AIRPORT
▶ TRAIN STATION
▶ SEA HARBOR
▶ INLAND PORT
▶ BORDER CROSSING

If you implemented foreign trade, you probably have CUSTOMS OFFICE definitions available, so you can complete border crossing details by adding the customs office code and office description. You can also define the length of stay at the particular point and a factory calendar; this information will be relevant for availability check calculations.

Define your connection point as a customer or vendor location, shipping point, plant, and a warehouse of a particular plant. If your connection point is a rail station, you can maintain additional information on the RAIL DATA tab. Here you can define the type of rail station, specify rail carrier account, train station number, and leg class. If your location has no reference, you can maintain the connection point address by clicking on the ADDRESS icon or pressing `Shift`+`F5`. If you're using reference to define connection point, this will be copied from the reference object.

Save your data to complete the definition process. Next, select ROUTES in the NAVIGATION PANE; on the main part, you'll get the list of defined routes ready for maintenance. Routes are defined using six alpha numeric characters (see Figure 2).

To change route data, click on the DETAILS icon or press `Ctrl`+`Shift`+`F2`. If you're adding a new route, click on NEW ENTRIES or press `F5`. Enter the route number if you're defining a new route, then DESCRIPTION and ROUTE ID. If you're not planning on using route stages, you can populate the data in the processing and scheduling sections such as:

▸ SHIPPING TYPE: Assign a shipping type to the route and preliminary and subsequent legs

▸ SERVICE AGENT: Account number for the vendor servicing the route

▸ DISTANCE: Specify the total distance or leave it blank if you use stages

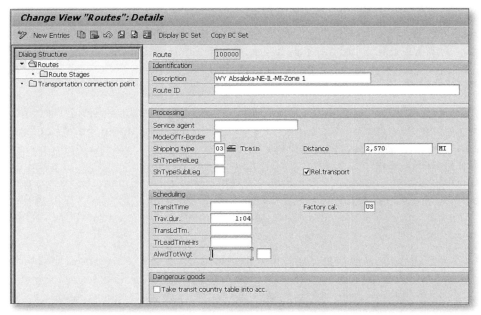

⟫ *Figure 2* *Route Definition Details*

▸ TRANSIT TIME: Maintain this field if no stages are used

▸ TRAVEL DURATION: Maintain this field if no stages are used

▸ TRANSPORTATION LEAD TIME: Specify the number of calendar days required for shipment preparation; accuracy of two decimal places is allowed

▸ TRANSPORTATION LEAD TIME HOURS: Lead time in hours/minutes is used to calculate the transportation planning date

▸ ALLOWED TOTAL WEIGHT: This will result in messages when route determination is executed

▸ FACTORY CALENDAR: Defines working days and influences planning dates

If you're using or planning on using stages (which give you more granular and detailed capabilities for shipment processing), maintain data for route stages. You can access the ROUTE STAGES folder in the NAVIGATION pane. If you maintained stages already, you'll get the list on the main part of the screen or click on the CREATE NEW ENTRY button.

The main stage list has two display options:

▶ SINGLE-COLUMN DISPLAY: Recommended if your route has only stages of type 1 (Transportation). You'll have the data showing the departure points where the beginning point of the next stage represents the destination point of the previous stage.

▶ DOUBLE-COLUMN DISPLAY: Shows the beginning point and the destination point of the stage in separate columns. Use this option if you have mixed stage types.

To maintain your stages, enter the departure connection point and the destination point and fill in the details like transportation service agent, distance, leg indicator, relevancy for shipment costing, pricing procedure default, and scheduling details (see Figure 3).

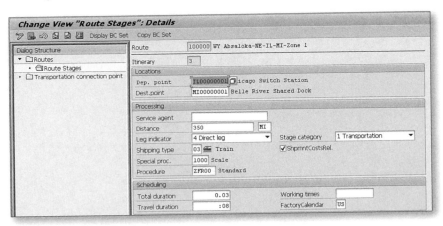

✿ **Figure 3** *Route Stage Details*

Remember that the system checks all stages in other routes with same departure and destination points and will propose the values for you. Once you're done maintaining stage details, you can go back to the route list and recalculate route duration and distances based on the updated stage data. Select the route that needs updating and run a check function using the pull-down menu path UTILITIES • CHECK. The system will compare values for transit time, driving time, and distance with the calculated totals from stages returning messages. Once you're satisfied with the check, you can copy the sum of stage values from the route stages by using menu path UTILITIES • ADOPT VALUES. The route overview screen will now be populated with totals from stages in your route.

Part 6
Billing

Things You'll Learn in this Section

Billing is part of Sales and Distribution in the order-to-cash process, and when we're talking about cash, it's always best to have as many tools as you can. In this part of the book, you'll find tips on how to better process and follow up on billing documents, as well as tricks to work with reports that we've found are very useful for the accounts receivable and the sales areas. You'll also find information on CO-PA transactions that are very helpful in solving issues with incomplete billing documents.

Processing Multiple Deliveries in a Billing Due List

You can save a lot of time and effort by processing multiple deliveries that are due for billing at once.

When your outbound deliveries are completely picked, packed, and goods issued, you can proceed with the billing. Billing is the follow-up process that creates the invoices to the customer, and when you have to bill several deliveries at the same time, it's always nice to find a transaction that can save you time with multiple processing.

✓ And Here's How ...

To process several sales documents at the same time, access Transaction VF04 or follow the menu path:

> LOGISTICS • SALES AND DISTRIBUTION • BILLING • BILLING DOCUMENT • PROCESS BILLING DUE LIST

Carefully select the document for processing so that you don't invoice something that shouldn't be.

As part of your selection criteria, you can include the BILLING TYPE, the SHIPPING POINT, or even a list of deliveries you want to process (see Figure 1) and click on the DISPLAY BILLING LIST button or press F8.

The resulting list will give you an opportunity to select individual deliveries or to select all and create invoices for all the deliveries. Highlight the deliveries you'd like to select as shown in Figure 2 and choose a button to push for processing, which we describe next.

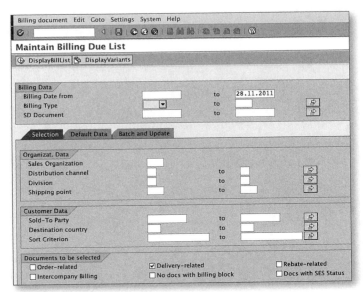

⏶ *Figure 1* Enter Your Selection Criteria for the Billing Due List

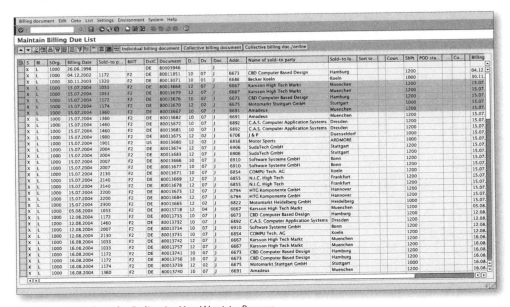

⏶ *Figure 2* Select the Deliveries You Want to Process

There are three ways in which you can process the deliveries; each has a button assigned:

▶ INDIVIDUAL BILLING DOCUMENT: Processes the deliveries you marked as selected and takes you through the individual creation of the billing document for each of them.

▶ COLLECTIVE BILLING DOCUMENT: Processes the selected deliveries in the background. It will generate one billing document per delivery.

▶ COLLECTIVE BILLING DOCUMENT/ONLINE: Processes the selected deliveries and takes you through the creation screens. This option comes in handy when you're having problems billing a delivery. By going through the individual screens, you'll be able to see the error as it happens.

After you've clicked the applicable button, the status of the deliveries will be updated on the screen shown in Figure 3. To the right, there's a column called STATUS, and it will have a checkmark when everything went well and a big red X if it failed.

⋩ *Figure 3* *Changed Status of the Deliveries*

After the run, you can click on the LOG DISPLAY button or press ⎡Shift⎤ + ⎡F4⎤, and you'll be able to look at the documents that were created.

Cancelling Multiple Billing Documents

You can easily cancel multiple invoices or billing documents with a standard transaction.

Cancelling any document is an essential part of the business process. Sometimes mistakes or changes in priorities make it necessary to cancel an invoice. In this tip, we'll show you how to do it. A word of caution: Canceling an invoice is activity that should always be done carefully and in close contact with the finance department (i.e., Accounts Receivable).

And Here's How ...

To cancel a billing document, use Transaction VF11 or follow the path:

> LOGISTICS • SALES AND DISTRIBUTION • BILLING • BILLING DOCUMENT • CANCEL

You'll immediately see a table in which you can enter the documents you want to cancel (see Figure 1). If you have a list of these documents in Excel, you can copy and paste them into this screen so that the data entry process is faster. Make sure you enter a posting date for the document; this is very important for the creation of the accounting document.

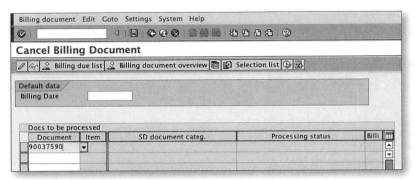

⌃ *Figure 1 Document Number Entry Screen to Cancel Billing Documents*

Once you've entered all the documents you need into the table, click on the BILL-ING DOCUMENT OVERVIEW button. This will display the basic information for each billing document and the amount that will be cancelled, as shown in Figure 2.

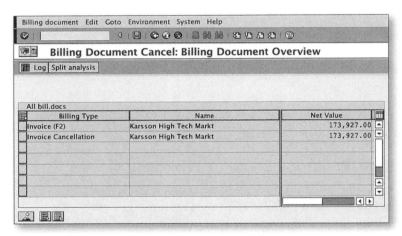

⌃ *Figure 2 Document Overview Showing Basic Information*

Select the documents you want to cancel and click POST. As the documents are saved, you'll receive confirmation that the document was successfully cancelled.

Go to Transaction VF03 to display the new document. It should match the original billing document so that it's totally cancelled (see Figure 3).

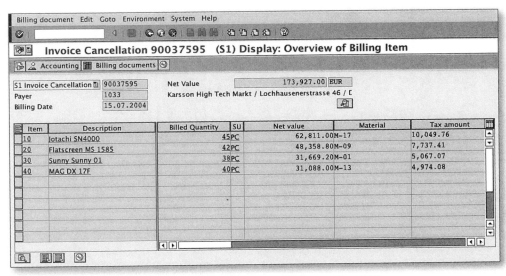

⌃ *Figure 3 Details of the Billing Cancellation Document in Transaction VF03*

The billing cancellation document updates the document flow of the outbound delivery. You can review this in Transaction VL03N (see Figure 4).

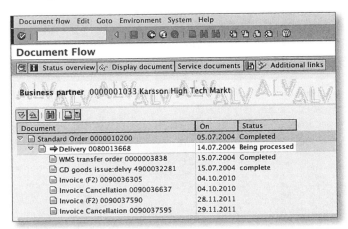

⌃ *Figure 4 The Updated Document Flow of the Delivery Document*

Tip **76**

Collectively Releasing Billing Documents to Accounting

When you have several billing documents that you need to release to accounting, you can do it collectively to save time and avoid errors.

During billing document creation, there can be a series of conditions that block the creation of the accounting documents such as pricing errors, closed posting periods, or lack of authorization. After solving the issue that blocked the accounting document creation, you need to go to the specific document and release it to accounting. However, releasing a large number of billing documents to accounting can be a very long and tedious process if you do it one by one. In this tip, we'll show you how to do it collectively to save time and effort.

✅ And Here's How ...

To be able to use the transaction described in this tip, you need to have already identified and solved the issues that prevented the accounting document from being created.

To release billing documents for accounting collectively, use Transaction VFX3 or follow the path:

> LOGISTICS • SALES AND DISTRIBUTION • BILLING • BILLING DOCUMENT • BLOCKED BILLING DOCS

This report releases several documents at the same time to accounting. As you can see from Figure 1, these billing documents show the accounting documents missing in the document flow, and the status of the billing document remains opened.

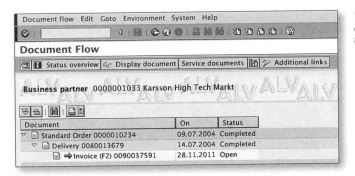

《 Figure 1 Billing Document Doesn't Show in the Document Flow

In the search screen (Figure 2), enter criteria that match your document needs.

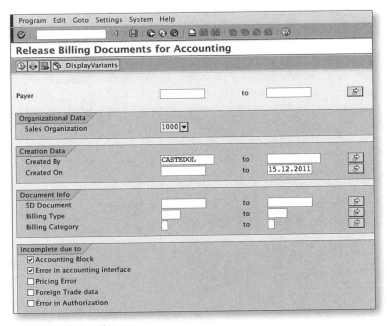

《 Figure 2 Search Screen

After you enter your search criteria, the system will display a list of the billing documents with an accounting block that fulfill your search, shown in Figure 3. From the list, you can select the ones you know have been fixed and then release them by clicking on the green flag button for RELEASE TO ACCOUNTING or pressing

Shift + F6. Look at the processing status in the PsST column to know why these documents were blocked. You can click on the column for a specific document and press F4 to see the description of the value you're looking at.

Before attempting to release the document, you need to fix any issues related to it.

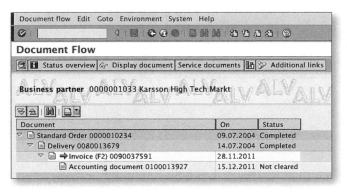

≫ **Figure 3** Select the Document(s) and Release to Accounting

Once the system attempts the release, it'll update the SELECTION column. You'll see an "X" if the error is still there and the document couldn't be processed or a number "1" if it was successfully released. No green color lines or success message will be displayed.

After attempting to release documents to accounting, the system creates a log that you can access by clicking on the NOTES button or pressing Shift + F5. This log will help you understand the errors, and the additional work you need to perform on the billing documents so they can be released.

If you display the document flow for the documents you released, this time you'll see the accounting document there (see Figure 4).

≪ **Figure 4** The Document Flow Now Includes the Accounting Document

Tip 77

Creating a List of Billing Documents

You can easily create a list of billing documents for analysis either by material or payer.

You may find that it's very difficult to compile all the billing information for a given material or customer to do sales or revenue analysis. In this tip, we'll show you a standard report that can help you find a specific customer invoice or look at its complete billing history for a given period of time; or you can look at who's been buying a certain material.

 And Here's How ...

To get to the list of billing documents, use Transaction VF05 or follow the path:

LOGISTICS • SALES AND DISTRIBUTION • BILLING • INFORMATION SYSTEM • BILLING DOCUMENTS • LIST BILLING DOCUMENTS

In the search screen for this transaction shown in Figure 1, enter a customer, material number, or a combination of both. As you see, the field to enter the customer number is labeled *payer*, as per the partner function for whom the bill was issued. If needed, you can click on the PARTNER FUNCTION button or press Ctrl+F10 to use the sold-to partner function instead.

You can also look at all the invoices or only those that are still opened. The latter will show you billing documents without accounting documents.

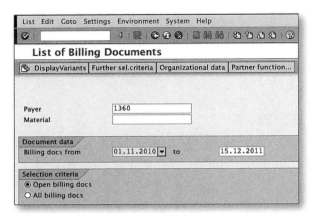

« *Figure 1 Select a Payer and/or a Material Number on the Search Screen*

If these fields aren't enough, you can always click on the FURTHER SEL. CRITERIA button or press Ctrl + F8. This will bring up a pop-up screen that will let you select up to three additional fields from a list of eight additional search fields (see Figure 2).

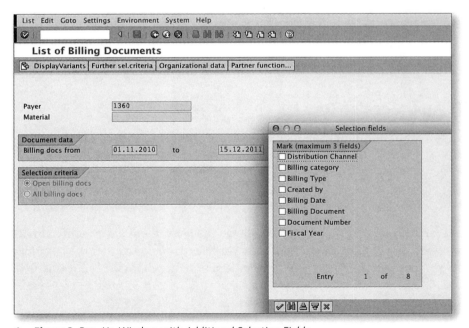

⌃ *Figure 2 Pop-Up Window with Additional Selection Fields*

Fill out your selection criteria and press ⌷Enter⌷. As you do that, another pop-up will come up on the screen and prompt you for the sales organization. Type it and press ⌷Enter⌷ again.

The resulting report will show you the invoice numbers, the detail of the materials billed along with quantities, unit prices, and totals (see Figure 3). The billing documents are summed up by date, but you can change the sorting and also include totals and subtotals. You can also change the layout by adding or removing fields. To export it your list, use the LIST • SAVE • FILE option from the menu.

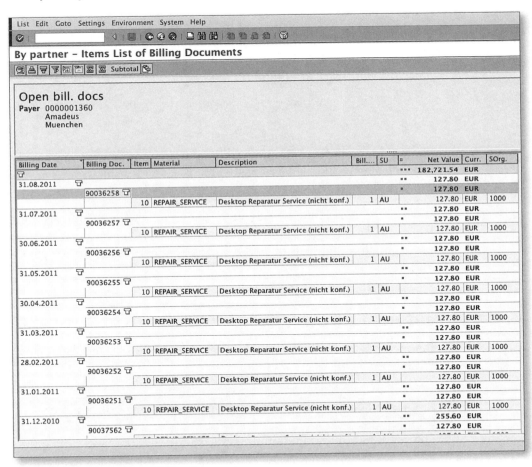

⌃ *Figure 3* *Resulting List of Billing Documents*

Tip 78

Making a Document Relevant for Billing by Finding the Configuration Error

When the SAP system tells you your sales order isn't relevant for delivery, you can easily check your order setup to find and fix the missing information.

After creating a sales order and its corresponding delivery, and then executing the picking, packing, and posting goods issue, you're faced with a small problem. The SAP system says that your document isn't relevant for billing.

This problem is normally found when you try to execute the billing due list for a certain delivery as described in Tip 77. What this error message means is that you missed a configuration step. This tip will help you complete the setup and get rid of the error.

And Here's How ...

Billing relevance is set at the item category level. To fix your issue, use Transaction VOV7 or follow the path:

> SALES AND DISTRIBUTION • SALES • SALES DOCUMENTS • SALES DOCUMENT ITEM • DEFINE ITEM CATEGORIES

When you execute the transaction, you'll see a list of all the delivery item categories that exist in your system. Select your item category from the list and double-click on it; this will take you to the details screen (as shown in Figure 1). When an item category isn't relevant for billing, it's because you have the wrong parameter in the BILLING RELEVANCE field. To fix this problem, enter "A" for a delivery-related billing document.

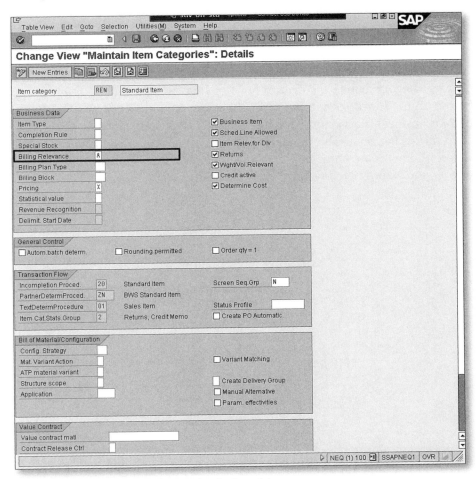

⌃ *Figure 1* *Set Up Billing Relevance for the Item Category*

Other very useful values you can enter in this field are:

▸ **B**: Relevant for order-related billing documents. The billing status is defined by the required quantity in the sales document. Item categories REN (returns) and BVN (cash sales) are examples of this setting.

- ▸ **C**: Relevant for order-related billing documents. The billing status is defined by the target quantity in the sales document. Item categories G2N (credit memo) and L2N (debit memo) are examples of this setting.

- ▸ **F**: Relevant for order-related billing documents; status according to the invoice receipt quantity. With this setting, orders are considered by the billing due list only after the invoice receipt for the purchase order has been processed. Item category TAS (third-party business transaction) is an example of this setting.

The item category defines the control functions for sales documents. The settings of these control functions determine the use of the different item categories in the different business transactions. For this reason, it's a good configuration practice not to make changes to the standard-delivered item categories. If you require a change, it's important that you instead make a copy of the standard-delivered item category you want to modify, and then modify the copy.

Tip (79)

Manually Posting CO-PA Documents if Automated Posting Fails

If your CO-PA documents aren't created due to errors in your billing processes, you can manually post them.

CO-PA documents should be generated as part of billing if they're configured correctly. They're generated along with the FI, CO, and profit center documents. However, sometimes there are errors in the accounting interface or in the ALE interfaces, which causes the CO-PA document posting to fail.

Failed CO-PA documents have to be posted manually and in this tip, we'll show you how to do this so that your records are complete and your Profitability Analysis is accurate.

And Here's How ...

To manually post CO-PA documents, run Report RKERV002 in Transaction SE38 or directly go to Transaction KE4S.

Once in the transaction, enter the document or list of the SD billing documents you want to transfer to CO-PA (see Figure 1). You can choose to do a test run before posting any documents, so that you're sure that you are submitting the right data.

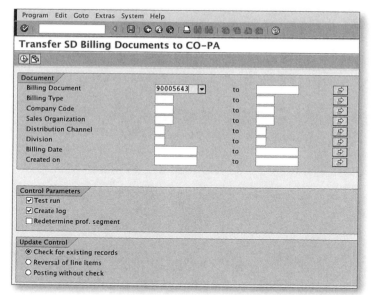

⚒ *Figure 1* *Transfer SD Billing Documents to CO-PA Selection Screen*

If the SD billing document is correct and hasn't been previously transferred, you'll see a message indicating that it simulated successfully (see Figure 2). Now you can remove the TEST RUN check in the selection screen and rerun to transfer the document.

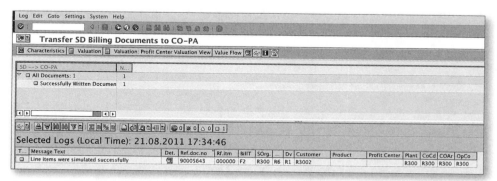

⚒ *Figure 2* *Successful Simulation*

After running without the TEST RUN indicator, the program will create the CO-PA documents for the SD billing documents you selected. You can review that the document is now there by checking the document flow of those SD billing documents in Transaction VF03.

Tip (80)

Cancelling CO-PA Line Items

When CO-PA items have been created with errors, you can quickly cancel them.

CO-PA documents can sometimes be created with errors. These errors can be duplicates, inconsistencies between FI and Profitability Analysis, or after you discover errors in Customizing. Another case when CO-PA documents need to be cancelled is when the FI invoice needs to be reversed and the CO-PA document isn't cancelled automatically.

As in most SAP documents these items can't be edited, so in this tip, we'll show you how to cancel these documents.

✓ And Here's How ...

To cancel a line item or a set of line items in Profitability Analysis, run Report RKECADL1 in Transaction SA38, or go to Transaction KE4S00.

The program selects the lines based on the operating concern, and an offsetting entry is posted in Tables CE1xxxx and CE3xxxx for the selected operating concern.

In this transaction, as shown in Figure 1, you have to at least enter the following data:

- ▶ Operating Concern
- ▶ Record Type
- ▶ Reference Document Number

You could alternatively enter the following parameters:

▶ OPERATING CONCERN

▶ RECORD TYPE

▶ PERIOD/YEAR

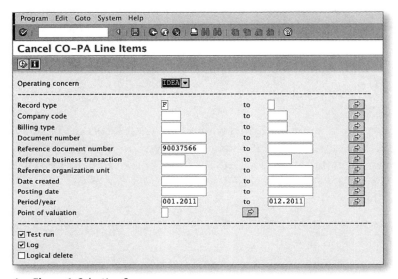

⌃ **Figure 1** Selection Screen

Note that if you use the period/year only, your search will be too broad and the search results too vague. It's much better to enter the reference document number directly to avoid cancelling the wrong posting.

This program has the option of running in test mode, which you should always do if you're trying to correct a large number of documents. It's also a good idea to first run this program in a test system.

When you're sure the resulting documents are the ones you want to cancel (see Figure 2), remove the TEST RUN flag from the selection screen.

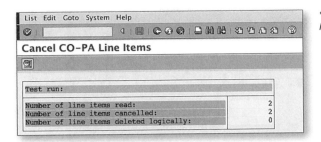

« *Figure 2* The Number of Line Items Found

If you select the LOGICAL DELETE field in Figure 1, then you won't be able to repost the document. When a line item generated by an SD billing document is logically deleted, it will no longer appear in the list of accounting documents for the transaction that created it. If you double-click on the previous screen's found document line, you get the list of CO-PA documents that will be cancelled (see Figure 3).

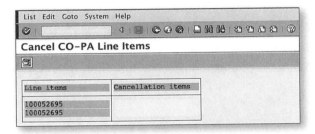

« *Figure 3* CO-PA List of Documents to Be Cancelled

Reviewing Invoice Lists en Masse

You can review multiple invoice lists to verify the processing status, dates, and what billing documents were on them.

In your daily work, you receive multiple inquiries either from internal departments (like customer service, credit, and shipping) or directly from your customers to verify status and other details of the customers' invoice lists. You may also want to verify other details by drilling into subsequent document display functions. You don't want to do it using time consuming, individual document transactions (VF22 or VF23); you want to do it en masse, per payer account number.

✔ And Here's How ...

To create a list of invoices, execute Transaction VF25 or follow the path:

> Logistics • Sales and Distribution • Billing • Information System • Invoice Lists • List of Invoice Lists

Now do the following:

▸ Enter the Payer account number on the initial screen.

▸ Populate the Document Data section with the range of dates you want to review.

▸ In the Selection Criteria section, select either Open Invoice Lists, or if you choose to review everything processed or not, select All Invoice Lists.

▸ Press ⌜Enter⌝ to continue. If you didn't specify your Organizational Data, a pop-up window will display where you have to specify the Sales Organization you're reviewing the data for. On the next screen, you'll see a list of invoice lists that met your criteria (see Figure 1).

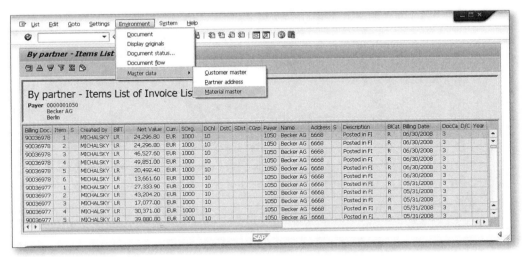

⚠ **Figure 1** *Invoice Lists*

You can export your report to Excel for further analysis or to share with your customers. In order to access additional details, use the ENVIRONMENT option on the pull-down menu as shown in Figure 1. Select the line and then choose your options. By selecting ENVIRONMENT • DOCUMENT you can access the INVOICE LIST CHANGE (this is an alternative to running Transaction VF22; see Figure 2).

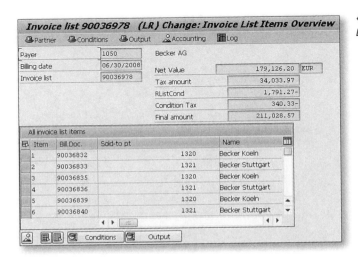

« **Figure 2** *Invoice List Items Overview*

You can also perform a variety of different tasks while in the invoicing list as long as your security settings permit you to do so, like access the individual invoices by clicking on the BILLING ITEMS OVERVIEW icon on the bottom left corner (see Figure 2) or one of the functions listed here:

► By selecting ENVIRONMENT • DISPLAY ORIGINALS, you'll access archived documents. If you don't have an archiving strategy, this action will return an information message.

► By choosing ENVIRONMENT • DOCUMENT STATUS, you'll get a pop-up showing you the document header status.

► Choosing ENVIRONMENT • DOCUMENT FLOW will access the document flow.

► ENVIRONMENT • MASTER DATA will provide you with access to maintain data for the customer master, partner address, and material master.

Once you've completed maintaining the data, simply return to the initial report list and then click on the BACK icon or press ⌐F3⌐ on your keyboard. Remember that your changes will impact one or all of the invoice lists and that may have to be reissued. And with that, you've successfully reviewed the invoice list report.

Reviewing a Collective Run Log for Invoice List Jobs

If your collective run invoice list didn't create the expected results, you can investigate the details to resolve the issues with a simple transaction.

All SAP collective runs create logs after a job is executed. The logs store all results—both the expected documents created and those with warnings and errors—and also gives you a good base for investigating issues and eventually reposting the desired documents. The same applies to an invoice list collective run, which is performed using Transaction VF24 (Work List for Invoice Lists). When you notice that the expected documents aren't generated, simply by comparing the number of daily volume of printed invoice lists, for example, you need a tool that will allow you to review past results and follow up with corrections

✓ And Here's How ...

To display a work list for invoice lists, execute Transaction V.24 or follow the path:

> LOGISTICS • SALES AND DISTRIBUTION • BILLING • INFORMATION SYSTEM • INVOICE LISTS • DISPLAY WORK LIST FOR INVOICE LISTS

On the initial screen shown in Figure 1, maintain the TYPE OF COLLECTIVE RUN field. Set it to R for invoice lists for the purpose of this tip. Then click on the EXECUTE icon or press F8 on your keyboard to continue.

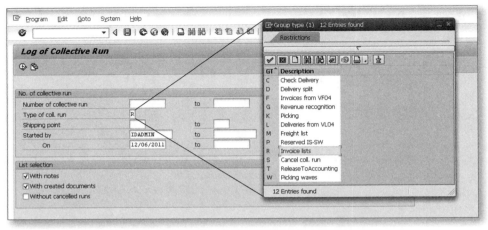

⩓ **Figure 1** *Log of Collective Run Initial Screen*

On the next screen you'll see a list of collective runs matching your selection criteria that are identified by a unique group number (see Figure 2).

« **Figure 2** *Collective Run List*

If you have any values in the CREATED DOCUMENT column (this will be marked in the NO. column), you know that the invoice list run completed successfully. To display the results, select the relevant line and click on the DOCUMENTS button or press F9 on your keyboard to see the generated invoice list numbers. If you have any entries in ERR. column, this means that your collective run failed to generate invoice lists. In order to review the errors, select the error line, and click on the NOTES icon or press Shift + F8 to continue.

On the next screen shown in Figure 3 you'll see the list showing the error summary and technical details needed for you to make corrections. Make sure you review all line items since each detail listed will provide additional data that could be crucial to successful reposting of the failed collective run.

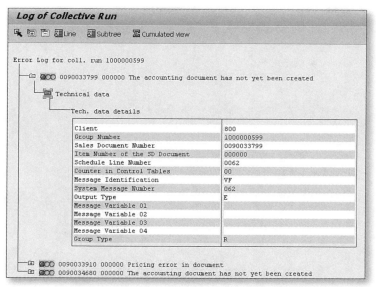

Log of Collective Run

⧉ 🔍 🗐 🗐 🖳 Line   🖳 Subtree   🗐 Cumulated view

Error Log for coll. run 1000000599

⊟ ◍◍◍ 0090033799 000000 The accounting document has not yet been created

🖳 Technical data

Tech. data details

Client	800
Group Number	1000000599
Sales Document Number	0090033799
Item Number of the SD Document	000000
Schedule Line Number	0062
Counter in Control Tables	00
Message Identification	VF
System Message Number	062
Output Type	E
Message Variable 01	
Message Variable 02	
Message Variable 03	
Message Variable 04	
Group Type	R

⊞ ◍◍◍ 0090033910 000000 Pricing error in document
⊞ ◍◍◍ 0090034680 000000 The accounting document has not yet been created

⌃ *Figure 3* *Error Log for Collective Run*

When done, click on the BACK icon or press [F3] on your keyboard. You've now successfully reviewed the collective run logs for invoice list jobs.

Part 7

Credit Management

Things You'll Learn in this Section

The SAP Credit Management application stands on guard in the SAP system, protecting your company from customers with unstable financial conditions, and helps you manage your own risk and exposure to uncollectable receivables. System configuration and maintaining credit master data are crucial in automating the process of catching the transactions at risk, and you can review them in several reports covered in the tips in this part of the book. We'll show you a number of transactions that can help monitor your customer's activities and look for warning signs. You'll also learn how to act on the information that the system provides and how to quickly make decisions to process orders by extending or denying credit based on the available data.

Releasing Blocked SD Documents to Process Sales Orders

You can quickly release blocked SD documents to process sales orders by running lists with a few select transactions.

Let's say your customer's credit limit has been exceeded and credit is building up rapidly. Many sales orders are entered daily, but they don't go through payment processing, meaning your ability to deliver products comes to an abrupt halt. What's confusing in this situation is the fact that a credit block doesn't show as an entry similar to the delivery or billing block. If the account in question is blocked due to a credit limit, you'll be notified about it in various stages of sales order processing in the form of messages.

You have to execute a report that will show you the list of affected documents and give you the ability to release these documents. There are a few transactions that allow you to run lists of blocked SD documents including orders, deliveries, or both. In this tip, we'll show you how to quickly release blocked sales orders.

✓ And Here's How ...

To find a list of blocked SD documents, execute Transaction VKM1 or follow the menu path:

> LOGISTICS • SALES AND DISTRIBUTION • CREDIT MANAGEMENT • EXCEPTIONS • BLOCKED SD DOCUMENTS

On the initial screen shown in Figure 1, enter your CREDIT CONTROL AREA number and any other criteria if possible to help narrow down your selection.

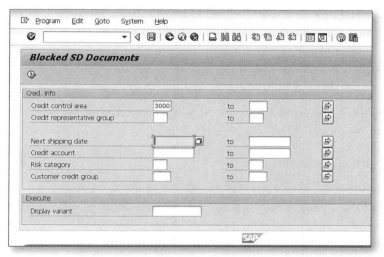

⌃ *Figure 1* Blocked SD Documents Selection Screen

Once you've filled in your criteria, click on EXECUTE or press ⌷F8⌷ to continue. On the next screen, you'll get a list of all blocked sales documents and billing documents that can include multiple documents waiting for credit release, as shown in Figure 2.

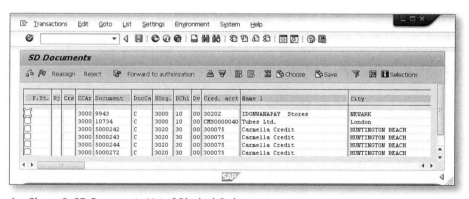

⌃ *Figure 2* SD Documents List of Blocked Orders

You can perform different actions from this screen, which you can see if you use the EDIT option pull-down menu or function buttons (see Figure 3).

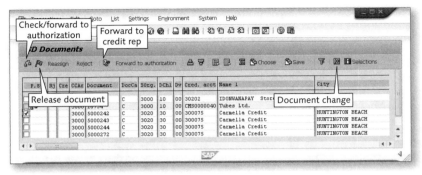

⌃ *Figure 3* *Credit Review Action Buttons*

The following functions can be performed:

▸ Release the sales document and approve the transaction. By releasing it, you post the approval for the full amount of the invoice, impacting customers' total credit exposure.

▸ Reject credit and cancel the document.

▸ Forward the blocked document to another processor.

▸ Re-check the blocked sales document.

Once you perform your action of choice by pressing the corresponding icon (see Figure 3 where all buttons are listed with callouts), your report will be updated with the status icon. The processing status icon is in the first column of your report next to the line selection checkbox, as shown in Figure 3. To check a legend describing all possible status icons, use the menu path SETTINGS • LEGEND.

Save the report in order to apply all of your actions. The end results will be logged in and displayed in the last window of the release transaction (see Figure 4).

≪ *Figure 4* *SD Documents Processing Log*

You'll now be able to process your sales documents in accounts that were previously blocked due to credit limit.

Tip 84

Displaying a List of Released SD Documents

When a customer's sales orders were delivered despite a credit limit block, you can investigate the situation to prevent it from happening again.

We're sure that the following scenario has happened to you before—sales orders seem to be magically delivered to customers, despite the credit blocks that should be preventing this from taking place. In this situation, it's more than likely that the sales documents were released from the credit block by using Transaction VKM1, which we talked about in Tip 83. In this tip, we'll show you how to review the historical document release data, extract the report to Excel, and access the document details. These functions will help you out to figure out the error and decide how to prevent this from happening again.

✅ And Here's How ...

First, execute Transaction VKM2 or follow the menu path:

> LOGISTICS • SALES AND DISTRIBUTION • CREDIT MANAGEMENT • SALES AND DISTRIBUTION DOCUMENTS • RELEASED SD DOCUMENTS

Populate the relevant data on the initial screen and then enter your credit control area number and customer credit account number to help to narrow down your selection. Press F8 or click on the EXECUTE icon to continue. On the next screen (see Figure 1), you'll see a list of all released documents. This can include sales contracts, sales orders, and deliveries.

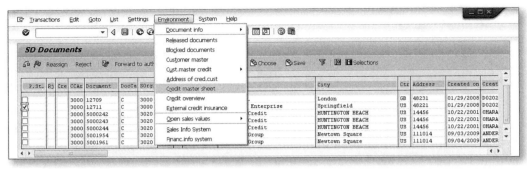

⌃ *Figure 1* SD Documents Additional Options

You can perform some additional actions from this screen, which you can see if you use the EDIT option pull-down menus or function buttons (reject credit and cancel the document and re-check blocked sales document).

This report also allows you to export the list to Excel to review sales documents; this includes open orders and open deliveries. Use the pull-down menu path LIST • EXPORT • SPREADSHEET or press $\boxed{\text{Shift}}$+$\boxed{\text{F4}}$ to initiate the extract. Next, specify the file name and location you'll be saving it to. This report will help you investigate your total credit exposure if, for example, multiple orders have been released by mistake to figure out the impact generated by faulty releases.

You can also access a number of additional reports using the ENVIRONMENT option from the pull-down menu (see Figure 1).

One of the useful investigative options is to display the credit master sheet, credit overview, and others. These functions are also available within Transaction VKM1, VKM3, VKM4, and VKM5. See Figure 2 for a sample of credit overview details.

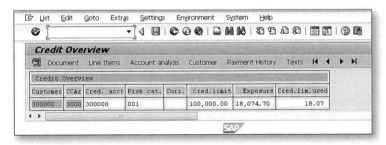

⌃ *Figure 2* Credit Overview Details

Releasing Individual or Grouped Blocked Sales Documents

You can view or release an individual order or a range of sales orders that have been blocked due to credit limit.

Let's say you need to release credit hold on a sales order, but don't have the account number available. You don't want to go through the sea of orders for a particular customer account number. You may also be running into security-related restrictions where you don't have access to Transaction VKM1 to display and release en masse orders that are blocked due to credit restrictions (see Tip 83). Therefore, you need a precise method of finding a single order or a group of only the orders of interest for immediate release. In this tip, we'll show you the easiest way to accomplish this.

And Here's How ...

Execute Transaction VKM3 or follow the menu path:

> LOGISTICS • SALES AND DISTRIBUTION • CREDIT MANAGEMENT • SALES AND DIS-
> TRIBUTION DOCUMENTS • SALES DOCUMENTS

Maintain the sales order data on the initial screen shown in Figure 1. Once you've filled in all relevant information, press F8 or click on the EXECUTE icon to continue.

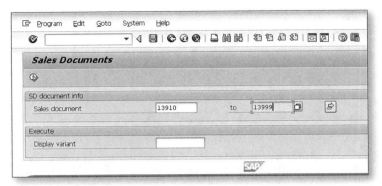

« *Figure 1* Sales Documents Selection Screen

Unlike Transaction VKM1, you'll now see *all* of the documents you specified in the selection screen (see Figure 2), regardless of whether they're blocked for credit check or not. In other words, you see a list of all released orders, some of which could be waiting for credit release. So remember that the difference between these two transactions (VKM1 versus VKM3) is related to overall credit status check; some orders listed won't be subject for release by any means.

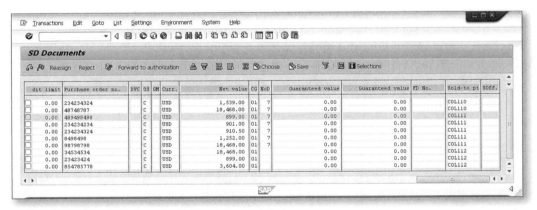

☆ *Figure 2* SD Documents List of Relevant Orders

You can also perform different actions from the screen shown in Figure 2 (see Tip 83 regarding Transaction VKM1). You can use the EDIT option pull-down menus or function buttons to access the following functions:

▶ Release the sales document and approve the transaction. By releasing it, you post the approval for the full amount of the invoice, impacting customers' total credit exposure.

▶ Reject credit and cancel the document.

▸ Forward the blocked document to another processor.

▸ Re-check the blocked sales document.

Use the screen scroll bars to review all data shown in this report such as the account's credit limit, order values, and other important information. If you release the sales orders from the credit block (like in Transaction VKM1 covered in Tip 83), your report will be updated to show the status icon in the first column of your report. Save the report to apply all of your actions. The end results will be logged in and displayed in the last window of the release transaction. You've successfully released or simply reviewed the individual sales orders blocked due to credit limit using the sales document numbers.

Tip 86

Using Credit Release to Immediately Process Deliveries and Sales Orders

You can list orders and deliveries blocked for a specific account that need to be released from credit hold for immediate processing.

Let's say you need to have both deliveries and sales orders listed for release on one report. You also have the customer number or a range of account numbers available to narrow down the selection. You want to release all of these documents from credit block en masse. How do we get this accomplished? You've tried all other transactions and none helped; you could only process either deliveries or sales orders or account numbers only. There is a way!

And Here's How ...

To access all sales documents, execute Transaction VKM4 or follow the path:

> LOGISTICS • SALES AND DISTRIBUTION • CREDIT MANAGEMENT • SALES AND DISTRIBUTION DOCUMENTS • ALL

Populate as much data as possible on the initial data selection screen (see Figure 1):

▶ CREDIT INFO: Specify credit control area and an account or range of accounts you want to review.

▶ DOCUMENT INFO: Pay attention to OVERALL DOCUMENT STATUS fields (defaulting to a range from A-NOT YET PROCESSED, to B-PARTIALLY PROCESSED) and OVERALL CREDIT STATUS; populate these fields *only* if you want to review documents in trouble with credit, and set the values to B-CREDIT CHECK WAS EXECUTED, DOCUMENT NOT OK and C-CREDIT CHECK WAS EXECUTED, DOCUMENT NOT OK, PARTIAL RELEASE, as shown on the sample screen (see Figure 1).

« *Figure 1* All SD Documents Selection Screen

▶ RANGE OF DOCUMENTS: Specify what type of documents you'd like to be subject for querying.

Press [F8] to continue. Depending on your selection criteria, you may receive a list of all documents, regardless of whether they're blocked for credit check or not. On the following screen (see Figure 2), you'll see a list of all released sales documents and deliveries that need credit release. You can perform different actions from this screen.

You can use the EDIT option pull-down menus or function buttons to access the following functions:

▶ Release the sales document and approve the transaction.

▶ Reject credit and cancel the document.

▶ Forward the blocked document to another processor.

▶ Re-check the blocked sales document.

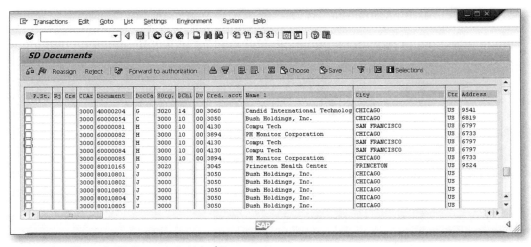

⚠ *Figure 2* SD Documents List of Documents

Use the screen scroll bars to review all data shown in this report such as credit limit and order value. If you release the sales orders from the credit block, your report will be updated with the status icon in the first column of your report.

Save the report and apply your selected action by clicking on the SAVE icon or pressing ⌷Ctrl⌷+⌷S⌷ on your keyboard. By saving and releasing, you're posting the approval for the full amount of the invoice, impacting customers' total credit exposure.

Tip 87

Listing Customer Balances to Review Credit Standings

You can quickly review customer balances to make sure there are no potential problems with credit down the road.

Whenever you're asked to update a customer's credit standing, a review of balances is always helpful and makes your decision process quick and easy. You have choices of several reports, but you need quick summary-level information in a clean and easy format. You also want to have the ability to investigate details of the balances listed, drilling into each category if necessary. Keep reading to find out how.

✓ And Here's How ...

Execute Transaction FD10N or follow the menu path:

> LOGISTICS • SALES AND DISTRIBUTION • CREDIT MANAGEMENT • ACCOUNT • DISPLAY BALANCES

Specify the mandatory fields CUSTOMER account number, COMPANY CODE, and FISCAL YEAR as shown in Figure 1, and click on the EXECUTE button or press F8.

On the following screen (see Figure 2), you'll see a BALANCES tab where you can find all balances listed per period. By double-clicking on a listed category or by selecting it with a single click and pressing F2, you can access line item details showing individual postings limited to just this category (credit/debit/balances).

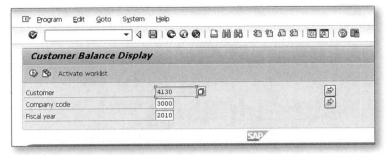

⩙ *Figure 1 Customer Balances Display Initial Screen*

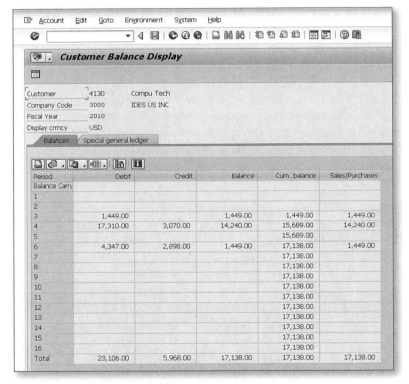

⩙ *Figure 2 Balances Detailed List*

If you're only interested in the summary level, go to the SPECIAL GENERAL LEDGER tab. Here you can also access line item detail using the same technique we just discussed. You can also print, export your report to Excel, and use graphics to present your data using standard SAP list viewer functions. When done, simply exit the report.

Tip 88

Quickly Displaying the Details of Customer Balances

When a customer calls and asks for details on dunning information, you can quickly review customer posting details to resolve the issue.

Your customer is calling to review their list of open items because they received a dunning letter. You therefore want to review balances, but you also need to see all the details behind them. The summary isn't enough to explain if a specific invoice has been paid or not. In this tip, you'll learn to how quickly access the details of customer accounts, as well as discover additional information such as who parked or changed these documents.

And Here's How ...

Execute Transaction FBL5N or follow the path:

> LOGISTICS • SALES AND DISTRIBUTION • CREDIT MANAGEMENT • ITEM • DISPLAY/
> CHANGE

On the initial screen, enter the relevant data in each of the selection sections:

- ▶ CUSTOMER SELECTION: Specify the account or range of account you want to review, and do the same for the COMPANY CODE data.
- ▶ SELECTION USING SEARCH HELP: Use this function if you need more granular selection criteria using defined help IDs and search strings, shown in Figure 1. It allows you to use multiple predefined criteria for extended document searches.

- ▶ STATUS: Specify what type of line items you'd like to pull into the report: open items, cleared items, or both.

- ▶ TYPE: Select all that apply to your search criteria; in our example, we selected all types of items.

- ▶ LIST OUTPUT: By selecting a layout, you can re-determine the look and contents of the report, and by selecting MAXIMUM NUMBER OF ITEMS, you can also alter the number of records presented.

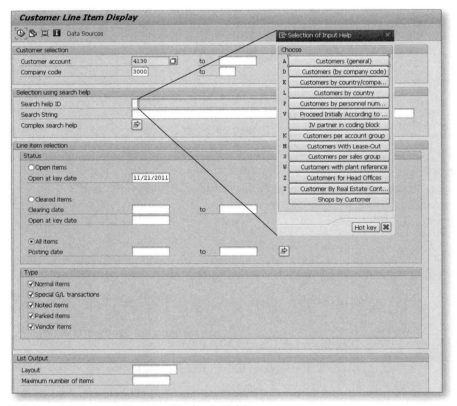

⌃ *Figure 1* *Customer Line Item Display Initial Screen*

When finished, click on the EXECUTE button or press ⌈F8⌋.

On the following screen you'll see a list of accounting documents that meet your selection criteria. You have several different options for a choice of action:

► You can display, change a document, and perform mass changes to selected documents.

► You can use standard list tools like sorting, filtering, and printing your report, or you can export it to Excel.

You probably also noticed the legend right below the toolbar; this can be turned on or off by using the pull-down menu following the path SETTINGS • LEGEND ON/ OFF • ICONS (see Figure 2).

Customer Line Item Display

	St	Assignment	DocumentNo	Typ	Doc. Date	S	DD	Amt in loc.cur.	LCurr	Clrng doc.	Text
		0080014998	100000001	RV	03/09/2010			1,449.00	USD		
		0080015011	100000000	RV	04/12/2010			14,490.00	USD		
		0080015012	100000014	RV	04/13/2010			1,285.00	USD		
		01000000052010	100000005	RV	04/13/2010			250.00-	USD		
		01000000082010	100000008	RV	04/14/2010			1,285.00-	USD		
		01000000092010	100000009	RV	06/04/2010			1,449.00	USD		
*								17,138.00	USD		
		01000000032010	100000003	RV	04/13/2010			250.00-	USD	100000004	
		01000000032010	100000004	AB	04/13/2010			250.00	USD	100000004	
		0080015012	100000006	RV	04/13/2010			1,285.00	USD	100000007	
		0080015012	100000007	AB	04/13/2010			1,285.00-	USD	100000007	
		01000000102010	100000010	RV	06/04/2010			1,449.00	USD	100000011	
		01000000102010	100000011	AB	06/04/2010			1,449.00-	USD	100000011	
		01000000122010	100000012	RV	06/04/2010			1,449.00	USD	100000013	
		01000000122010	100000013	AB	06/04/2010			1,449.00-	USD	100000013	
		0080004814	100000002	RV	02/24/1999			64,240.96	USD	1400000794	
		14000007941999	1400000794	DZ	03/10/1999			64,240.96-	USD	1400000794	
*								0.00	USD		
**	Account 4130							17,138.00	USD		
***								17,138.00	USD		

Status: open Parked Cleared
Due date: Overdue Due Not due

Customer: 4130
Company Code: 3000

Name: Compu Tech
City: SAN FRANCISCO

⌃ *Figure 2* Customer Line Items Details

The body of the report contains the line items. By using the DISPLAY or CHANGE icons from the toolbar, you can access the accounting document line item details. You can also display details simply by double-clicking on a line.

On the DISPLAY DOCUMENT view you'll see the summary of the billing document transaction you decided to review. On this screen, click on the DOCUMENT OVERVIEW icon or press F9 to see FI posting details, credits and debits, and G/L account details (see Figure 3).

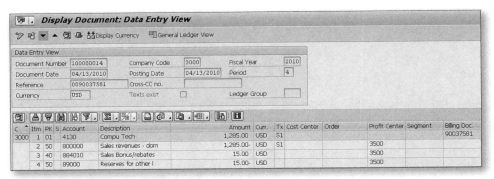

⌃ *Figure 3* Display Document Line Item Details

To discover who entered or parked the document, click on the DISPLAY DOCUMENT HEADER icon or press F5 (see the pop-up window in Figure 4).

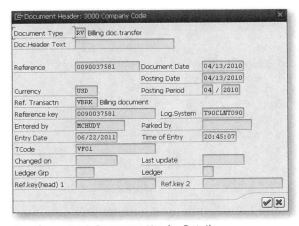

⌃ *Figure 4* AR Document Header Details

You can use command /n in the command window to close the transaction and return to the SAP menu. You've successfully processed a customer request for open items status and verified who processed the accounting documents and when it was done.

Changing Customer Credit Master Data

You can maintain credit master data for a customer and change the credit risk category, credit limits, or maintain account blocks all in one place.

Let's say that your customer acquired a new business unit. This means that their business activity will increase, and with it, you need to update the customer's credit management master data, including the credit limit. You can also update risk category, credit representative groups, and blocking/unblocking of the account. This is absolutely necessary to avoid the frequent block of sales documents due to credit limits that no longer have appropriate levels for the increased volumes.

Since this transaction is usually maintained by the FI team, a person from the SD team will have a difficult time maintaining this data when needed. This can happen often in the training and testing systems when large numbers of orders are processed but receivables are usually never performed.

✓ And Here's How ...

To change your customer's credit master data, execute Transaction FD32 or follow the path:

> LOGISTICS • SALES AND DISTRIBUTION • CREDIT MANAGEMENT • MASTER DATA • CHANGE

On the initial screen, complete the following steps:

▶ Enter the payer account number in the CUSTOMER field. Whenever you need to update credit master data, remember that all credit management settings are related to the payer partner function within individual credit control areas.

▶ Specify the appropriate code in the CREDIT CONTROL AREA.

▶ Mark the individual checkboxes for the changes you wish to make, marking in sections OVERVIEW, GENERAL DATA, or CREDIT CONTROL AREA DATA.

To continue, click on the ENTER icon or press ⟨Enter⟩ on your keyboard. The initial screen is an overview of credit information for the account. The only thing you can update on this screen is the HORIZON field. This date is defaulted for the customer and the risk category from configuration in the IMG.

Click on the NEXT icon or press ⟨Shift⟩+⟨F1⟩. The next screen shows the address data from the customer master record; note that you can't make any changes to it using this transaction, but instead have to run Transactions VD02 or XD02. To continue on to credit data status screens, click NEXT.

The next screen (see Figure 1) displays CREDIT MANAGEMENT CENTRAL DATA, showing current total credit limits for the account, as well as the highest individual limit in a credit area, if defined.

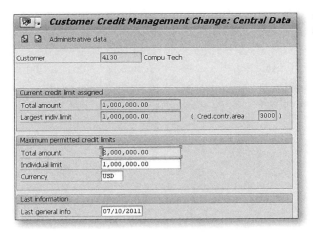

《 Figure 1 *Customer Credit Management Central Data*

To extend the total credit limit of the customer across all credit control areas, specify the desired value in the TOTAL AMOUNT field in the MAXIMUM PERMITTED CREDIT LIMITS section (see Figure 1).

Click on NEXT or press `Shift`+`F1` to continue to the STATUS screen and maintain additional data like credit limit, risk category, and credit rep group. You can also review AR activity and access TEXTS, where you can maintain internal and external notes and actions (see Figure 2).

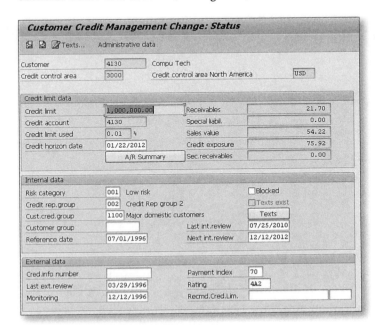

« **Figure 2** Credit Management Status Details

You can maintain the credit limit for the specific credit control area in the CREDIT LIMIT DATA section, which simply translates to a limit for the total receivables from the customer. Below that you can also see the percentage of credit limit used, which normally drives the credit checks. On this screen you can also set the BLOCK flag, which will set the block for all credit transactions like sales orders, deliveries, and goods movements except for invoices for completed deliveries.

Running the Credit Overview to Create a Tracking List

There's an easy way to create a list that allows you to monitor critical customers' open items older than your credit policy allows, as well as other credit management relevant data.

You need to quickly identify customers with constant credit problems. You have customers that are on the credit critical customers watch list and won't pass certain credit checks such as oldest open items, overdue open items, or credit limit used. It's important to proactively identify accounts that may need to have their credit limits managed more strictly. In this tip, we'll show you a report that allows you to review data for critical customers due to the credit checks settings in Sales and Distribution.

✓ And Here's How ...

Run Transaction F.31 or follow the menu path:

> Logistics • Sales and Distribution • Credit Management • Credit Management Info System • Overview

In order for this transaction to have all the required data, create an A/R summary for the selected group of customers within the credit control area by running Transaction FCV1 (Create A/R Summary) first. Then you can fill in data on the F.31 Credit Overview initial screen, shown in Figure 1.

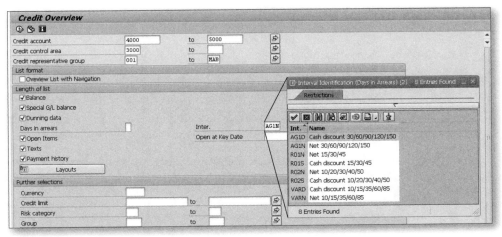

⌃ *Figure 1* Credit Overview Initial Screen

Enter the CREDIT ACCOUNT number or range of accounts, and then specify the code for the CREDIT CONTROL AREA. Next, fill in data for CREDIT REPRESENTATIVE GROUP. In the LENGTH OF THE LIST section, specify all details you'd like to see in the relevant category listed. Select the INTERVAL indicator, which is used to divide the customer open items by arrears interval. Select the required interval from the pop-up window (see Figure 1). You can also use many other fields to narrow down your selection listed in the FURTHER SELECTION section such as currency, credit limit, risk category, blocked indicator, or rating.

When finished, click on the EXECUTE icon or press F8 on your keyboard. If chose the OVERVIEW LIST WITH NAVIGATION field in the LIST FORMAT section, you'll be presented with the list of credit accounts sorted by credit account and the credit control area.

If you need more data than what's presented in the list, select one of the report lines and do one of the following:

▶ Click on the DISPLAY button or press Shift + F1 to display the document.

▶ Click on the LINE ITEMS button or press Shift + F2 to display line items.

▶ Click on the ACCOUNT ANALYSIS button or press Shift + F4 to display the account analysis.

▶ Click on the CUSTOMER button or press Shift + F5 to display the customer master record.

▶ Click on the PAYMENT HISTORY button or press ⎡Shift⎤+⎡F8⎤ to display payment history.

▶ Click on the TEXTS button or press ⎡F9⎤ to display customer credit master texts.

If you didn't mark the OVERVIEW LIST WITH NAVIGATION field on the initial screen in the LIST FORMAT section, your list will include details requested in the LENGTH OF THE LIST section (see Figure 2).

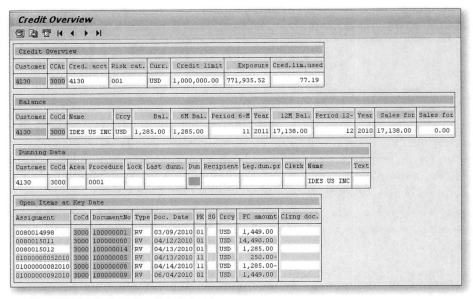

⌃ **Figure 2** *Credit Overview Detailed List*

You can now print your results or export to Microsoft Excel, and then exit the transaction.

Displaying Changes to Credit Management Master Data

If unexpected or incorrect changes were made to a credit account, you can verify who made the changes and what fields were modified.

It happens in any business: there's a fast-triggered action, or you switch to other activities. You save your data, and the worst case scenario is waiting to happen: a customer with a bad score is granted a credit line it doesn't deserve, risking the creation of uncollectable receivables. In the credit management area, this isn't a welcomed scenario, and you need to quickly create a report to display changes that were made to either an individual account or a range of accounts.

✓ And Here's How ...

To create such a report, run Transaction S_ALR_87012215 or follow the path:

> LOGISTICS • SALES AND DISTRIBUTION • CREDIT MANAGEMENT • CREDIT MANAGE-
> MENT INFO SYSTEM • DISPLAY CHANGES TO CREDIT MANAGEMENT

On the initial screen shown in Figure 1, enter your selection data in each section, starting with GENERAL SELECTION:

▶ In the CUSTOMER field(s), specify the account number or range of accounts.

▶ In CHANGED ON, enter the date range in which the suspected change occurred.

▶ If you know the user responsible for the modifications, populate the user name in the CHANGED BY field(s).

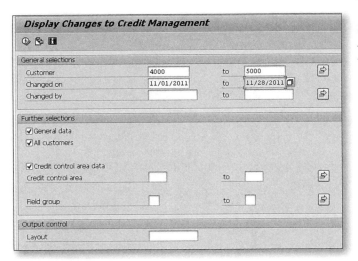

« Figure 1 *Display Changes to Credit Management Initial Screen*

In the FURTHER SELECTION section, check the boxes for the data types you want to review. Then click on the EXECUTE icon or press F8. The screen shown in Figure 2 will appear where you can see the list showing all relevant data changes recorded for your review, sorted by account.

Credit Overview

Customer	CCAr	Cred. acct	Risk cat.	Curr.	Credit limit	Exposure	Cred.lim.used
4000	3000	4000	001	CAD	500,000.00	62,068.46	12.41
4100	3000	4100	001		500,000.00	0.00	0.00
4130	3000	4130	001	USD	1,000,000.00	771,935.52	77.19
4140	3000	4140	001	USD	1,000,000.00	0.00	0.00
4150	3000	4150	001	USD	1,000,000.00	0.00	0.00
4250	3000	4250	001	USD	1,000,000.00	1,696.90	0.17
4251	3000	4251	001	USD	1,000,000.00	0.00	0.00
4252	3000	4252	001	USD	1,000,000.00	7,276.00	0.73
4253	3000	4253	001	USD	1,000,000.00	1,520.93	0.15
4254	3000	4254	001	USD	1,000,000.00	1,165.54-	0.00
4255	3000	4255	001	USD	1,000,000.00	0.00	0.00
4256	3000	4256	001	USD	1,000,000.00	0.00	0.00
4711	3000	4711	001	USD	1,000,000.00	0.00	0.00

⌃ Figure 2 *Display Changes to Credit Management Details*

You can print your results or export the list to Excel. You've successfully displayed changes made to credit management master data.

Creating a Credit Master Sheet for a Customer Credit Review

When performing a customer credit review, you can create a credit master sheet that displays all activities.

Let's say that you need to produce a report for a credit standing review to share during meetings. You therefore need a summary of all activities for a customer's account. This data is stored in multiple different tables; building a report like this could take a long time.

SAP provides a transaction that we'll cover in this tip that will help you bypass this issue. We'll show you how to run a detailed report that shows all credit-relevant data you'll need to successfully review a customer's credit master.

And Here's How ...

To open the credit master sheet, run Transaction S_ALR_87012218 or follow the menu path:

> LOGISTICS • SALES AND DISTRIBUTION • CREDIT MANAGEMENT • CREDIT MANAGEMENT INFO SYSTEM • CREDIT MASTER SHEET

On the initial screen shown in Figure 1, enter the customer number and the credit control area you're reviewing.

Next, choose the interval in the DISPLAY OF DAYS IN ARREARS section. To do this, simply select the required interval from the popup window and click on the EXECUTE icon or press [F8] on your keyboard.

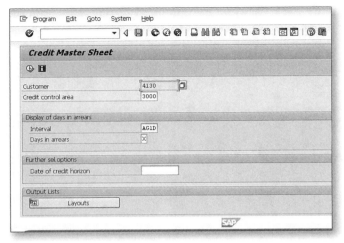

⌃ *Figure 1* Credit Master Sheet Initial Screen

On the next screen shown in Figure 2, you'll see all your detailed data sorted by category starting with CREDIT MANAGEMENT MASTER DATA. Here you'll find a summary of what you would see in Transaction FD32, which we covered Tip 89.

Credit Master Sheet

🖳 Line Items   Account Analysis   Customer   Payment History   Texts 🗔 🗗 |◄ ◄ ► ►|

Credit Management Master Data

Medium Field Label	Value	Medium Field Label	Value
Customer	0000004130	Telephone 1	
Name	Compu Tech	Fax Number	
City	SAN FRANCISCO	Created by	VAN DIJK
Created on	03/06/1996		
Cred.contr.area	3000	Created by	SCHOEPFEL
Risk category	001	Created on	11/22/1994
Cred.rep.grp	002	Changed by	MCHUDY
Cust.cred.grp	1100	Changed on	11/28/2011
Customer group		Text changed	07/25/1996
Other areas	No		
Last int.review	07/25/1996	Cred.info no.	
Next int.review	12/12/2012	Payment index	70
Last ext.review	03/29/1996	Rating	4A2
Referen.date	01/01/2005		
Credit limit	1,500,000.00	Receivables	17,138.00
Credit limit used	771,935.52	Special liabil.	0.00
Over/under	728,064.48	Open delivery value	21,603.52
Cred.lim.used	51.46 %	Open order value	730,296.00
Credit horizon date		Open billing doc.val	2,898.00
DSO	9999		
Exceeded			
Last payment	12/19/1996	Last payment	318.75 USD
Total limit	2,500,000.00	Currency	USD
Individ.limit	1,500,000.00	Last gen.info	07/10/1996

⌃ *Figure 2* Credit Master Sheet Credit Management Master Data

If you scroll down, you can see a summary of balances, similar to the summary provided in Transaction F.31, covered in Tip 90.

If you keep scrolling, you'll see a grid summary as shown in Figure 3 that shows you the number of days open items are, or will be overdue.

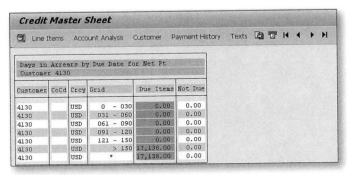

⌃ *Figure 3 Credit Master Sheet Days in Arrears*

This report can be printed or sent to Excel. If you need to drill into more details, you can do so by selecting one of the following options from the menu or using available buttons:

▶ Click on the LINE ITEMS button or press ⌈Shift⌉+⌈F1⌉ to display line items.

▶ Click on the ACCOUNT ANALYSIS button or press ⌈Shift⌉+⌈F2⌉ to display account analysis.

▶ Click on the CUSTOMER button or press ⌈Shift⌉+⌈F4⌉ to display the customer master record.

▶ Click on the PAYMENT HISTORY button or press ⌈Shift⌉+⌈F5⌉ to display the payment history.

▶ Click on the TEXTS button or press ⌈F9⌉ to display customer credit master texts.

When done, you can return to the selection screen to repeat these steps for another customer or exit the transaction.

Part 8

Sales Information System

Things You'll Learn in this Section

In this part of the book, we cover four of what we consider to be the most useful and valuable of the reports in the Sales Information System (SIS). The tips included in this section were selected to help you incorporate reports and analyses into your daily operation to improve your knowledge of your customer's credit and sales situation. You'll be able to do analysis on sales volumes by customer or material, display extensive credit information for customers, examine price lists, and search for blocked orders.

Tip 93

Using the Credit Master Sheet to Discover Customer Credit Information

When you need to quickly find credit information on a customer, you can use the credit master sheet report to give you essential information.

Sales activities require information about a customer's credit to know how well they're managing their payments and also how much you can sell them. In this tip, we'll show you how to get this information from the customer's credit master sheet.

✔ And Here's How ...

The credit master sheet shows the current credit limit and the current exposure or the part of the credit that has been used. It also shows any delays in payments (arrears), if any. To run this report, use Transaction F.35 or follow the path:

> LOGISTICS • SALES AND DISTRIBUTION • SALES INFORMATION SYSTEM • ENVIRONMENT • MASTER DATA • CREDIT MANAGEMENT • CREDIT MASTER SHEET

When you reach the selection screen shown in Figure 1, enter a customer and a credit control area. Keep in mind that a credit control area could be responsible for several company codes, so that when you look at the report the numbers don't surprise you.

Choose the interval according to the arrears information you want displayed. You can also enter a date for credit horizon, which will set a date after which all deliveries that are still opened for GI will be ignored. Only opened items and deliveries pending billing will be listed.

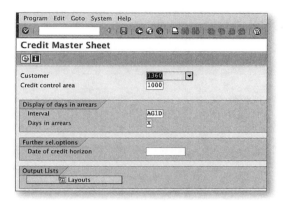

« *Figure 1* Search Criteria for the Credit Master Sheet Report

Execute the report and look at the data. The report is divided into several sections (see Figure 2).

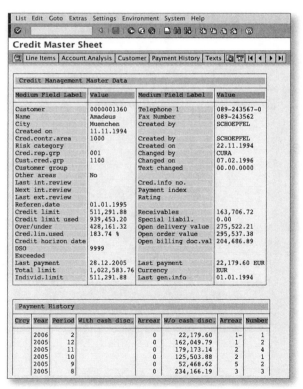

« *Figure 2* Credit Master Sheet

You can double-click on any line and the system will take you to the credit management information for this customer. You can also look at the opened and cleared items for this customer by clicking on the LINE ITEMS button or pressing ⌷Shift⌷+⌷F1⌷ (see Figure 3), as described in Tip 77.

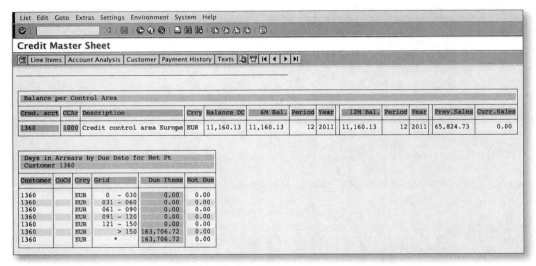

⌃ **Figure 3** *Days in Arrears Listed by Time Range*

The report's length will vary depending on how much information there is to display for the customer, and you'll have to page up and down to look at all the information.

Tip **94**

Displaying the Sales Price List

You can easily display and sort sales price lists based on a specific requirement.

Price lists are provided by the SAP system to allow you to put together several products that can be offered at different prices to different customers. For example, you can have a group of products that are sold at a different price when sold to retail customers than when sold to wholesale customers.

However, if you're working for a large company in particular, it can sometimes be difficult to remember which price lists exist for each sales area, which ones are still valid, and which condition types are used in each one. In this tip, we'll show you how to create lists depending on your specific question or requirement.

✓ And Here's How ...

Before you use this transaction, make sure that you've made the necessary settings in Customizing to assign a pricing procedure to your required price list type, and already created price lists in the system.

To get to this report, use Transaction MCV5 or follow the path:

> LOGISTICS • SALES AND DISTRIBUTION • SALES INFORMATION SYSTEMS • ENVIRONMENT • CONDITIONS • PRICE LIST

In the search screen for this report, enter your sales organization at the minimum, as well as the validity period for the price lists. If you want to make the search more specific, enter the distribution channel, the price list type, or a specific condition type to look for in your price lists.

315

In the list screen section shown in Figure 1, select the fields and columns you want to display in the report. You can choose from the following:

▶ DISPLAY SCALES

▶ DISPLAY VALIDITY PERIOD

▶ ADDITIONAL CONDITION FIELDS

▶ COND. MARKED FOR DELETION

▶ EXCLUSIVE

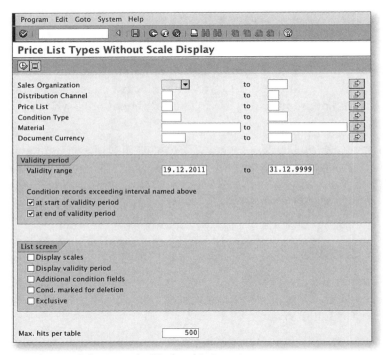

⌃ *Figure 1* *Selection to be Displayed in Report*

Click EXECUTE, and you'll be presented with a list of price lists that fulfill your search criteria (see Figure 2). The display may vary depending on the fields you selected on the search screen.

Double-click on any line, and you'll be taken to a detail screen for that condition type, as shown in Figure 3.

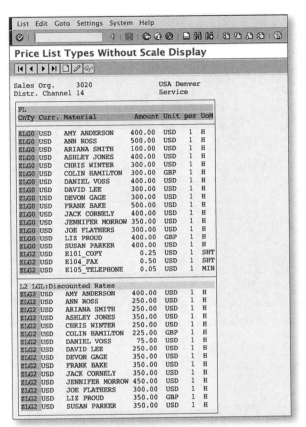

≫ *Figure 2 Price Lists That Fulfill Your Search Criteria*

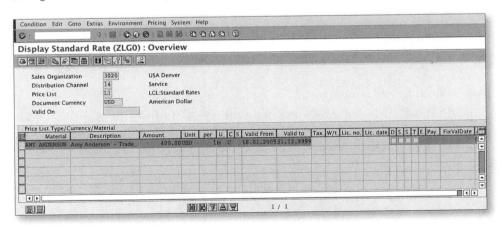

≫ *Figure 3 Condition Type Screen*

Tip 95

Analyzing Sales Volumes with the Sales Information System

You can use the Sales Information System to perform multidimensional sales volume analysis for customers and materials.

Analytic reports aren't easy to develop, and one that gives you totals by customer, material, sales area, and period could be a real nightmare due to the volume of data and the number of tables that it would need to read. In this tip, we'll show you how to use standard, delivered analyses to create reports for customers and materials.

✓ And Here's How ...

As a prerequisite to working with this tip, you need to have activated the Sales Information System (SIS) in Customizing and made sure it's configured to collect statistical information about all your sales transactions.

This tip will discuss two reports. One presents an analysis of the sales volume by customer, and the other by material.

Sales Volume by Customer
The SIS is a component of the Logistic Information System that allows for data analysis. This tool is composed of several info structures that collect statistical information from the transactional data as those transactions are executed.

To get to the first analysis, use Transaction MC+E or follow the path:

> INFORMATION SYSTEMS • LOGISTICS • SALES AND DISTRIBUTION • CUSTOMER • SALES

This report takes the statistical information collected in the info structure S001 and summarizes different concepts or key figures so that you're able to display these totals by different drill-down levels such as month, sales organization, distribution channel, division, sold-to party, and material.

Enter your search criteria in the selection screen shown in Figure 1. In this case, the less specific you are, the more chances you have of drilling down and seeing different total levels. As an example, you could alternatively enter all the sales organizations in the same company code and look at the sales information for the past three months.

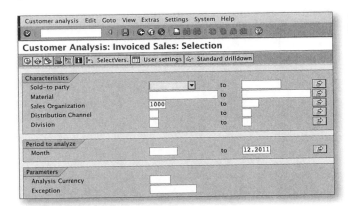

« *Figure 1 Report Selection Screen*

Keep in mind that this report can't be more granular than a month; this is because you're looking at statistical data and not an on-line transactional report.

Sales Volume by Material

To get to the second analysis, use Transaction MC+Q or follow the path:

> INFORMATION SYSTEMS • LOGISTICS • SALES AND DISTRIBUTION • MATERIAL • SALES

This report takes the statistical information collected in the info structure S004 and summarizes different concepts or key figures so that you're able to display these totals by different drill-down levels, such as month, sales organization, distribution channel, division, and material.

In the selection screen shown in Figure 2, enter your search criteria similar to the customer report.

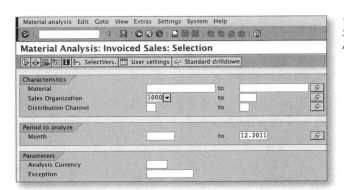

《 Figure 2
Selection Screen for
Material Analysis

The data in both analyses is displayed in columns that represent key figures. If you double-click on any of these key figures' data, a pop-up screen will display with all the key figures for the line you clicked on (see Figure 3).

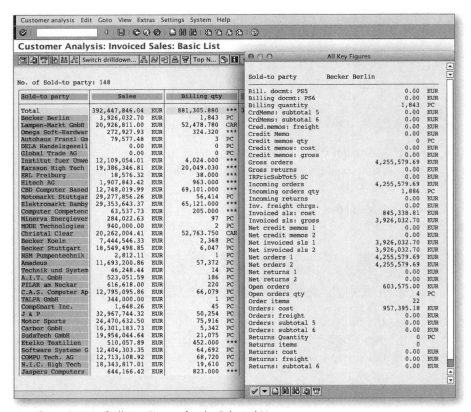

≋ Figure 3 *List of All Key Figures for the Selected Line*

In both reports you can adjust the displayed columns and create display variants. You can switch the drill-down level by double-clicking on any line of the first column. If, for example, you double-click on one of them on the initial sold-to list, you'll see the sales organization totals; if you double-click on one of these sales organizations, then it will take you to the division totals, and so on.

You can also select the drill-down level by clicking on the SWITCH DRILLDOWN button.

If you want to list the top-N lines of any drill-down level, select the pivot key figure, click on the TOP-N button, and enter the number of N lines it will display. The resulting list will only have the top-N elements, as shown in Figure 4.

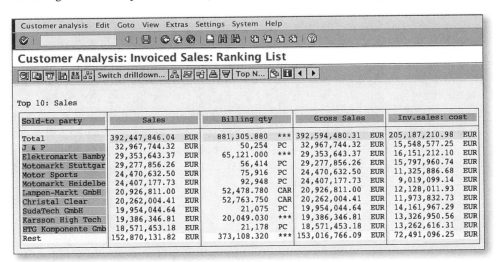

Figure 4 *List of the Top 10 Sold-To by Sales Totals*

You can save these analyses so that they don't have to be recalculated in the future by clicking on the SAVE As button. The key figures on the layout of your report can be changed by clicking on the CHOOSE KEY FIGURES button or pressing F6 .

Monitoring Blocked Sales Orders

If your company processes large numbers of sales orders, you can set up your system to run a report in the background to monitor blocked orders in a timely manner.

In high-volume operations, there are always orders that are blocked for various reasons. You may have incompletion procedures that are blocking the order because it still requires data to be entered. There might be delivery blocks, credit management blocks, and in case you're using payment cards, there's the chance that the card wasn't approved or the approval expired and now the block is set. For all these reasons, you need to keep an eye on your system for blocked orders so that they don't just stay there without being processed until your customer calls to complain about not having their goods. In this tip, we'll show you how to find blocked orders so they can be analyzed.

 And Here's How ...

To get to the blocked orders report, use Transaction V.14 or follow the path:

> LOGISTICS • SALES AND DISTRIBUTION • SALES INFORMATION SYSTEM • ENVIRONMENT • DOCUMENT INFORMATION • ORDERS • BLOCKED ORDERS

This report shows you a list of blocked sales orders along with the blocking reason and the total amount of the order.

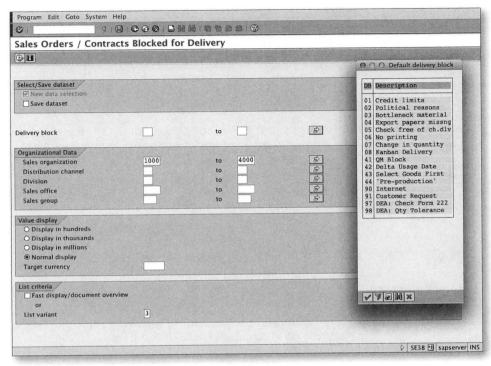

⩟ *Figure 1* List of Blocking Reasons in the Selection Screen

From the selection screen shown in Figure 1, you can select the blocking reasons by opening the match-code for delivery block. Select the sales areas, the display mode for the order amounts, and the list criteria. The list criteria refers to the information that will be listed and has two modes:

▶ FAST DISPLAY/DOCUMENT OVERVIEW
Shown in Figure 2, this is a very brief screen that shows a list of the documents and the blocking reason. From here you can double-click on any line and display the sales order.

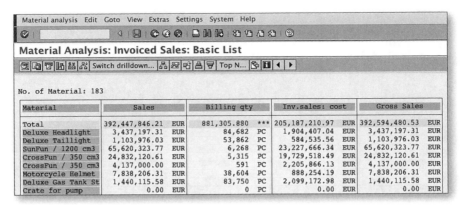

⌃ *Figure 2 Fast Display Lists Sales Orders That Are Blocked*

1. LIST VARIANT

   Shown in Figure 3, this is a detailed report that will tell you how many sales orders are blocked by sales order date. You can select a list variant for customer, material, or both.

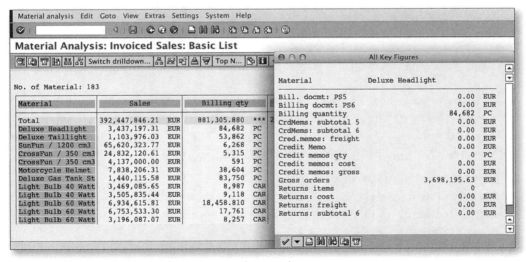

⌃ *Figure 3 List Display for Customer and Material*

You can schedule this report to run in the background by creating a selection variant and asking your basis group to schedule a background job for Report RVSPERAU. We recommend scheduling it to run periodically so that you're always on top of this subject.

Part 9

Other Tools

Things You'll Learn in this Section

While the other parts of this book are grouped by specific areas of tools, the book wouldn't be complete without mentioning a few tools that don't particularly belong to the Sales and Distribution component, but will prove to be very valuable in the day-to-day operations of a systems analyst. The ability to browse and query tables, find IDoc documentation, reprocess IDocs, and use the SAP Mail tool for executing workflow tasks is something you will definitely find valuable in extracting information from the system, writing functional specifications, troubleshooting interfaces, and looking at system messages that require an analyst's intervention.

Tip **97**

Building Reports Using QuickViewer

You can build a report without any ABAP programming by putting together a few different tables.

SAP provides a large number of out-of-the-box reports, but sometimes you have requests to provide data in the format that is familiar to the end users and not provided by any of the available choices. Most of the complicated reports where calculations and multiple look-ups are performed are prime candidates for your ABAP technical team. As a functional user you should have enough knowledge to navigate the basic SAP tables. We've provided a compilation of the most important and frequently-used tables in Appendix A for your reference. Some reports are as simple as a single table and should be very easy to generate without any programming knowledge by connecting a few tables.

And Here's How ...

Execute Transaction SQVI or follow the menu path:

> TOOLS • ABAP WORKBENCH • UTILITIES • QUICKVIEWER

On the initial screen shown in Figure 1, populate the name for your Quickview report by filling out the TITLE and COMMENTS fields.

Next, specify the type of DATA SOURCE; in our example, we'll use TABLE JOIN to use data from order header, item, and schedule lines. Press ⌷Enter⌷ or click on the ✓ icon to continue. On the next screen, add the tables required for your report.

Click on the INSERT TABLE icon (⊞) or press ⟨Shift⟩+⟨F1⟩ on your keyboard. A pop-up window will show up where you need to type in the table name, then press ⟨Enter⟩ to continue. Remember that only transparent tables are allowed in Transaction SQVI, so choose your tables wisely. Repeat these steps until all the required tables are dropped into your screen (see Figure 2).

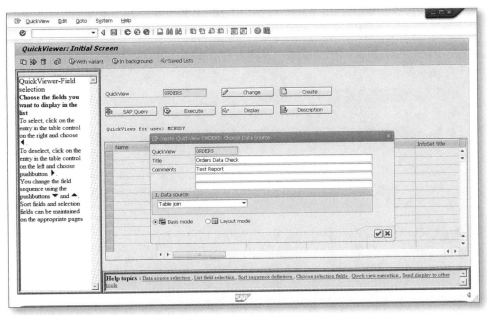

≫ **Figure 1** QuickViewer Initial Screen

Click on the BACK icon or press ⟨F3⟩. Back on the initial screen, select each of the tabs we'll discuss here and complete your setup process:

▶ LIST FIELDS SELECTION

On the first tab (see Figure 3), specify the fields you want to see on the actual report list. Pick the fields from the right side (see AVAILABLE FIELDS), select them, and use the left arrow to move them over to the FIELDS IN LIST section. If you want to change the sequence of the LIST FIELDS, select the field you want to move and use the UP or DOWN arrow buttons located to the left of the FIELDS LIST section. Another feature is the ability to add mulple lines if you're planning on displaying a large amount of data; simply click on ⊞ (add) or ⊟ (remove).

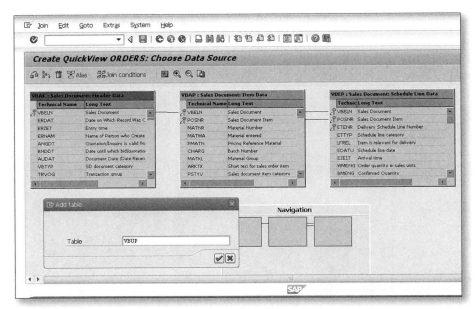

⋏ *Figure 2* *Create QuickView Data Source*

≪ *Figure 3* List
Fields Selection

▶ SORT SEQUENCE
On the second tab, specify the fields for sort sequence. The same building block
as in the first tab applies here.

▶ SELECTION FIELDS
These will be the selection fields you'd like to see at the start of your report for
your initial selection criteria.

▶ DATA SOURCE
This tab allows you to access the table join data you've initially created.

There's another way to complete tasks you've completed on the LIST FIELDS SELECTION and SELECTION FIELDS tabs. In the DATA FIELDS navigation pane on the left, you have all your tables listed. By expanding the table contents, you can maintain the fields for lists and for the selection screen there instead of the tabs (see Figure 4).

« Figure 4 Data Fields Navigation Pane

Execute a test run by pressing F8 or clicking on the EXECUTE icon. Once you're happy with your newly constructed report, click SAVE or press Ctrl+S. Next time you want to run the QuickViewer, start Transaction SQVI, select the line, and click on the EXECUTE button (see Figure 5).

« Figure 5 QuickViewer Initial Screen

The report will show the data in the sequence you've defined and will look exactly like many other SAP reports that feature the same tools and icons you're familiar with. Figure 6 shows our sample report defined in earlier steps.

« Figure 6 QuickViewer Report Details

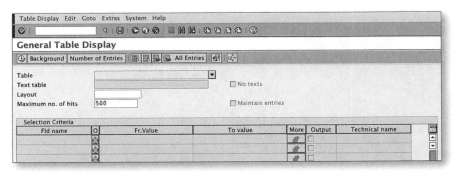

Tip 98

Browsing Sales Tables with Transaction SE16N

SAP provides a new transaction that will help every analyst browse tables to find the data more easily.

Table browsing is a regular activity among systems analysts. For years we've been using Transaction SE16, but you may not be aware that now the SAP ERP system has a more recent version of this transaction—SE16N, which is a more versatile and easy-to-use transaction. In this tip, we'll go over some of the new functions and displays of this transaction.

✅ And Here's How ...

To get to the transaction, use Transaction SE16N directly on the command line (there's no menu path to get to this transaction). The transaction will first prompt you for a table to browse; enter the table name and press ⌈Enter⌉ to see the screen shown in Figure 1.

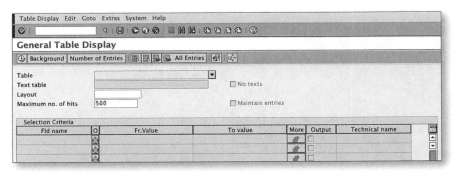

⌃ *Figure 1* Select a Table to Browse on the Main Screen

Ease of Use

Next, the system will present you a list with all the fields for the chosen table. This list is also the selection screen; here you can enter the search values on any field and they'll be used to query the table (see Figure 2).

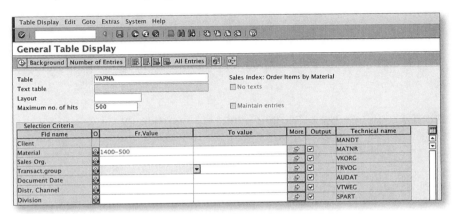

⌃ *Figure 2 All Fields Are Available on the Selection Screen*

The new search input design allows you to easily enter search values. As opposed to the older transaction, you won't need to go to the menu and add search fields, and all of the fields in the table will appear on the selection screen. Key fields are marked in bold blue font.

Useful User Interface

When you execute, the contents of the table that match your search criteria are presented using ALV (ABAP List Viewer), which is a grid view that also allows you to sum columns, calculate subtotals, filter content, and even graph your data (see Figure 3).

⌃ *Figure 3 Search Results Displayed in ALV Grid Mode*

If you double-click on any record, the system displays a pop-up window with all the fields in the table, not only the ones visible on the current layout.

Fld Name	Val.	Technical Field Name	Value Unconverted
Client	800	MANDT	800
Material	1400–500	MATNR	1400–500
Sales Organization	1000	VKORG	1000
Transaction group	0	TRVOG	0
Document Date	09.05.2010	AUDAT	09.05.2010
Distribution Channel	10	VTWEG	10
Division	00	SPART	00

≫ *Figure 4* *Total Contents of the Table Records Presented in a Pop-Up Window*

In the pop-up window shown in Figure 4, there's a column with the field names; now you can see the field description and the field name at the same time. If you need to have the field names on the search screen, you can change the settings by clicking on the SETTINGS button or pressing ⌈Shift⌉+⌈F12⌉ and selecting TECHNICAL COLUMN NAME LEADS, as shown in Figure 5.

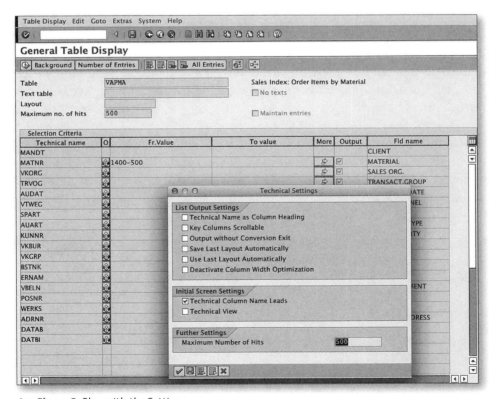

≫ *Figure 5* *Play with the Settings*

Tip 99

Accessing IDoc Documentation

In order to build interfaces with external systems, you need to know about IDocs and the segments that form them.

Most people, including savvy system users, don't know that the SAP system includes detailed IDoc documentation.

The best way to understand the structure of an IDoc and the different segments that form it is to read its documentation. The documentation includes the control record description, the data record description, and the status record description. There's also the segment structure. In this tip, we'll explain each of these documentation areas, how to access it, and how it's structured.

✓ And Here's How ...

Use Transaction WE60 or follow the path:

> LOGISTICS • LOGISTICS EXECUTION • INTERNAL WHSE PROCESSES • COMMUNICATION WITH EXTERNAL SYSTEMS • ALE ADMINISTRATION • SERVICES • DOCUMENTATION • IDOC TYPES AND SEGMENTS

Enter the name of the IDoc in the initial screen shown in Figure 1. You can also select what information you want displayed: CONTROL RECORD, DATA RECORD, or STATUS RECORD.

The Control Record

The control record is the part of an IDoc that does the hand-shaking with the external system. It tells it which system it comes from, what kind of document it is, which version it conforms to, and other technical information. One IDoc has only *one* control record.

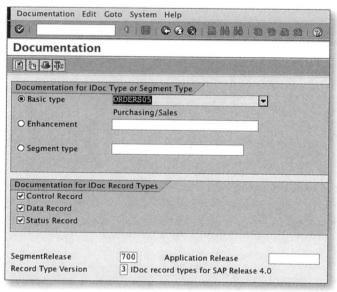

⪢ *Figure 1* *Initial Selection*

The Data Record

The data record describes each segment in the IDoc. It describes the segment name, the document it belongs to, the segment number, and the hierarchy it belongs to: it can have a higher level segment it belongs to or it can have lower level segments that belong to it. One IDoc can have one or many segments.

The Status Record

The status record basically tells what happened to the document after it was created. It keeps track of the document that it refers to and tells you if it was successful or failed, and which was the result of posting it or attempting to post it.

The Segment Structure

This documentation (shown in Figure 2) refers to the actual structure of each and every segment that's available in the IDoc. Normally, according to the standard SAP structure, there are header segments and item segments. You'll be able to see this hierarchy in the documentation. Each segment is formed by fields which are also described in the documentation.

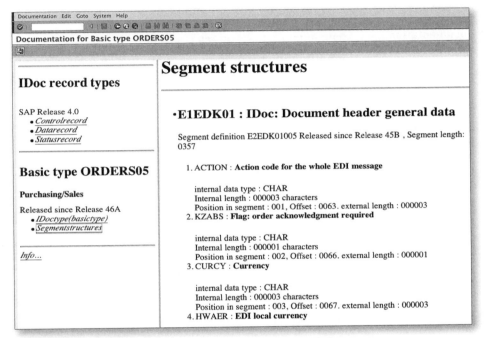

⌃ *Figure 2 Segment Structure Documentation from the Hyperlink*

Displaying the IDOC Documentation

To display the IDoc documentation, click on the HTML FORMAT button or press F8 . This will take you to the documentation.

Depending on the information you input at the beginning, you'll have different hyperlinks available at the top left frame of the document to switch between the CONTROL RECORD, DATA RECORD, and STATUS RECORD. On the right frame, you can see a manual with the description of the different elements of the IDoc.

When you click on the different hyperlinks, the corresponding documentation is brought up into the main frame on the right side. When you scroll down, you'll be able to read through the documentation. You'll also see the IDoc name, its description, the release, and two more hyperlinks: IDOC TYPE and SEGMENT STRUCTURE on the left frame.

If you click on the segment structure in Figure 2, you'll see the detailed documentation for each of the IDoc segments on the main frame on the right.

It's from this segment documentation that you can choose which fields you need to communicate with the external system. The documentation will tell you the data type, length, and offset for the field, which you'll use to specify interfaces between the SAP system and other external systems.

IDocs in Sales and Distribution

For your convenience, some of the most commonly used IDocs are:

Direction	Document	Message Type	IDoc Basic Type
Inbound	Inquiry	REQOTE	ORDERS05
Inbound	Sales order	ORDERS	ORDERS05
Inbound	Sales order change	ORDCHG	ORDERS05
Inbound	Delivery order	DELORD	ORDERS05
Inbound	Forecast delivery schedule	DELINS	DELFOR01
Outbound	Shipping notification	DESADV	DELVRY01
Outbound	Shipment notification	SHPMNT	SHPMNT01
Outbound	Invoice	INVOIC	INVOIC02

Using SAP Mail/Inbox for Monitoring System Events and IDoc Failures

You can use the SAP Mail tool to follow up on Sales and Distribution system events.

The SAP ERP system uses SAP Mail to communicate with you. However, it isn't commonly known how the SAP system communicates IDoc errors, workflow events, or other system messages. Workflow, for example, sends notifications for action on tasks using your inbox. Also, when severe problems occur that prevent the system from posting a transaction, it sends you a notification describing the problem.

SAP Mail is used by the Sales and Distribution interface system to communicate any problem posting inbound or outbound IDocs. You'll see the detail of the failure in your inbox, and you'll know that you have a message in there because you'll see a pop-up window telling you that you've received an express message. In this tip, we'll show you how this communication is sent using SAP Mail.

✅ And Here's How ...

To get to your inbox, use Transaction SBWP or click OFFICE • WORKPLACE.

You can also reach this transaction from the SAP EASY ACCESS screen (main menu). There you'll find a button with a little IN-tray labeled SAP BUSINESS WORKPLACE `Ctrl`+`F12`, and then click on the Inbox.

Your inbox is organized in several sections:

- ▶ UNREAD DOCUMENTS: System notifications and messages that you haven't read
- ▶ DOCUMENTS: System notifications and messages that you've already read
- ▶ WORKFLOW: Actions required on workflow tasks
- ▶ OVERDUE ENTRIES: Workflow tasks that you haven't worked on yet
- ▶ DEADLINE MESSAGES: Also related to workflow items that have to be worked on before a certain date/time

Maybe the most important pieces of information you'll get in the SAP inbox are the workflow items. Click on a work item from the WORKFLOW item list, and the message is displayed in the message section of the screen; you can click on the EXECUTE button on the work item detail screen. When you click on the EXECUTE button, it makes you the owner of this work item, and it disappears from the inbox of any other agents. Executing a work item starts the task behind it.

IDocs are reported also as workflow tasks. When an IDoc fails to post or to send data, it will create a workflow task for whoever was defined as agent in the partner's profile.

Another kind of very important messages are update terminations (see Figure 1). These are events in which the system was unable to post the data to all the databases involved in a transaction. When the system finds an error that prevents it from successfully completing the updates, it rolls back the postings from the tables that were already affected and sends a message to your inbox.

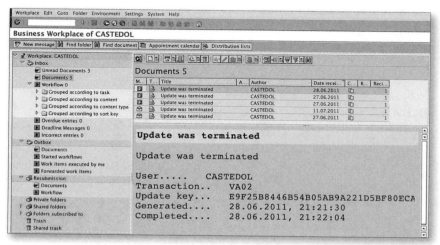

▲ **Figure 1** View of the SAP Mail Inbox

Most of the time these errors happen because there was a change in configuration that caused a conflict or the basis group needs to do some technical maintenance to the SAP system.

When you get these kinds of messages, check if any configuration changes have been made to your productive system. You may also want to check with the basis team if they've identified any problems with the system.

In many cases, you won't be able to successfully complete your transaction until the configuration change has been reversed or fixed and/or the basis problem has been resolved.

When you select NEW MESSAGE on your inbox screen, you'll be taken to a new screen where you can enter a subject, type your message, and select the recipients of the message.

If you started this new message functionality from a report transaction, then the report is automatically attached. Otherwise, if you started it from your inbox, you can attach a document to it by clicking on the little paper and clip icon at the top labeled CREATE ATTACHMENT or by pressing Control + Shift + F3.

To send the message, click on the SEND button or press Shift + F8.

Tables and Quick References

SAP Logistics Tables: Tables and Quick References

SAP functionality revolves around a multitude of tables and structures crisscrossing all types of modules, capturing the business in motion as it happens. Sometimes you need to connect the dots, but this can be a daunting task to start. This appendix illustrates some of the most important logistics tables used in Sales and Distribution and depicts the relationship, showing the common reference data fields shared amongst them per module. You can use this information to build the QuickView queries we covered in Tip 97, and when searching for data using Transaction SE16N, which we covered in Tip 98.

Customer Master Data

Transaction	Description
KNA1	Customer General Data
KNAS	Customer Master - VAT Registration
KNB1	Customer Master - Company Code Data
KNB4	Customer Payment History
KNB5	Customer Master - Dunning Info
KNBK	Customer Master Bank Data
KNKA	Customer Master Credit Management
KNKK	Customer Master Credit Control Area Data - Credit Limits
KNVA	Customer Master Unloading Points
KNVH	Customer Hierarchies
KNVI	Customer Master Tax Indicator
KNVK	Customer Master Contact Partner
KNVL	Customer Master Licenses
KNVP	Customer Master Partner Functions
KNVS	Customer Master Shipping Data
KNVT	Customer Master Record Texts for Sales

Transaction	Description
KNVV	Customer Master Sales Data
KLPA	Customer/Vendor Link Data
KNVH	Customer Hierarchies

Sales Documents Data

Transaction	Description
VBAK	Sales Document Header Data
VBAP	Sales Document Item Data
VBBE	Sales Requirements Individual Records
VBEH	Schedule Line History
VBEP	Sales Document Schedule Line Data
VBFA	Sales Document Flow
VBLB	Sales Document Release Order Data
VBLK	SD Document Delivery Note Header
VBPA	Sales Document Partner
VBUK	Sales Document Header Status and Administrative Data
VBUP	Sales Document Item Status

Pricing Data

Transaction	Description
KONV	Conditions for Transaction Data
KONP	Conditions for Items

Shipping Documents Data

Transaction	Description
LIKP	SD Document: Delivery Header Data
LIPS	SD Document: Delivery: Item Data
VBFS	Error Log for Collective Processing
VBLK	SD Document: Delivery Note Header
VLKPA	SD Index: Deliveries by Partner Functions
VLPMA	SD Index: Delivery Items by Material

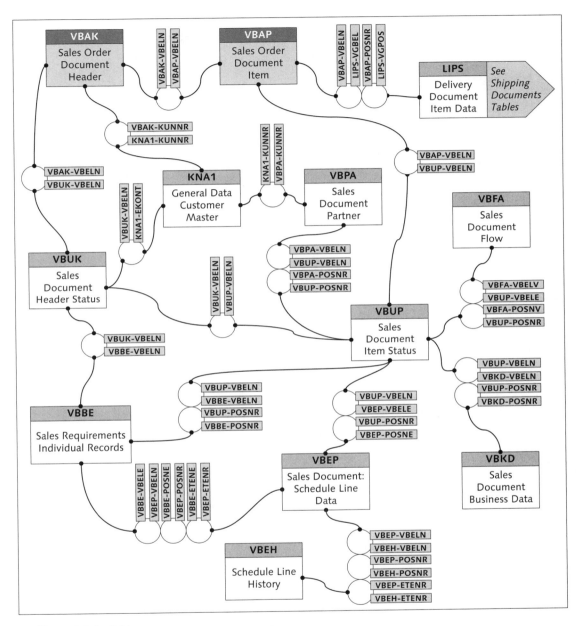

⌃ *Figure 1* *Sales Tables*

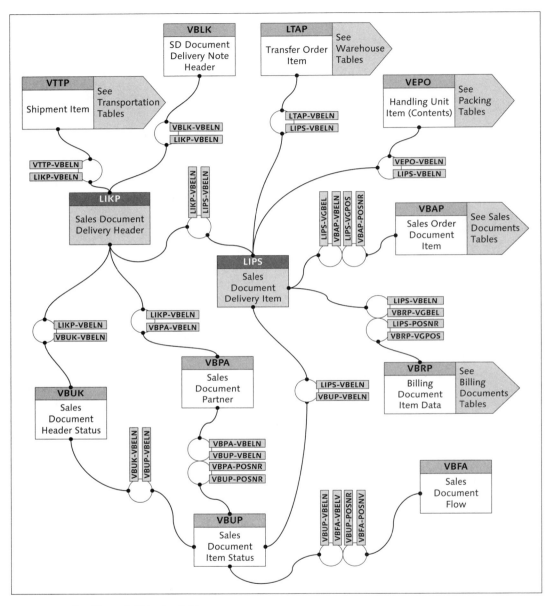

⌃ Figure 2 Shipping Tables

Warehouse Management Data

Transaction	Description
LAGP	Storage Bins
LEIN	Storage Unit Header Records
LINK	Inventory Document Header in WM
LINP	Inventory Document Item in WM
LINV	Inventory Data per Quant
LQUA	Quants
LQUAB	Total Quant Counts for Certain Strategies
LTAK	WM Transfer Order Header
LTAP	Transfer Order Item
LTBK	Transfer Requirement Header
LTBP	Transfer Requirement Item
LTHU	Assignment of Pick-HUs to Transfer Orders
LUBU	Posting Change Document

Transportation Management Tables

Table Name	Description
TVKN	Routes: Transportation Connection Points
TVKNT	Routes: Transportation Connection Points: Texts
TVRAB	Route Stages
TVRO	Routes
TVROT	Routes: Texts
TVRSZ	Routes: Legs for Each Route
TVSR	Routes: Legs

≫ **Table 1** *Routes Tables*

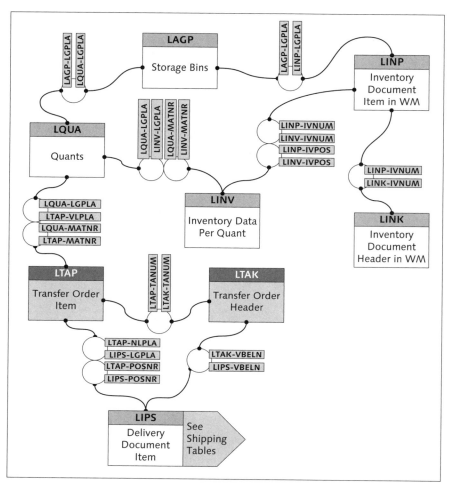

⌃ *Figure 3* Warehouse Management Tables

Table Name	Description
VTSP	Stage of Transport/Item Allocation
VTTK	Shipment Header
VTTP	Shipment Item
VTTS	Stage of Shipment

⌃ *Table 2* Shipment Document Tables

Table Name	Description
VFKK	Shipment Costs: Header Data
VFKN	Account Determination in Shipment Costs Item
VFKP	Shipment Costs: Item Data
VFPA	Partner for Shipment Costs
VFSI	Shipment Costs: Sub-Item Data
VFZP	Correct Original Assignment of Conditions

☆ *Table 3* *Shipment Cost Document Tables*

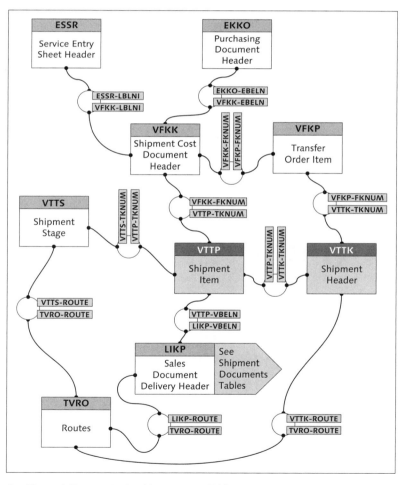

☆ *Figure 4* *Transportation Management Tables*

Tables in Billing

Table Name	Description
VBRK	Billing Document: Header Data
VBRL	Sales Document: Invoice List
VBRP	Billing Document: Item Data
VBSK	Collective Processing for a Sales Document Header
VBSS	Collective Processing: Sales Documents
VRKPA	Sales Index: Bills by Partner Functions
VRPMA	SD Index: Billing Items per Material

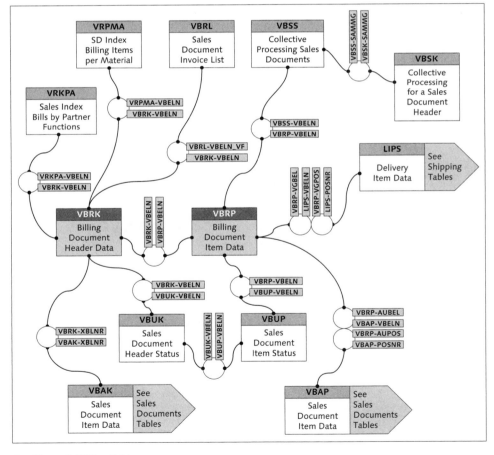

≽ *Figure 5* *Billing Tables*

Tables in Packing

Table Name	Description
VEKP	Handling Unit - Header Table
VEPO	Packing: Handling Unit Item (Contents)
VEVW	Where-Used List for Handling Units
HUEXIDV	Table with Key 'External ID'
HUSSTAT	Individual Status for Each Handling Unit
HUSTOBJ	Information about HU Status Object

» *Table 4* Handling Units: Main Data

Table Name	Description
HUINV_HDR	Handling Unit: Phys. Inv. Document Header
HUINV_ITEM	Handling Unit: Physical Inventory Document Item
HUINV_SERNR	Handling Unit Phys. Inv. Doc. - Serial Numbers for Item

» *Table 5* Handling Units: Physical Inventory

Table Name	Description
HUMSEG	Reference-HU-Item for Material Doc.Item that was Posted Last
HUMSEG_SER	Serial Numbers for the HUMSEG Table
HUSSTAT	Individual Status for Each Handling Unit
THUBEW2 - HU	Movement Types for Stock Category Posting Change
THUBEW3 - HU	Movement Types for Pack and Unpack with Posting Chg

» *Table 6* Handling Units: Movements

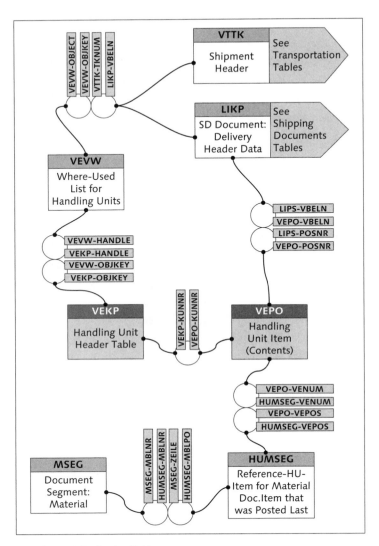

⌃ *Figure 6* Packaging Tables

Additional Resources

For further reference in any of the subjects we covered in this book, we suggest that you refer to the following resources:

SAP Help: *http://help.sap.com/*

SAP Developers Network: *http://www.sdn.sap.com/*

Chudy, Matt and Luis Castedo. *Sales and Distribution in SAP ERP—Practical Guide* (Boston, MA: SAP PRESS, 2011).

Iyer, D. Rajen. *Effective SAP SD* (Boston, MA: SAP PRESS, 2007).

Mohapatra, Ashish. *Optimizing Sales and Distribution in SAP ERP: Functionality and Configuration* (Boston, MA: SAP PRESS, 2010).

The Authors

Matt Chudy is an independent SAP Logistics consulting lead. He has more than 12 years of experience in SD, MM, and Logistics, spanning project administration, design, gap-analysis, testing, implementation, and supporting and training. He has been a strong team leader and covered several SAP project lifecycles. His specialties include Logistics Execution System, Transportation Management, Sales and Distribution, Inventory and Warehouse Management, Materials Management, and Production Planning. He currently lives in the greater Chicago area.

Luis Castedo is an independent systems and business consultant with more than 20 years of experience. For the past 15 years, he has been focused on SAP implementations. He has experience working with Fortune 500 companies and on multisite projects. He is a certified SAP MM consultant, and his specialties include Sales and Distribution, Materials Management, Inventory and Warehouse Management, Shipping, and Transportation. He currently lives in the Mexico City area.

Together, Matt and Luis have written the bestselling SAP PRESS book *Sales and Distribution in SAP ERP—Practical Guide*.

Index

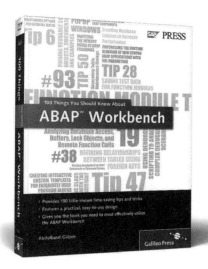

Provides 100 little-known time-saving tips and workarounds for developers

Features a practical, easy-to-use design

Gives you the tools you need to most effectively and efficiently utilize the ABAP Workbench

Abdulbasıt Gülşen

100 Things You Should Know About the ABAP Workbench

Don't hesitate in learning how to perform ABAP Workbench tasks more easily and efficiently than ever before! Whether you're a beginner or advanced user, this book provides tips and tricks that give you different and valuable ways of working with the tool. Based on your specific needs, you'll easily navigate the 100 tips and workarounds to help you increase productivity, save time, and improve the overall ease-of-use of working with the ABAP Workbench.

approx. 350 pp., 49,95 Euro / US$ 49.95
ISBN 978-1-59229-427-5, July 2012

>> www.sap-press.com

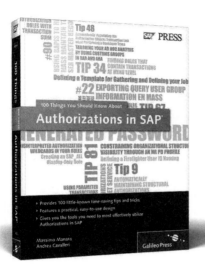

Provides 100 little-known time-saving tips and workarounds for administrators working on SAP authorizations

Teaches you how to improve the security of your SAP system

Gives you the tools you need to master authorizations in your SAP system

Andrea Cavalleri, Massimo Manara

100 Things You Should Know About Authorizations in SAP

Unlock the secrets of working with authorizations in the SAP Basis system! In this book, you'll find 100 tips and workarounds you can use to improve the security of your SAP system. The tips are grouped together based on the area of authorizations they cover, such as development security, Profile Generator, upgrades, and more. They have been carefully selected to provide a collection of the best, most useful, and rarest information.

approx. 348 pp., 59,95 Euro / US$ 59.95
ISBN 978-1-59229-406-0, March 2012

>> www.sap-press.com

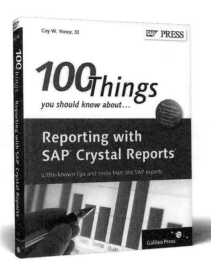

Provides 100 little-known time-saving tips and workarounds for SAP Crystal Reports users, super-users, and business analysts

Learn quickly with hands-on instructions and many screenshots

Gives you the tools for increasing efficiency and getting the most out of SAP Crystal Reports

Coy W. Yonce, III

100 Things You Should Know About Reporting with SAP Crystal Reports

Have you ever spent hours on a report only to discover that you could have saved time with a simple tip? If so, you'll be delighted with this book, which unlocks the secrets of reporting with SAP Crystal Reports. Its 100 tips and workarounds will help you increase productivity, save time, and improve the overall ease-of-use of SAP Crystal Reports. With this book, you will accomplish your reporting needs faster, more easily, and more effectively.

338 pp., 2012, 49,95 Euro / US$ 49.95
ISBN 978-1-59229-390-2

>> www.sap-press.com

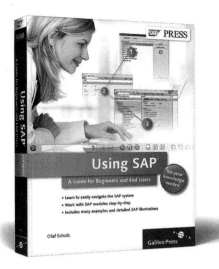

Learn to easily navigate the SAP system

Work with SAP modules step-by-step

Includes many examples and detailed SAP illustrations

Olaf Schulz

Using SAP:
A Guide for Beginners and End Users

This book helps end users and beginners get started in SAP ERP and provides readers with the basic knowledge they need for their daily work. Readers will get to know the essentials of working with the SAP system, learn about the SAP systems' structures and functions, and discover how SAP connects to critical business processes. Whether this book is used as an exercise book or as a reference book, readers will find what they need to help them become more comfortable with SAP ERP.

388 pp., 39,95 Euro / US$ 39.95
ISBN 978-1-59229-408-4

>> www.sap-press.com